Interpersonal
Conflict

Joyce Hocker Frost
University of Montana

William W. Wilmot
University of Montana

Interpersonal Conflict

wcb
WM. C. BROWN COMPANY PUBLISHERS
Dubuque, Iowa

To each other
and
all who love, honor, and negotiate

Contents

Preface

People are troubled, intrigued, and perplexed by their interpersonal conflicts and are often convinced that nothing can be done to improve them. Our approach to conflict is that "we do not have to stay the way we are"; we all have more choices in conflicts than we assume. We have seen people change the destructive patterns in their conflicts into productive outcomes. However, because the conflict process is complex, simple exhortations to "stop fighting" or "be nice" are not sufficient to open up new ways for doing conflict. We are convinced that a more complete understanding of the factors that contribute to the entire conflict process can lead to more successful conflict management by all of us. This book is a systematic examination of those factors, with the central focus on the communicative behavior of the conflict participants. Our communication approach assumes that conflict and communication are intrinsically tied to one another and this work is an attempt to demonstrate that notion.

Communication choices can be changed. It is through a fuller understanding of the role of communication in interpersonal conflict that we can come to understand how the process works and begin seeing more options for ourselves and others.

The book is written primarily for courses that focus on the conflict process as part of normal, ongoing communication relationships. Persons interested in small groups, communication in organizations, marriage communication, male and female communication, management, counseling, and organizational development will find this book helpful as a primary text or supplement to another text.

Chapter 1 examines the views of conflict that most of us are taught as cultural values, sets forth the elements that exist in all conflicts and distinguishes between productive and destructive conflicts. After this groundwork, styles that people use in conflicts are explained in the second chapter. People who find themselves and others repeating the same conflict behaviors will find the information particularly useful. Additionally, the conflict style differences between men and women are discussed. Research supporting differences in conflict patterns is cited. Suggestions are then given for changing patterns in male-female relationships.

One of the central determinants of all conflicts, power, is thoroughly treated in Chapter 3. Power is one of the most important yet least understood elements present in all conflicts. After explicating the nature of power we give specific suggestions that will aid you in assessing your power in specific kinds of conflicts. The "currencies" that conflict parties offer to others as the basis of their power are systematically examined.

Following the discussion of power, we demonstrate in Chapter 4 how the structure of a conflict influences the outcome. Game theory buffs will be attracted to this chapter, and if you previously have not found game theory relevant, we think you may find this treatment to be enjoyable. The prime contributions from game theory are placed into the perspective of everyday conflicts and discussed in meaningful terms.

One of the keys to gaining clarity about your conflicts is understanding how goals are formulated and how they guide conflict episodes. Chapter 5 is one of the few treatments of goals currently available that does not treat goals simply as "objective" statements made before a conflict starts. Goals are treated as statements evolving throughout the conflict process, changing along with other aspects of the relationship. You will also find valuable suggestions for using goal clarity in your conflicts.

Persons embroiled in conflicts all use strategies and tactics to accomplish their goals. Chapter 6 provides a perspective on moves that conflict participants make to escalate, avoid, maintain, or deescalate conflicts. If you find yourself reluctant to say, "I use tactics in my conflicts," we hope this chapter can help you see tactical choices as necessary and desirable.

The final chapter offers specific advice about the use of your new found information for productive ends. We discuss in Chapter 7 principles of effective intervention for aiding others in managing their conflicts. The focus of the chapter is on strategies of intervention that change the structure of the conflicts. The role of the third party is discussed. We end the book by suggesting that you can effectively intervene in your own conflicts.

We are optimistic about the possibility of genuine productive learning about conflict management. Over a five-year-period we have seen others change dramatically. We have changed in our own interactions. You can too!

Acknowledgments

The life of a book parallels the growth of a relationship. Writing requires faith and the ability to keep trying when the road looks blocked. Some very special people helped us stay with this project since the early speculation of "let's do a book on conflict." Eldon Baker had a significant impact on the book because of his confidence in us. His professionalism and departmental leadership was an essential element assisting us to fully concentrate on the project. We also had a disparate cast of "backseat editors" who closely followed the progress primarily from honkey-tonks and airports and provided their pseudoeditorial activities in incomprehensible letters and etchings on hershey bars. Our reviewers, John Stewart, Dennis Alexander, and Philip Emmert served as well throughout the entire process. Their helpful comments kept us writing with an eye toward improvement. Natalie Gould, of Wm. C. Brown, took on this adopted child and led it to completion.

Anne DeVore deserves an extra special thank you for guiding us through our own conflicts with patience and understanding. Elaine Yarbrough agreed to use the book in a trial run in her classes at the University of Colorado even before she read parts of the manuscript—for that confidence and her ebullient friendship, analysis of monster dreams, and sustaining love, we thank her. And finally, we thank students at the University of Colorado and University of Montana who actively participated in our conflict classes and provided moral support, anecdotes, and sharpened our analysis throughout.

I, Bill, wish to pay tribute to people who have become central in my changing view of myself. Mac Parks has remained my true and loyal friend while constantly serving as an appreciated intellectual thorn. John Means added perspective and confidence at some crucial turning points and I warmly appreciate him. Jason and Carina are a source of joy and satisfaction and emerged as central, important people. Joyce has been very patient with my impatience and has been invaluable in many realms.

I, Joyce, wish to thank Richard Douthitt, an early teacher and continuing friend, whose exciting and maddening classes at Texas Christian University first sparked an interest in the idea of conflict and the communication process. Much of him will be found here, transformed, no doubt, but essentially the same. My family has been more than routinely influential. Jean and Lamar Hocker as a team of parents taught both the necessity for speaking out and escalating conflict and the healing skills of the peacemaker to me when I was growing up. The early church experiences are emotionally part and parcel of every page of this book. Janice provides sisterly support and encouragement in every personal and professional endeavor. Ed is one of my models for the person who chooses "the way of peace" as a way of life. And my grandmother, Freddie Lightfoot, helped condition me for years by insisting that I would grow up to be an author. Earl Koile modelled for me the behaviors written about in Chapter 7, and his warm, effective intervention style inspired much of that section. The Conflict and Peace Studies Program at the University of Colorado provided collegial support, a summer of writing time, and ongoing encouragement for the development of work in conflict management. I thank especially Elise Boulding, Paul Wehr, and Frank Beer for their help. The "Boulder Gang," Elaine, Sandy, Mike, Rick, Tom, Wayne, and Chuck provided all kinds of crazy and wonderful help and personal support through all the writing stages. Lillian Davis, although not physically present during any part of the writing, was important—her belief in me as a potential writer about conflict carried me through many blank pages and late nights. And Bill, my cofriend, helped most of all by hanging in there. Maybe on the next project we will get our work times coordinated.

The Nature of Conflict

1

Wife:	I just came back from campus, and I've found that I can still register for Fall quarter. I want to send the forms in tonight.
Husband:	I don't think we can afford it. You agreed that my new business had to take priority, and we need your income. You could go back to school in two or three years.
Wife:	When we agreed that you would start the business, we never mentioned my not being able to go back to school! You know I've been counting on it, and now you're backing out. I've been working at this boring job since we got married, and it's time for me to do something more rewarding.
Husband:	Fine time you pick to better yourself! What are we supposed to use for money while you're becoming a coed again?

The husband and wife are engaged in one of the most pervasive and confounding of all human activities—conflict. Their conflict, like all conflicts, is a product of the communication behavior they choose to use. The husband and wife are in a bind. They face the problem of reconciling their individual needs for power, success, attainment, and winning with their relationship needs for trust, affection, collective benefits, and mutual growth. Differing needs all too often set up seemingly impossible dilemmas for people. However, when a conscious direction of energy is aimed at the productive management of conflict, people can discover options previously hidden to them and can more effectively accomplish both their individual and relationship goals. This book is designed to help you "do" conflict productively. We will use the phrase "doing conflict" often throughout the book to underscore one of our basic principles—conflict is a demanding activity, a process, a series of reciprocal communication behaviors. You may choose to change some of your communication behavior as a result of reading this book. At the very least, we hope that by reading it you will be able to understand your conflict behavior and that your communicative choices will influence your conflicts. A good starting point for our discussion of communication and conflict is a look at attitudes about conflict as an activity. We will then present our view of the essential elements that occur in communication transactions that are defined as "conflict."

Cultural Attitudes Toward Conflict

Recently one of us was asked to present a workshop on conflict management for a large corporation. The agreed-upon topic was "Conflict on the Job: Making it Work Productively." Three days before the workshop was to begin, a worried vice-president called. He said the proposed topic "certainly sounded interesting," and he was "sure everyone needed help in the area," but wondered if the leader would take a more "positive" approach to the subject. He urged a title change to "Better Communication in Business" and explained that his company didn't really have "conflicts," just problems in communicating. He felt conflict was such a negative subject that spending concentrated time on it might make matters worse. The executive's apprehensions about conflict were mirrored by a participant in a recent course called "Managing Conflicts Productively," who said she came to the course because she had never seen a productive conflict—all the conflicts she had witnessed were destructive. Further, her statement suggested that such a thing as a helpful conflict probably did not exist.

If you were asked to list the words that come to your mind when you hear the word "conflict," what would you list? Common responses people have given us when we asked them to do this were:

destruction	anxiety
anger	tension
disagreement	alienation
hostility	violence
war	competition

Many people view conflict as an activity that is almost totally negative and has no redeeming qualities. They take the attitude that "what the world needs now is love"; that if people just could understand each other better, they wouldn't have to have conflicts at all. Some people do not go that far, but they still see nothing particularly good about conflict, either. Would you list such words as the following when you hear the word "conflict"?

exciting	creative
strengthening	intimate
helpful	courageous
stimulating	clarifying

One of the assumptions we hold is that conflict can be related to all of the above words, both the negative ones and the positive ones. But society has encouraged us to believe that conflict is primarily negative.

Several well-known cultural clichés present a fairly clear picture of how many of us were raised to think about conflict. Some sayings we learned when we were small were: "If you can't say anything nice, don't say anything at all"; "Pick on somebody your own size"; "Don't hit girls"; "Don't rock the boat"; "Children should be seen and not heard"; "Act your age!" (which means act my age, not like a child); "Be a man, fight back"; and "Sticks and stones may break my bones, but words will never hurt me!" All of these sayings give a bit of philosophy about conflict: with whom to fight, permissible conflict behavior, injunctions about when to engage in conflict, and the power of words in conflict behavior. All of the sayings make assumptions that we think are not helpful to persons who want to learn to carry out productive conflict behavior.

The System View

One of the common teachings about conflicts reflects a view that protects already estbalished systems—what is good for the existing structure is good for the individual (Simons 1972). Many of us have been taught to be polite, patient, and nonthreatening because rude, impatient, and threatening behaviors are usually disruptive to those in power. Persons in power often are invested in the status quo—change is seen as the enemy, and conflict brings change. A nice boy or girl is one who knows his or her place and subordinates individual interests to the common good. The system being protected may be the family structure, a business, a classroom, a substructure of society, or an interpersonal relationship. Whatever the existing system is, conflict is suppressed because it threatens the very structure of the system. Take the common conflict between parents and children over cleaning up a room. A vivid first lesson in the system view of conflict for one of us occurred when the father said, "I don't care if you don't have time to clean up your room. The rest of us are tired of seeing your messy room, and we don't want to look at it." The child's retort of "why don't you close the door, then?" was rejected as unacceptable by the power figure of the establishment! In this system, conflict threatened the established order, so it was suppressed. The system view of conflict supports the notion that what is good for the overall system should be good for the individual.

The Actor View

One alternative to the system orientation toward conflict is an actor orientation. An actor orientation supports the idea that conflict may be necessary and desirable for those who are oppressed or are "one down" (or five down!) in society. Therefore, if you support the actor orientation toward conflict, you might say, "Well, conflict may not always be desirable, and it does cause disruption and havoc sometimes, but it's only destructive because you people in power don't know how to handle it. And I am being stepped on, so the system will have to put up with conflict I am causing.''

An advertisement placed by the Gallo Wine Company in national magazines illustrates both the system and actor perspectives. The representatives of Gallo Wine Company (or their ad writers) placed an ''Open Letter to Cesar Chavez.'' In it they emphasized the ''legally binding contract with the Teamsters Union,'' and that the ''answer to this problem is in legislation—not marches, boycotts, and demonstrations.'' Cesar Chavez had been using actor-oriented forms of dramatizing the conflict he and his followers perceived with the wine company, employing the marches, demonstrations, picketing, and boycotting mentioned in the advertisement. Both parties were convinced their way was right. The issue was not only over whether the farm workers were to be represented by the Teamsters Union, Chavez's independent union, or no union, but also over how the conflict was to be waged. Gallo, representing the establishment, denied that there was a conflict, calling it instead a ''problem.'' The system view tends to reinforce existing systems by avoiding and suppressing conflict (Bowers and Ochs 1971). But Chavez, representing the actor orientation, gained power by escalating and defining the situation as a true conflict.

Both the system and actor orientations to conflict have been taught in our society, but most of us have had more exposure to a system orientation. For example, think back to a typical day in your elementary school career, maybe the third grade. Some of these practices may have been standard operating procedure for you and your classmates and teachers. Children lined up to go everywhere. They were not allowed to interact for fear that fights would break out. Boys and girls played on separate areas of the playground—everyone knows that boys and girls cannot get along at that age! Perhaps strict procedures were set out for passing out materials and cleaning up. People who ''talked back'' or ''caused trouble'' were kept in school. The teacher may have used the threat of the principal as a third party, calling him in when activities got too hot for the teacher to handle. Instruments of control, such as instructions given over the public-address system may have been used (''room 302 is to proceed in an orderly manner to the auditorium for the program on good citizenship''). ''No talking in the halls'' was often a rule, and hall passes may have been used by those in power (anyone bigger than you) to regulate potential conflict. The overall philosophy was that order was all important, and anything that messed up the system was bad.

Just as with early school experiences, most of us have been taught that conflict in an interpersonal relationship is a sign of a deteriorating relationship. Most communication training has emphasized techniques for ''resolving'' or ''suppressing'' conflict, clearly a system orientation. Our purpose in this book is not to argue that either the system or actor perspective on conflict is superior, but that your culturally learned views of conflict affect the choices that you make. A student not believing he or she "has the right" to disagree openly with a teacher will make a predictable choice of avoiding the conflict. Our views of conflict affect how we do it.

Dysfunctional Teachings About Conflict

Many societies, including our own, express contradictory views of conflict—sometimes it is bad, sometimes it is good. Therefore, we grow up with a confusing perspective on when conflict is helpful and OK or when it should be avoided. We learn few strategies for changing situations from harmful ones into productive ones. In a pilot study of how children initiate and terminate friendships, Bell and Hadas (1977) found that children had twice as many ideas for how to get other children to be friends ("ask where they sit so you can sit next to them," "just walk up and say that you want to play!") than they did about how to end a friendship. The ending strategies relied heavily on such ideas as "ignore them," "you tell them to go away, or you move," and "beat them up." They also noticed uneasy silences when children were asked to tell how they ended friendships, or what they did when they wanted to make up after an argument. A poignant comment was made by one youngster who commented that friendships were over at the end of the school year anyway, so you did not have to make up.

Children receive confusing messages about their conduct of conflict. Sports are all right, random violence is not. Conflicts with peers are all right if you have been stepped on and you are a boy, but talking back to parents when they step on you is not all right. Having a conflict over a promotion is acceptable, but openly vying for recognition is not. Competing over a girl (if you're a boy) is admirable, but having a conflict over a boy (if you're a girl) is catty. And on and on. Double bind situations are set up in which persons in power send two different messages: (1) fight and stand up for yourself, but (2) only when it is acceptable (Bateson 1972). Thus, persons emerge with a schizophreniclike feeling about conflict, and many simply learn to avoid the whole subject. Clearly, one of the overall dysfunctional teachings about conflict is that you need to check with those in power to determine if you should have a conflict; and, if so, how to carry it out.

In addition, most of the writing about conflcit expresses assumptions that we feel work against a balanced view of the process. Communication scholars have generally presented conflict as negative, something to be avoided and altogether undesirable (Simons 1972). Some recent texts are beginning to present conflict as functional under certain circumstances and as a force that can provide beneficial results.[1] We agree with this reevalua-

---

1. *See,* for example, Miller and Steinberg (1975) and Stewart and D'Angelo (1975).

tion. But many assumptions that work against a potentially positive view of conflict still appear in texts. We discuss some of the most common misconceptions below.

1. One of the most common dysfunctional teachings about conflict is that *harmony is normal and conflict is abnormal.* Hawes and Smith (1973) refer to this treatment of conflict as the *time* disruption in an otherwise peaceful system, whether the system be interpersonal or a large organization. Coser (1967) and Simmel (1953) support the idea that conflict is actually the normal state of affairs in a relationship that endures over time. Conflict is cyclical, rising and falling. No one expects relationships or organizations to be in a constant state of upheaval, or else they would reach the "critical limit in a regressive communication spiral and disintegrate" (Wilmot 1975). But conflict is not an aberration. Fisher (1974) for instance, seems to assume that the maintenance of stable group norms is the status quo, and that when a group member "deviates," that deviance causes conflict, which is then effectively reduced by the group's pressure to conform. Aside from Simons, no one we reviewed considered conflict the norm and harmony an aberration—a position that is obviously also too extreme. Conflict normally emerges, subsides, and reemerges in ongoing relationships. Neither peace nor conflict is the norm.

2. Another popular assumption in communication texts is that *conflicts and disagreements are the same phenomena.* Simons (1972) notes the extensive use of the term "communication breakdown" to describe conflict situations. Stewart and D'Angelo (1975, p. 247) assume that "conflicts can be synonymous with disagreements." The problem with calling conflicts and disagreements the same thing is that people often assume that if a situation is "simply a disagreement," it can and should be solved by reaching a better understanding. As we argue later in this chapter, conflicts are more serious than disagreements, involving incompatible goals, while disagreements may often be solved by an understanding of terms and the other person's point of view.

3. Another common conception of conflict is that *conflict is pathological.* People who exhibit conflict behavior in a group situation, for instance, are "frustrated," "anxious," "blocked," or "neurotic" (Barnlund and Haiman 1960). This view ignores the

reality that many times people are indeed angry and frustrated, and legitimately so, when they are unable to progress toward the goals they desire. A student came fuming into a class late one day, exclaiming that she would never go back to a certain therapist. When asked why, she described a true conflict situation she was having with her parents who were going to cut off her income if she did not major in law as they wanted her to do. She wanted to go into business. The therapist had said that he was sure she was "troubled" by the situation and probably was feeling that she was "misunderstood." Of course empathy is important in therapeutic situations, but the student felt that the therapist did not understand that the conflict was caused by real opposing goals and could not be talked away by more understanding or by the right amounts of empathy from the counselor. Teaching people that conflict is dysfunctional does not make conflicts go away—they simply continue, but participants think *they* are abnormal.

4. Another treatment of conflict is that texts and articles often present only ways to *manage and reduce or avoid conflict, never ways to escalate or foment it when the cause seems right* (Simons 1972). Goldhaber (1975, pp. 230ff), for instance, while citing evidence of the productive nature of conflict, then lists only suggestions for reducing it. The proestablishment bias is maintained. Although conflict can be made to be productive, you would have to assume from reading the texts that it is better not to let it happen at all. Filley (1975) maintains that, "The opposite of conflict is problem-solving. Conflict generally ends in loss; problem-solving . . . ends in satisfactory achievement of the needs of the involved parties." Weiss (1974, p. 30), writing from a management perspective, presents "three ways to minimize conflict the next time it arises and rechannel the energy." Thus, the conflict process is not seen as a productive use of energy.

   Additionally, "conflict management" methods are often addressed only to the manager or supervisor, the high power person in the relationship. Again, this approach serves to reinforce the establishment, system orientation to conflict. Weiss (1974) suggests that the *manager* (italics ours) decide: (1) what the problem is, (2) who should be involved in its discussion, and (3) what the process of resolution should be.

5. *Conflict is presented as the result of "personality problems."* A typical section on conflict presents the phenomenon as a

mysterious, unfathomable, unresolvable entity stemming from "personality problems." For instance:

> There are some people who just cannot get along with each other. If, after trying such techniques as counseling and discipline, you still find two people battling with each other, physically separate them. . . . It's usually futile to try to convert such people to cooperative relations with others. On-the-job counseling can never be intensive enough and the effects of discipline will be short-lived at best. Do keep them away from the rest of your subordinates to the greatest extent possible. You will be doing everyone—including the battler himself—a favor (Weiss 1974, p. 33).

"Personality problems" are the result of learned human behavior, therefore they can be changed. People are creatures of their environment, which they can usually affect to some degree. As Fisher (1974, p. 104) has noted, "personalities don't conflict—behaviors that people *do* conflict."

6. The final misconception of conflict we noticed in a review of conflict literature aimed at students and practitioners is the *merging of conflict with emotions of anger.* Most people, when asked the difference between conflict and disagreements, will say something similar to the response of a woman in a recent seminar: "I can *feel* conflict. My blood boils and I get mad. I care about what's going on. Adrenaline flows. But in a disagreement, I'm calmer. It doesn't matter so much who wins, but in a conflict— watch out!" Often, types of conflicts are separated into "affective" (emotionally involving questions produced by how-to-do-it conflicts) or "substantive" conflicts, over "intellectual" opposition to content of ideas or issues (Miller and Steinberg 1975, p. 105).

The distinctions between emotionally involving and nonemotionally involving conflicts are not very useful. They further the idea that one must be angry and showing that anger if a "real" conflict is going on. Emotion does usually accompany conflicts, but often the emotion is sadness, bitterness, the desire to win, or sarcasm, as well as anger. And some conflicts, such as court battles between two primary attorneys, may involve little angry emotion at all.

Conflict is inevitable in human relationships. Far from being abnormal and undesirable, it serves, or can serve, a useful purpose in the growth of relationships. We are all familiar with the kind of strange coalition that can form among "enemies"—two people who work together, do not like each other much, but have mutual respect based on the feeling, "Well, Harry and I may not like each other much, but at least we know where each other stands. I can trust him to tell me where he is."

The Elements of Conflict

All interpersonal conflicts, whether they occur in a family, between a student and teacher, between worker and supervisor, or between groups have elements in common. We will illustrate what those underlying elements are by first providing a definition of conflict, then systematically examining the central elements.

Not surprisingly, scholars disagree about what conflict is (Fink 1968). One of the most popular definitions of conflict is Coser's (1967, p. 8), who says conflict is "a struggle over values and claims to scarce status, power and resources in which the aims of the opponents are to neutralize, injure, or eliminate the rivals." Deutsch (1973, p. 156) maintains that "*conflict* exists whenever *incompatible* activities occur. . . . An action which is incompatible with another action prevents, obstructs, interferes with, injures, or in some way makes it less likely or less effective." Mack and Snyder (1973) say that two or more parties must be present, there must be "position scarcity" or "resource scarcity," and that conflictual behaviors "destroy, injure, thwart, or otherwise control another party or parties, and a conflict relationship is one in which the parties can gain (relatively) only at each other's expense." They further state that conflict requires interaction and always involves attempts to acquire or exercise power. All of these definitions add important elements to a process definition of conflict and properly avoid the overly simple identification of conflict with "strain," "disagreement," or "controversy" (Simons 1972; Schmidt and Kochan 1972). One of the key elements in all conflicts is, however, the recognition that the parties are interdependent; they have some degree of mutual interest. As a result, there is the perceived opportunity for interfering with the other's goal attainment (Schmidt and Kochan 1972). Parties who perceive that the other can interfere with their goal attainment likewise perceive that there are scarce resources—money, land, status, power, or others. From a communication perspective, *conflict is an expressed struggle between at least two interdependent parties, who perceive incompatible goals, scarce rewards, and interference from the other party in achieving their goals. They are in a position of opposition in conjunction with cooperation.*

An Expressed Struggle

People often say, "I'm in a conflict but the other person doesn't know it." Sometimes they leave home, resign, get divorces, change professions, and have nervous breakdowns without other persons close to them knowing that they were "having a conflict." In Bergmann's film, *Scenes From a Marriage,* for instance, Johann came home one night, told his wife of ten years that he had fallen in love with another woman, and was leaving the next morning. He then related "conflicts" in their marriage that had built up to an intolerable level, while Marianne watched, shocked, trying to absorb the new reality of Johann's definition of their relationship as a relationship of conflict. Internal, one-person conflicts certainly exist. We have all experienced them—agonizing choices that have to be weighed carefully before life can go on. But as communication scholars, we are not primarily interested in these inner conflicts, important as they may be. This book deals with *expressed* conflicts, between at least two people. Relational conflict *is* communicative behavior; it is impossible to have conflict without either verbal or nonverbal behavior, or both. The "expression" may be very subtle, but it must be present for the activity to be interpersonal conflict. Therefore, although other conditions must exist also before we label an activity "conflict," we agree with Jandt (1973, p. 2) when he asserts, "Conflict exists when the parties involved agree in some way that the behaviors associated with their relationship are labelled as 'conflict' behavior." Often, the communicative behavior is easily identified with conflict, such as when one party openly disagrees with the other. Other times, however, an interpersonal conflict may be operating at a more subtle level. Two friends, for instance, may both be avoiding the other and aware that they are engaging in avoidance because, "I don't want to see him for a few days because of what he did." The interpersonal struggle is being expressed by the avoidance.

Interestingly enough, whenever parties are in an interpersonal conflict, there is usually internal conflict occurring within each of the parties. However, each could have internal conflicts unrelated to the activities of the other. We are taking a *communication perspective* on conflict because expressed struggles involve communication behavior. It is through communication behavior that conflicts are recognized, expressed, and experienced.

Finally, most expressed struggles have a "triggering event" (Walton 1969). When the worker says, "I don't like this job" to his boss, the wife stays out late, or the teenager says, "why do you always pick on me?" such events are often triggering events. While a conflict is often over issues that are longer lasting than the triggering event, the event makes it clear to all that an expressed struggle is occurring. All interpersonal conflicts are expressed struggles, even if that expression is nonverbal or very subtle.

Perceived Incompatible Goals

What do people fight about? (We use the word "fight" to mean verbal conflict, not physical violence.) The safest statement is that people usually engage in conflict over goals they might deny as important to them. One company with which we consulted had an extreme morale problem. The head cashier said, "all our problems would be solved if we could just get some carpet, since everyone's feet get tired—we're the ones who have to stand up all day. But management won't spend a penny for us." Her statement of incompatible goals was clear—carpet vs. no carpet. But as the interview progressed, another goal emerged. She began to talk about how no one noticed when her staff had done good work, and how the "higher-ups" only noticed when lines were long and mistakes were made. There was a silence, then she blurted, "How about some compliments once in a while? No one ever says anything nice. They don't even know we're here." Her stated goals then changed to include not only carpet, but self-esteem and increased notice by management—a significant deepening of the goal statement. Both goals were real, carpets and self-esteem, but the first goal desire may be incompatible with management's desire, while the second might not, and the goal of recognition could be more important than the carpet. We are not so naive as to assume that all incompatible goals are really just *perceived* as incompatible—some really are. Many, however, are not incompatible when other goals are identified or when mutuality is stressed. Careful identification is the key. Goal analysis will be discussed in greater detail in Chapter 5.

Perceived Scarce Rewards

A reward can be defined as "any positively perceived physical, economic or social consequence" (Miller and Steinberg 1975, p. 65). The rewards, or resources, may be "real" or perceived as real by the person. And the perception of scarcity, or being limited, may be apparent or real. For example, people in love often think that if their romantic partner loves someone else too, then the "supply" of love available to the original partner will diminish. This may or may not be so for the person in the love relationship—but a perception that love is "scarce" may well create genuine conflict between the partners. Sometimes, then, the most appropriate behavior for a party to initiate is trying to change the other person's *perception* of the reward or resource, instead of trying to reallocate the resource. Ultimately, one person can never force another to change his or her valuing of a reward or the perception of "how much" of the reward is available, but the persuasion coupled with supportive responses for the party fearful of losing the reward can help.

Everyone is familiar with money, oil, land, promotions, jobs, and positions in a business being seen as scarce rewards. But as we have discussed, intangible "commodities" such as love, esteem, attention, respect, and caring may indeed be scarce or *may be seen as scarce*. A poignant example is of dropouts in the school system. Videotapes installed in classrooms documented the fact that researchers could predict by the fourth grade which students would later drop out of school. The future dropouts were those students who received, either by their own doing or the teacher's, very limited eye contact from the teacher. They became, nonverbally, a nonperson. The glances, looks, smiles, and eye contact with the important person in the room became a scarce resource on which the students were highly dependent. Whether the eye contact is really scarce, or just perceived as scarce, such conditions lead to conflict. When the rewards are perceived as scarce, an expressed struggle is often on its way.

In interpersonal struggles, two rewards are often perceived as scarce: (1) power and (2) self-esteem. Whether the parties are in conflict over a desired romantic partner or after a coveted raise, power and self-esteem are often seen as scarce. For instance, people engaged in conflict often say things that are easily interpreted as power and self-esteem needs. In the following scenarios, the verbal expressions are translated into what rewards are seen as scarce.

She always gets her way.
  (she has more power than I do)

He is so sarcastic I can't stand him.
  (he is interfering with my self-esteem when I'm around him)

My boss doesn't appreciate me. I think I'll steal from the company.
  (I don't have enough impact around here. If I steal, I'll feel better and my self-esteem will increase.)

We maintain that in interpersonal conflicts, regardless of the content issue involved, the parties usually perceive a shortage of power and/or self-esteem rewards. And, the key is the perception of the scarcity.

Interdependence and Independence

Conflict parties engage in an expressed struggle because they are *interdependent*. Each person's choices affect the other because conflict is a mutual activity. People are seldom ever totally opposed to each other. Even two people who are having an "intellectual conflict" over whether a community should limit its growth and resource development are to some extent cooperating with each other. They have, in effect, said, "Look, we are going to have this verbal argument, and we aren't going to hit each other, and both of us will get certain rewards for participating in this flexing of our intellectual muscles. We'll play by the rules, which we both understand." Schelling (1960) calls strategic conflict (that conflict where parties have choices as opposed to conflict where the power is so disparate that there are virtually no choices) a "theory of precarious partnership" or "incomplete antagonism." In other words, even these informal debaters concerned with a city's growth cannot formulate their verbal tactics until they know the "moves" made by the other party.

Parties in strategic conflict, therefore, are never totally antagonistic and must have mutual interests, even if the interest is only in keeping the conflict going. Without openly saying so, they often are thinking, "How can we do this conflict in a way that increases the benefit to me?" These decisions are complex, with parties reacting not in a linear, cause-effect manner, but in a series of interdependent decisions. Bateson (1972) calls this ongoing process an "ecological" view of patterns in relationships. As in the natural environment, where a decision to eliminate coyotes because they are a menace to sheep affects the overall balance of animals and plants, so no one party in a conflict can make a decision that is totally "separate"—each decision affects the other conflict participants. In all conflicts, therefore, interdependence carries elements of cooperation and elements of competition.

Even though conflict parties are always interdependent to some degree, their perceptions of the interdependence affects the choices they make. They will decide whether they are acting as (1) *relatively independent agents* or (2) *relatively interdependent agents.* Is it desirable to say something to the effect of, "I am making my choices and doing my thing with very little regard for your choices?" or "We are in this together— neither of us can decide what we want to do without taking the other into account?"

If we are to study conflicts based on the degree of interdependence, we must look at (1) how the parties themselves perceive their interdependence, and (2) how parties outside the primary conflict perceive the interdependence of the conflict unit. The "facts" of their connectedness depend on mutual perception and metaperception. A group of university students recently discovered their degrees of interdependence in an unwelcome way. One program unit showed the film, "Hearts and Minds," a documentary about the human side of the Viet Nam war. Another group of students, representing another student government committee, organized pickets protesting the use of money deriving from the showing for anything other than refugee relief. Both groups then embroiled themselves in a constitutional struggle over large policy-making issues. The issue originally defined as an ethical struggle between two student groups later involved hundreds of members of the university community. The reference groups of the primary conflict unit refused to let the original committees define themselves as independent of the larger system. Conflict always takes place in an encompassing system—when intimates enter into conflict, their conflict affects their personal worlds to some degree. Not only, then, must persons decide how much they want to be involved with each other, they must respond to the larger society, whether that society is a family or a racial group or a corporation.

In a conflict in one of our classes recently, one student challenged the teacher's choices about the most appropriate way to run the class. This conversation went on for several class periods, with the rest of the large class becoming very restless and annoyed. Finally, a representative of a coalition of students spoke up and said, "Look, you are taking our time to work on this personal conflict, and we are really getting angry. We're not able to do what we came to this class to do. Don't involve us in your personal hassles." The students initiating the challenge said "But you're involved— you're in the class and you ought to be concerned about how the sessions are run. You're in this just as much as I am." They proceeded to carry on a short-term conflict based not only on the issues of class goals, but on the issues of "How interdependent are we?" The most salient issue at that point was how the parties perceived themselves in relationship to each other—the issues of power and class goals had to wait until the first-order issue was settled. The basic question, then, in any conflict is, *"How much are we willing to allow each other to influence or interfere with our choices?"*

As you can tell from the examples above, when parties are interdependent and want incompatible goals, their actions often interfere with the goals of others. If an employer and employee have incompatible goals, the employer wants all employees to volunteer extra work time and the employee wants to spend no extra time at the job, when they each pursue their goal, someone will be interfering with the other. Interference occurs because parties are interdependent and want scarce rewards or have incompatible goals. Interdependence brings with it the possibility for joint action and for discord.

Sometimes parties are locked into a position of mutual interdependence whether they want to be or not. Not all interdependent units choose to be interdependent, but are for other compelling reasons. Some colleagues in an office, for instance, got into a conflict over when they were to be in their offices available to receive calls and speak with customers. One group took the position that "What we do doesn't affect you—it's none of your business." The other group convinced the first group that they could not define themselves as nonconnected since the rest of the group had to be available to fill in for them when they were not available. They were inescapably locked into interdependence. Therefore, the first mutual decision that must be made in any conflict is the mutual influence issue. Then other procedural and goal-oriented decisions can be made after the relationship issue is solved. The issue, may, of course, have to be compromised. But a decision must be made, or the parties have almost guaranteed getting themselves into an unproductive conflict, with one party acting and making choices as if they are only tenuously connected.

Persons who define themselves as interdependent in some way must enter into the process of determining *who they are as a unit* after they decide individually how much influence they want the other person to have with them. (Sometimes, as we have stated, these choices are not available.) They must decide, tacitly or overtly which rules bind them, how they will communicate, where "belt-lines" are (Bach and Wyden 1968), and dozens of other relationship issues that proceed to define them as a conflict unit at the same time they are proceeding toward mutual and individual goals. Persons who see themselves as relatively independent are primarily concerned with *acting* issues—where will I go, what will I get, or how can I win? But persons who view themselves as highly interdependent must, in addition, decide *being* issues—who are we, and how will this relationship be defined? For instance, two persons in competition for a job are more interested in maximizing their own gains than the gains of the ephemeral relationship. They want to win—separately. But the same two individuals, one year later after both being hired by the company, perceive themselves as highly interdependent when asked to come up with a plan for implementing an environmental inpact study together. They want to win—together. And in the second relationship, while still in competition with each other for promotions, they also must define for themselves a workable relationship that gains desired goals for them both.

The elements we have discussed, an expressed struggle, perceived incompatible goals or scarce rewards, and interdependent parties who also cooperate with each other, are the essential elements of all interpersonal conflicts.

Assessing Conflicts

We have examined cultural attitudes toward conflict and noted that they often portray conflict in a negative light. Then, we specified the component elements inherent in conflicts in order to further clarify our communication perspective. We will now turn to an examination of what constitutes destructive and productive conflicts.

Destructive Conflicts

The challenging and frightening aspects of conflicts and crises are always present when one is thrust into a conflict situation. O'Neill and O'Neill (1974, p. 93) express the duality well in *Shifting Gears:*

> Out of every crisis comes the chance to be reborn, to reconceive ourselves as individuals, to choose the kind of change that will help us grow and to fulfill ourselves more completely. This potential, . . . is nowhere better expressed than in the Chinese language. The written character for crisis in Chinese is made up of two equal symbols: one which stands for *danger* and one which stands for *opportunity.*

How can people learn to recognize the danger existing in conflict interactions?

Most simply, conflicts are destructive if all the participants are dissatisfied with the outcomes and all feel they have lost as a result of the conflict (Deutsch 1973, p. 158). Sometimes, an outside observer might think a party had "won," but the person involved might feel that a loss had taken place. A church in a large city was involved in a bitter dispute that took place in an extremely divisive manner over a three-year period. Two dissident groups fought over what kind of leadership they wanted in the church. Both sides think they will have "won" if they can get the other side so angry they will leave. Although both sides are still involved in bitter fighting, including shouting and screaming at each other in meetings, and even have on occasion called the police to maintain order, both sides now feel hopeless about the situation. Because of financial interdependence, neither side can survive without the other. They are locked into a destructive conflict and have not been able to see how to make the situation a productive one. Everyone is dissatisfied.

Destructive conflicts often seem to have only one direction—upward and onward. Participants choose to escalate even when other options are available. One acquaintance of ours seems to have only one conflict style—escalation. Small details become major battles. He continues developing a destructive style, people soon learn to avoid him, and he is shut out of the information flow and the informal socializing around him. In these escalating conflicts, the issues become more important than they previously were, extra parties get dragged in, and normal rules of behavior are forgotten in the giant feud that results (Deutsch 1973, p. 160). Escalation is sometimes an appropriate conflict option to choose, as we will discuss in Chapter 6. In destructive conflicts, however, the participants are forced into an upward spiral without really choosing the direction or considering its consequences.

Specific behaviors can be pinpointed as typical in a destructive conflict. Deutsch (1973) lists a few—heavy reliance is placed on overt power manipulation, threats, coercion, and deception. There is a shift away from persuasion, conciliation, minimizing differences, and enhancing goodwill. When groups are conflicting with each other, they place a high premium on conformity—deviance is not allowed, and the "outside enemey" becomes all important (Deutsch 1973, p. 160). In a fight between two campus groups over whether affirmative action guidelines were followed adequately, the dissident group physically threatened the director, wore sunglasses to meetings to minimize nonverbal interaction, and attempted to falsify records of previous decisions. Additionally, they informally "expelled" other members of the minority group on campus who refused to support their friends, creating a clear climate or "If you're not with us, you're against us."

In conflicts among intimates, several kinds of actions paint a clear picture of destructive conflict. Often, the conflict is covert. False issues or red herring issues become the object of exaggerated or inappropriate display (Villard and Whipple 1976). For instance, one couple we know was having a fight over what the wife did with her free time—she usually was reluctant to accompany her husband on outdoor expeditions and preferred to stay home by herself and read or sleep. The husband insisted she was not "having enough fun with her free time" and kept bringing up hobbies she could take up. Finally the deeper issue emerged. Since the wife had recently become highly involved in a demanding job, the husband felt that he was going to become permanently left out of her recreation time. When they began to deal with the underlying issue of commitment to one another, the conflict was satisfactorily managed.

Other patterns of behavior emerge when people who are highly interdependent enter into conflict with each other. Bach and Wyden, in their popular book *The Intimate Enemy* (1968), suggest that intimates be on the guard for behavior such as "hitting below the belt"—violating special sensitive areas the other person maintains. Other destructive activities include the "hit and run tactic" of the uninvolved fighter. Nothing is more frustrating than to be involved in a conflict and then have the other party decide they really do not care one way or the other. The injunction "don't fight unless you mean it" is often violated in harmful conflicts. The purpose of a conflict should be, especially among intimates, to bring them closer after the fight. If no such movement is desired, then the conflict might reasonably be avoided.

The key to understanding destructive conflicts is that one party attempts to unilaterally change the structure, restrict the choices, and gain a one-party advantage in the payoffs.

Productive Conflicts

Conflict can have highly desirable, productive functions in a relationship. As Coser has pointed out, conflict is only threatening to a society when there are no avenues to handle it. Elastic systems, which allow the open and direct expression of conflict and adjust to shifting power balances are not likely to be highly threatened by explosions in their midst (Coser 1970, p. 29). In a family where the father's word is law, since there are no channels to deal with conflict, no opposition from the children is tolerated. When systems create channels for handling conflict, they further the possibility that the system will continue to exist. A friend of ours has instituted a democratic voting system in his family council. The family is made up of highly individualistic children and parents who all have strong identities. Since the children are growing up, the possibility for disruptive and highly threatening conflict is present—so the family set up a "council" system of government. Even though all the members are not always happy with the results, thus far, it has kept the family functioning well as a unit.

True openness occurs when, like in the above family, the power balances have a possibility of shifting. Often, high power parties promote an illusion of openness. A corporation, for example, often prides itself on its openness and lack of conflict citing the "suggestion box" and "open door policy" as proof. The low power participants are allowed to express themselves, but the corporation makes sure that no changes in the power relationship are forthcoming. True openness is present when all parties to a conflict can influence the structure of the relationship in addition to expressing frustrations.

Other societies sometimes recognize the potential threat of conflict and allow for an "acting out" of possible conflicts, which seems to serve as a catharsis preventing violent outbreaks. In the Zulu tribe in Africa, traditional rituals included insults of in-laws. *The prospective wife* would sit with her head down while potential in-laws talked about how much trouble she was going to cause. Then the wife would run away and the new husband would catch her. Then everyone would go off and feast with each other (Gluckman 1956, p. 119). The dramatization of possible conflicts helped the tribal members feel more sure of the new roles they were going to assume. The United States culture, however, has few rituals other than athletics to dramatize conflict.

Another way conflict can be used productively in societies is to capitalize on strong loyalties. Members of a corporation prizing loyalty often stress their interdependence, thus promoting the possibility they will learn to work together. In Gluckman's (1956, p. 809) discussion of conflict in Africa, he refers to the highly practical custom of people from the same village fighting each other with clubs, not spears, while men of different villages fight with spears. Additionally, the "blood tie" has been used throughout history as a conflict deterrent. Children are traded to foster parents for a while in differing tribes to assure that war will not be made on the other village. Modern people have furthered the "blood tie" concept by insisting that we are all related; "brothers and sisters" imagery, for instance, has been strongly utilized by the churches.

Realistic conflict tends to be productive, while unrealistic conflict is not. Coser (1956, pp. 48-55) identifies realistic conflict as directly related to a goal, while unrealistic conflict often leads to random, meaningless violence. For instance, a Chicano student tried to get medical help through the student health center. He had been, however, suspended as a regular student because of failing grades, and the health center would not admit him. The ombudsman of the university was called, along with a mediator from the center on campus set up to handle disputes with minority students and the university. They intervened on the students' behalf with the People's Clinic—an alternative to the student medical center. Upon leaving the administration building, the student threw a bottle through the large plate glass window, and the police were called. In Coser's view, this action would be *unrealistic* conflict, since the action was not taken to further any identifiable goal. The student, however, may have had a covert goal of relieving frustration against the establishment that observers were unable to determine. Observers have to take the participant's point of view into account when determining realistic and unrealistic conflict.

Productive conflicts can *size up the power of another* party so you can decide whether you want to get involved in a conflict or not (Filley 1975). Faculty meetings, for instance, often involve much discussion—seemingly nongoal directed. Yet at the time all the discussion is taking place and conflicts are being hashed out, individuals are deciding whether or not to promote a certain issue. The opposition is "sized up"; judgments about their power are made.

Coser (1956), one of the first to write extensively on the positive functions of conflict, documents that conflict can bind groups closer together, can preserve the group by providing a "safety valve" for blowups, can unite a group against a common "outside enemy," and can further group cohesiveness by helping them define their structure, and can promote helpful associations and coalitions. Additionally, strong group cohesiveness as a result of conflict, both internal and external, can set up a functional "balance of power" among groups so that one group finds it harder to totally dominate. Everyone is familiar with the feeling of "you and me against the world"; "if we survived this, we can survive anything"; "united we stand, divided we fall"; and other expressions of group unity that come from experiencing conflict and surviving it. The same benefits are derived from individuals in dyadic relations and small, informal groups who learn to experience conflict productively.

Summary

Conflict is an event that occurs between people because they are interdependent and perceive some incompatible goals or scarce rewards. It is neither "good" nor "bad"; it is a communication event in which people participate. The rest of this book will explore the styles people use to do conflict, how to assess power in conflict, how to identify the structure of conflicts, and how to set goals and utilize strategies and tactics in conflicts. The final section will discuss the role of conflict intervention and outline some useful techniques for intervening in other's conflicts as well as your own.

Bibliography

Ackoff, Russell, and Emery, Fred E. *On Purposeful Systems.* Chicago: Aldine-Atherton, Inc., 1972.

Alinsky, Saul D. *Rules for Radicals: A Practical Primer for Realistic Radicals.* New York: Random House, Inc., 1971.

Bach, George R., and Wyden, Peter. *The Intimate Enemy: How to Fight Fair in Love and Marriage.* New York: Avon Books, 1968.

Bardwick, Judith M. "Androgyny and Humanistic Goals, or Goodbye, Cardboard People." In *The American Woman—Who Will She Be?* edited by Mary Louise McBee and Kathryn A. Blake, pp. 49-63. Beverly Hills, Ca.: Glencoe Press, 1974.

———. *Psychology of Woman: A Study of Biocultural Conflicts.* New York: Harper & Row, Publishers, 1971.

Barnlund, Dean C., and Haiman, Franklin S. *The Dynamics of Discussion.* Boston: Houghton Mifflin Company, 1960.

Bateson, Gregory. *Steps to An Ecology of Mind.* New York: Ballantine Books, 1972.

Bell, Jeff, and Hadas, Aza. "On Friendship," paper presented at Wyotana Conference, University of Montana, June, 1977.

Bettinghaus, Erwin P. *Persuasive Communication.* 2d ed. New York: Holt, Rinehart and Winston, Inc., 1973.

Boulding, Kenneth. Publicity for "Center for Dispute Settlement" Conference, Boulder, Colo., Apr. 16, 1975.

Bowers, John W., and Ochs, Donovan J. *The Rhetoric of Agitation and Control.* Reading, Mass.: Addison-Wesley Publishing Co., Inc., 1971.

Coser, Lewis A. *Continuities in the Study of Social Conflict.* New York: The Free Press, 1967.

———. *The Functions of Social Conflict.* New York: The Free Press, 1956.

Deutsch, Morton. "Conflicts: Productive and Destructive." In *Conflict Resolution Through Communication.* edited by Fred E. Jandt, pp. 155-197. New York: Harper & Row, Publishers, 1973.

Duke, James T. *Conflict and Power in Social Life.* Provo, Utah: Brigham Young University Press, 1976.

Emerson, R. M. "Power-Dependence Relations." *American Sociological Review.* IXVII (1962):31-41.

Filley, Alan C. *Interpersonal Conflict Resolution.* Glenview, Ill.: Scott, Foresman and Company, 1975.

Fink, Clinton. "Some Conceptual Difficulties in the Theory of Social Conflict." *Journal of Conflict Resolution* XII (1968):412-460.

Fisher, B. Aubrey. *Small Group Decision Making: Communication and the Group Process.* New York: McGraw-Hill Book Company, 1974.

Goldhaber, Gerald M. *Organizational Communication.* Dubuque, Ia.: Wm. C. Brown Company Publishers, 1974.

Gluckman, Max. *Custom and Conflict in Africa.* New York: The Free Press, 1956.

Haley, Jay. *Strategies of Psychotherapy.* New York: Grune & Stratton, Inc., 1963.

Hawes, Leonard C., and Smith, David. "A Critique of Assumptions Underlying the Study of Communication in Conflict," *Quarterly Journal of Speech* 59 (1973):423-435.

Hesse, Hermann. *Siddhartha.* New York: Bantam Books, Inc., 1974.

Jacobson, Wally D. *Power and Interpersonal Relations.* Belmont, Ca.: Wadsworth Publishing Co., Inc., 1972.

Jandt, Fred E., ed. *Conflict Resolution Through Comnunication.* New York: Harper & Row, Publishers, 1973.

Mack, Raymond M., and Snyder, Richard C. "The Analysis of Social Conflict— Toward an Overview and Synthesis." In *Conflict Resolution Through Communication* edited by Fred E. Jandt, pp. 25-87. New York: Harper & Row, Publishers, 1973.

Miller, Gerald R., and Simons, Herbert W. eds. *Perspectives on Communication in Social Conflict.* Englewood Cliffs, N.J.: Prentice-Hall, Inc., 1974.

―――, and Steinberg, Mark. *Between People: A New Analysis of Interpersonal Communication.* Chicago: Science Research Associates, 1975.

Mortensen, C. David. "A Transactional Paradign of Verbalized Social Conflict." In *Perspectives on Communication in Social Conflict* edited by Miller and Simons, pp. 90-124, Englewood Cliffs, N.J.: Prentice-Hall, Inc., 1974.

O'Neill, Nena, and O'Neill, George. *Shifting Gears: Finding Security in a Changing World.* New York: Avon Books, 1974.

Rogers, Carl R. *On Becoming a Person: A Therapist's View of Psychotherapy.* Boston: Houghton Mifflin Company, 1961.

Scheflen, Albert (with Alice Scheflen). *Body Language and the Social Order.* Englewood Cliffs, N.J.: Prentice-Hall, Inc., 1972.

Schelling, Thomas C. *The Strategy of Conflict.* Cambridge, Mass.: Harvard University Press, 1960.

Schmidt, Stuart M., and Kochan, Thomas A. "Conflict: Toward Conceptual Clarity." *Administrative Science Quarterly* 17 (1972):359-370.

Simmel, George. *Conflict and the Web of Group Affiliations.* Translated by Kurt H. Wolff. New York: The Free Press, 1953.

Simons, Herbert. "Persuasion in Social Conflicts: A Critique of Prevailing Conceptions and A Framework for Future Research." *Speech Monographs* 39 (1972):227-247.

Stewart, John, and D'Angelo, Gary. *Together: Communicating Interpersonally.* Reading, Mass.: Addison-Wesley Publishing Co., Inc., 1975.

Vickers, Geoffrey. "Is Adaptability Enough?" In *Modern Systems Research for the Behavioral Scientist* edited by Walter Buckley, pp. 460-473. Chicago: Aldine Publishing Company, 1968.

Villard, K., and Whipple, L. J. *Beginnings in Relational Communication.* New York: John Wiley & Sons, Inc., 1976.

Waller, Willard, and Hill, Reuben. *The Family: A Dynamic Interpretation.* New York: Dryden Press, 1951.

Walton, Richard E. *Interpersonal Peacemaking: Confrontations and Third Party Consultation.* Reading, Mass.: Addison-Wesley Publishing Co., Inc., 1969.

Watzlawick, Paul *et al. Pragmatics of Human Communication.* New York: W. W. Norton & Company, Inc., 1967.

Weick, Karl E. *The Social Psychology of Organizing.* Reading, Mass.: Addison-Wesley Publishing Co., Inc., 1969.

Weiss, Alan. "Conflict: It's What You Make It." *Supervisory Management, 19* (6), June 1974, pp. 29-36.

Wilmot, William W. *Dyadic Communication: A Transactional Perspective.* Reading, Mass.: Addison-Wesley Publishing Co., Inc., 1975.

Conflict Styles

2

I Guess my boss is mad at me. I have left three messages for her to return my phone calls and she hasn't. I wonder why she is avoiding me.

My boyfriend is really a case. Everytime I ask him to change something, like the time to begin our date, he blows his top.

John is a good manager. He can sit and listen to our disagreements without being defensive. He is (as far as managers go), easy to talk to.

I handle conflicts with my wife by not involving her in them. If I tell her that she is doing something I don't like, she pouts for two days. It's just better to avoid the whole thing.

The above scenarios exemplify different ways people interpret conflict behavior for themselves and for people with whom they live, work, or interact in other ways. They are making statements about *styles* people use in conflict interactions. The purpose of this chapter is to examine different styles people develop for handling conflicts—styles they themselves prefer to use, develop because they seem to work, or develop because they fit the situation at the time. In addition, we will discuss male and female conflict styles and "relational styles"—that is, ways of handling conflicts that people-in-relationship develop for the same reasons that individuals do.

Several assumptions underlie this chapter. (1) We assume that *people have characteristic approaches to conflicts,* or, at least, have *preferred* approaches to conflicts, even if they often use other styles because necessity dictates that a certain style, such as "getting things out on the table," would work best in a special situation. Often when we ask people to describe their preferred or habitual conflict style, they respond, "I just do whatever the situation suggests," "I never thought about my conflict style," or "I usually avoid conflict even though I know I shouldn't." We have noticed that individuals can isolate some aspects of their personal styles. For instance, on a scale ranging from one to ten, with one being descriptive of people who, given a choice, prefer peace, harmony, and getting along with others, and ten being descriptive of persons who enjoy a good verbal fight, like to confront, and feel exhilarated and excited about engaging in conflict, where would you be? If you ranked yourself as about a six, a person who likes conflicts when they are productive, usually chooses a mediating or compromise style, and doesn't mind the process of conflict if it is done productively, how would your friends respond to your ranking? Do other people see you the same way you see yourself? While we assume that people have preferred styles of conflict, we would suggest at this point that you ask people around you how they see you as a conflict participant. This informal information will be helpful in your own decisions about your conflict style.

Another assumption is (2) *people develop conflict styles for reasons that make sense to them.* A person's experiences provide a background for judging what will and will not work in a certain conflict. If you work in an organization of ten associates who depend upon each other for creative approaches to your work, such as a group of city planners in a medium-sized community, you may well have developed an "office style" of managing conflict by accommodating each other when possible, taking each other's wishes into account most of the time, holding frequent meetings to check out your progress, and spending some time over coffee testing out new ideas on each other before "springing" them in more formal planning meetings. This style, which might be labeled "accommodation," was developed for good reasons and may be highly appropriate for your work group. We, therefore, assume that since styles develop for good reasons, that (3) *no one style is automatically better than another.* Schuetz (1975) discussed bargaining styles in terms of "reasonableness, rationality, and logic," giving a different connotation to these words than usually is taken. In her viewpoint, everyone's conflict behavior is reasonable to that person—the behavior is chosen, consciously or unconsciously, because it makes sense to that person in that situation. "Rationality" then becomes important—a person's conflict behavior is seen as rational not by some outside standard of what constitutes rational behavior such as reliance on formal logic, use of expert evidence, and a calm, unemotional approach. Rationality is judged by how well a person's choice of behavior moves him or her toward desired goals given the facts of the persons involved in the conflict, their particular relationship to each other, and the requirements of the situation at that time. Therefore, compromise might be appropriate to the office situation involving the planners mentioned above, while if the same people were involved in arguing for a growth-management plan on which they had worked for two years in front of the county commissioners, compromise could be disastrous for their goals. Assertive, strong argumentation aimed at gaining adherence to their point of view would be more approrpiate for those people, in that relationship, and in that specific situation (experts arguing their case in front of policymakers).

Our fourth and final assumption about styles of engaging in conflict is that (4) *people's styles undergo change in order to adapt to the rationality demands of new situations.* If rewards are available for changing, people do change. They can change if they want to and are willing to practice new communication skills in given situations.

People who can change and adapt are more likely to be effective conflict participants, gaining private and group goals better than people who avoid change. Hart and Burks (1972), in their article "Rhetorical Sensitivity and Social Interaction," discuss the concept of rhetorical sensitivity—of persons who have skills in goal-directed communication. They give the following five characteristics of persons who are rhetorically sensitive:

1. They are able to alter their roles in response to the behaviors of others and accept their alteration of roles in response to someone else.

2. They avoid stylizing their communication behavior so they are able to adapt.

3. They are able to withstand the pressure and ambiguity of constant adaptation and will develop skills of dealing with different audiences.

4. They are able to monitor talk with others to make it purposive rather than expressive. They speak not so much to "spill their guts" as to solve problems.

5. They alter behaviors and carry on adaptation in a rational and orderly way.

In other words, effective interpersonal communicators expect change and adapt to change in their communication with others. They avoid getting "stuck" in certain conflict styles.

Why should you try to change your conflict style so you will not get "stuck?" As we have discussed, people present themselves in conflicts according to what they take to be a suitable manner (Harre and Secord 1973). But if this presentation seldom changes, problems occur. For instance, some people are committed to solving conflicts by searching for "objective" solutions that are best for everyone. Such an approach often ignores the uncomfortable reality that objectivity is in the eye of the beholder. Majority voting, for instance, is usually seen as an objective way to solve a conflict in a group. After all, the American way of life is based upon majority voting—who could object? But if the people in the losing faction feel that the majority block forced their own way and that the people in the majority were "overbearing" and inconsiderate, then the minority's judgment about the *style* employed by the majority will affect the outcome of the decision. Other people in the majority might not have run into trouble because their style of using majority vote might have been different—more considerate of the feelings of the minority. In the former case, the minority group will often wage a campaign against the majority decision by halfheartedly working for the decision, postponing the implementation of the decision, or even actively (although subversively) working against the decision. Then the majority members accuse the minority members of not playing fair, of backstabbing, and similar heinous offenses. Clearly, the style of the parties doing conflict has an impact on the subsequent development of the conflict. Overreliance on tried and true conflict styles, whether that style is majority vote or accommodation, has built-in problems.

One clear reward for developing a *repertoire* of conflict styles is that we are then able to see the behavior of others in a different, more rational light. When we have a wide repertoire of conflict behaviors, then we assume that other people do, too. We are far less likely to judge the behavior of others as automatically having evil intent, being "childish," or being "improper." For example, Terry grew up in a family where conflicts between father and mother were never expressed openly in front of the children. He grew up believing that a happy marriage meant that one could not have open disagreement. He internalized a rule that said, "Ignore hostile feelings and do not openly argue." Perhaps to compensate for the suppression at home, he adopted a different style of conflict for public, nonfamily episodes. In public, if he disagreed with someone and saw that that person was in the way of his accomplishing his goals, he was quick to argue forcefully, express his hostile feelings, and behave in an overbearing manner. The corollary to the rule about avoiding conflict at home was, "While behaving passively at home is appropriate, acting aggressively in public is also appropriate."

People often stick themselves into behaviors that fit what we call their "Golden Age." The golden age is that period in which you felt best about yourself and from which you possibly still draw many positive feelings. The person who still looks back to high school athletics, even though he may be a forty-five-year-old history teacher, might operate from the rule that, "The way to handle conflict is to get out there and give it everything you've got, fight to win, pull with the team, and never let anything move you from your goal." This rule probably worked beautifully when trying to win a football game, but may cause real havoc when the man is faced with a principal who does not want to work with aggressive teachers and recommends his transfer to another school.

We know a man who is "stuck" in the style of the 1960s protestor. Everything is an antiestablishment fight for Carl. He identifies with the underdog (without thinking clearly about whether the underdog is right) and plots ways to make the people at the top take notice of the less powerful people. This style became dysfunctional when Carl was suddenly elected chairperson of his department. He looks for enemies at the top, while having to work in a problem-solving, cooperative manner with them. Others may have internalized a conflict style appropriate for a scared child. We recall with amusement and understanding the young man who mistakenly set fire to a neighbor's garage, ran madly into his room and hid under his bed, only to be pulled out by the inevitable strong arm of his father. When this young man "hides" from situations and assumes there is no way to save himself except escape, he uses behavior appropriate for the scared child but not for the competent young professional.

A final reason for actively working to widen one's repertoire of conflict styles is that many styles were developed from rules of etiquette (Harre 1974) that may also be outdated. These rules often help us make sense out of social situations—without some expectations of what constitutes appropriate behavior, we would be confused much of the time. However, while it may well be appropriate to "respect your elders" when you are eight years old, overgeneralizing that rule to include not bringing up situations that might cause conflict with respected elders when you are an adult is not so appropriate. Learning to seek permission to speak might be fine for behavior in the third grade, but waiting for permission to speak in a bargaining session, whether informal or formal, may well assure that you will never be heard. Rules of manners or etiquette have to be tempered with the exigencies of adult conflict behavior.

In conclusion, we assume that people do have conflict styles and that they can and should work to change these styles when such change provides rewards for them. In the next section, we will discuss one way of assessing your personal style so that you will have more complete information about which styles work for you and which styles might be due for an update. Then we will discuss ways in which men and women learn conflict styles in a different manner, and how these and other learnings interact in developing relational styles of conflict.

Assessment of Personal Conflict Styles

If you are going to be able to make effective choices about how to engage in conflict, then the first step is to understand your present conflict style. Conflict styles can be classified several ways,[1] and we are choosing one that

---

1. Styles can be assessed by various techniques. Those interested in observing and coding the conflict behavior of others should consult Rausch et al. 1974; Valentine and Fisher 1974; Ellis and Fisher 1975; Tedeschi et al. 1973; and Rogers and Farace 1975. While some of these were not specifically designed to code conflict behaviors, they can be adapted to such use. The other major way of assessing the conflict styles comes from self-report measures where the person reports on his or her typical conflict behavior. The most extensively used are those of Blake and Mouton 1964; Lawrence and Lorsch 1967; Hall 1969; and Thomas and Kilman 1973. Glick and Gross 1975 provide a comprehensive review of observation systems for marital conflict.

will assist you in seeing what your present style is and how it can be compared to other available styles.

Kilmann and Thomas (1975) provide the following diagram to help you compare your conflict style with styles of others. The system is based on the notion that each style is composed of two partially competing goals—*concern for self* and *concern for the other*. We noted in Chapter 1 that every conflict has degrees of cooperation and competition and that conflict parties are necessarily interdependent. The chart in Figure 1 uses those ideas as the basis for classifying the modes of doing conflict.

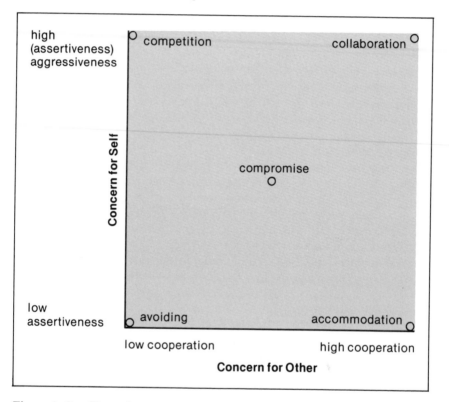

Figure 1. Conflict styles.

If your style is "competitive," it is characterized by being aggressive and uncooperative—pursuing your own concerns at the expense of another. Competitive styles attempt to gain power by direct confrontation, by trying to "win" the argument without adjusting to the other's goals and desires. The most extreme example of a competitive style would be a person who usually feels it is necessary to engage the other participant in overt disagreement. The competitor would typically see the conflict as a battleground, where winning is the goal and concern for the other is of little or no importance. Usually, someone who adopts a competitive style in conflicts would agree with statements such as "once I get wound up in a heated discussion, I find it difficult to stop" and "I like the excitement of engaging in verbal fights." These forms of competitiveness are probably best labeled as "aggressive" rather than "assertive."[2] If you are trying to win against other parties, destroy them in some way, or actively work against them, such behavior is aggressive rather than assertive. Alberti and Emmons (1974) provide a useful classification for the different degrees of assertiveness that are not specified in Figure 1. While nonassertive persons deny themselves and inhibit their expression of feelings and open striving for goals, assertive persons enhance the self, work toward achieving desired goals, and are expressive. The aggressive person, however, carries the desire for self-expression to the extreme. His or her goals are accomplished at the expense of others. The aggressive style results in a "put down" of others', actively working against the goals of others. The assertive person can be competitive without berating, ridiculing, or damaging the other. The aggressive person is competitive primarily by trying to destroy the opponent.

The following quote from a student paper exemplifies the aggressive style of conflict:

> When I get into an argument with a person over something I really stand for, then I really like to get involved and have a good battle. If my competitor has a good stand on his issues then I like to "rip" at him until he breaks or if things go wrong, I break. The excitement of confrontation when I'm battling it out with another person has a tremendous thrill for me if I come out as the victor.

Later in the paper, the student even referred to his conflict partner as his "foe," "my adversary," and said how he enjoys "being at each other's throats." Obviously, the student is operating from an aggressive conflict style.

The competitive style of doing conflict is not necessarily "bad." One can openly compete to accomplish individual goals without destroying the other person. Furthermore, such a style of conflict is often very appropriate. Intimates often report that "we fight hard, and really actively work to achieve

---

2. We have taken the liberty of changing Thomas and Kilmann's original designation of "assertiveness" to "aggressiveness," since we believe that assertiveness has come to connote a highly desirable manner of behavior with the growth of the "assertiveness training" movement. "Aggressiveness" describes the more self-centered behavior better than the term "assertiveness," which has come to mean appropriately insistent behavior that also does not deprive others of their rights. Thus, we change the designation for our purposes in this book.

our own goals. And the process works for us.'' Such an approach can often be productively used in conflict, especially if the participants are in agreement over the amount of assertiveness that can legitimately be used in their styles of conflict.

When high assertiveness aimed at reaching one's own goals gets tempered with a high concern for the other person, a *collaboration* style is the result. Collaboration is characterized by statements such as "when I get in conflict with someone, I try to work creatively with them to find new options" or "I like to assert myself and I also like to cooperate with others." Collaboration differs from compromise because in compromise, one looks for some intermediate position that partially satisfies both parties. In collaboration, the two people or parties work creatively to find new solutions that will maximize goals for both. An example would be a married couple who have a conflict about their priorities. For the wife, the husband works too much and does not spend enough time with her. For the husband, the wife is not interested enough in his work. A simple lowering of his working hours and spending more time with the wife and an increase of her interest would be one possible way to manage the conflict. But if the two parties collaborate, they work together on the conflict to identify the underlying concerns of both parties. It may be, for example, that both of them want more warmth and affection in the relationship, and the conflict arose because each one's way of attempting to get affection was not working. Through such collaborative effort, they explore the disagreement in order to learn from one another's insights. They may discover, for instance, that the time of day for taking time together makes a big difference. They may be able to meet for lunch occasionally and then the husband can work at home late on an evening. Collaboration as a style means that one person asserts individual goals while being concerned with the goals of the other also.

Compromise is intermediate between assertiveness and cooperativeness. If one uses a compromise style, conflict behavior is characterized by beliefs such as "not everyone can get their own way, you have to be satisfied with part of the pie" or "when disagreements occur, you each have to give a little." As you can tell by Figure 1, in a compromise style you address the issue more directly than in the avoiding style, but do not explore it in as much depth as would someone using a collaborative style. Some sample management tactics consistent with the compromise style would be to get two parties to split the difference, exchange equal concessions, or seek any middle-ground position. For instance, if a person is buying a used car from a dealer and the asking price is $3,000, the potential buyer may offer $2,900, knowing that he wants to pay only $2,800, but the dealer has to make a profit before he will sell. So, the buyer estimates the loss to both the dealer and herself and makes a compromise offer.

Wage and fringe benefit disputes in industry often are settled in a compromise manner, sometimes by third parties like an arbitrator. When both parties can't agree on terms yet want to avert a strike, they will sometimes submit to a third party to specify the terms of the compromise.

The problem with the compromise style is that persons sometimes give in too easily and fail to seek a solution that gives significant gains to either party. The "giving in" can become so habitual that it becomes a goal in itself.

Avoidance is a style often characterized by being nonassertive, passive, and not actively seeking cooperation. The person does not openly pursue his own concerns or those of the other person. The person effectively "goes limp," refusing to engage openly in the conflict. The person may sidestep the issue by changing the topic or simply withdrawing from open dealing with the issue. Interestingly enough, just as the competitive style does not mean you will get what you want (remember, you are interdependent with the other party), avoidance as a style does not mean the person will not accomplish the set goals. For instance, if a person is having a conflict with a large organization (they overcharged for some goods), the organization can enhance its position by not responding to correspondence on the matter. By pretending that the conflict does not exist, the high power party then is freed from dealing with the low power party. Avoidance can serve similar functions in interpersonal conflicts as well. If two roommates are both dating the same girl, they may refuse to discuss the subject openly even if both of them are aware of the problem. Avoidance is a way of dealing with conflict by trying to not recognize its existence or your part in its creation. As a final example, in intimate relationships the style of avoidance is often invoked on sensitive matters. If a couple is having some difficulty in dealing with each other's families, they may not feel free to discuss the difficulty. Avoiding a conflict, however, does not prevent it from happening. Conflict occurs when parties have the perception of incompatible goals, regardless of the style they choose to use in responding to it.

Accommodation occurs when one is nonassertive and cooperative, the opposite of competing. When adopting the accommodating style the individual neglects his or her own concerns in order to satisfy the concerns of the other person. It can, like the other styles, take many forms. One may obey another's directives when preferring not to do so, or, one may yield to another's point of view. Individuals in groups often succumb to pressures to make decisions by not pushing their point of view. Then, when the group reaches consensus and agrees on a decision, the individuals will later say they did not agree but "the group had to reach a decision."

Conflict styles can be examined from many perspectives. This section has presented just one of the many possible conceptual schemes for classifying conflict styles. This system is currently receiving support for its utility (Ruble and Thomas 1976), but, like any scheme, has limitations. For example, self-reports on your own conflict style may not accurately capture how others see your actual conflict behavior. And, of course, there are varying degrees of each one of the five styles. We noted that competitiveness can take many forms and other styles are also variable. All of the forms of avoidance, for example, have not been catalogued or described, and it may well be that some forms of conflict avoidance do not reflect unassertive, uncooperative behavior. In any event, these five styles are not exhaustive of all possible responses.

Gender-Related Conflict Differences

In this section, we will explore some of the conflict differences resulting from our socialization as males and females. We are often asked if we really think men and women fight differently. We certainly do! Individual differences are more important than simple assumptions about sex roles, but we most definitely concur with some of the recent research on sex-related communication differences. Intuitively, people report to us that they notice differences in the way men and women do conflict. For instance, men tend to say that women "get emotional," and women tend to say that men "are overly competitive." In any discussion about conflict styles, we should remember that one sex's *perception* of differences in the opposite sex is just as important as research reporting on specific differences. Self-fulfilling prophecies come into play—men and women choose behaviors in conflict situations partially because they are expected to choose those behaviors. Therefore we must look not only at relatively objective data giving a picture of what men and women do differently, but at what they *think* they do differently.

In a recent class in conflict, students were asked to reflect on how conflict was handled in their homes and to think about how their individual attitudes toward conflict developed. Women overwhelmingly reported the experience of learning to *avoid* conflict. Bardwick (1971) has noted that girls are socialized into drastically lower levels of activity in conflict. This was emphasized by some of the responses from the class. One woman reported:

> As a child, I was forbidden to "talk back." As a result, I stifled all my replies until I was of sufficient age to walk out and did so. That was fifteen years ago—I have never been back. . . . Thus, my strategy has been one of avoidance of a conflict to which I can see no resolution. As I had been raised by my father and

stepmother, I scarcely knew my mother. When I was seventeen, I went to live with her. She wanted a mother-daughter relationship to which I could not respond. Legally bound to her, my attempts at confrontation ended in failure. Once again I walked out—this time into marriage. After seven years of marriage and abortive attempts at communication, I again walked out—this time with two children.

Another student reported that she was raised in a gentle, peaceful family where there was little conflict and "never saw my parents angry with each other, and seldom with us four children." Thus she reported she has been trying to live up to what she now views as an unreal expectation of peace and harmony.

Not only was avoidance the primary tactic used by these women, but they also discussed the inability to even sense the feelings that *might* lead to conflict. Another student said:

In our home, conflict was avoided or denied at all costs, so I grew up without having the experience of seeing conflicts managed in a satisfactory way, and I felt that conflict was somehow "bad" and would never be resolved. This experience fitted well with the rewards of being a "good" girl (compliant), combining to make a pattern for me in which I was not even sensitive to wishes and desires which might lead to conflict.

Thus, the fear of conflict combined with female role stereotyping produced an avoidance pattern.

Another common pattern remembered by some of the women in the class was the *temper tantrum*. Girls were not punished as severely as boys for exhibiting uncontrollable emotion. This behavior, which seems incongruous for a grown woman, was reported by many women. Pouting, angry crying, and screaming is a method women said they sometimes used when the felt that they were in a low power situation. Grown women, feeling a lack of power by little practice in and reinforcement for dealing with conflicts productively, have traditionally been expected to resort to tactics more appropriate for children. It is common for texts and readers for elementary school children to show girls in conflict throwing tantrums then giving up. A typical frame will show a boy saying to his mother about his sister, who has just fallen on her skates, "She's just like a girl—she gives up!"

As we stated earlier, however, both men and women suffer from stereotypic styles used in dealing with conflicts, especially with each other. The following example illustrates the boxes both men and women get into in their conflict relationships.

A prime example of conflict was my recently ended twenty-nine year marriage. We never raised our voices. I felt I was the keeper of the peace over the years. I always avoided "scenes." In the last few years my desire to develop my abilities and make use of them in a part-time job . . . created a conflict situation. At that time belligerant words were exchanged, if not in raised voices. At such times, he would say, "There's no point in talking about it now; it will only make matters worse." (His saying *that* made matters worse!) To proceed to do what I wanted to do against his will was a frightening thing (not because of fear of any physical violence, but because of disappproval.) My former husband became my main "proving ground" for my newer strategies in conflict. I finally succeeded in standing up to him.

The losses both parties accured in this conflict are evident. The man was unwilling or afraid to discuss the woman's feelings. The woman was so used to the role of "peacekeeper" for the dyad that she could not change her role without getting out of the relationship altogether. They were caught in a *regressive communication spiral* (Wilmot 1975) with no useful strategies for continuing the relationship in spite of the conflict. All the woman could do was repeat the adolescent cycle of rebelling against "father" and walk out.

Just as with women, men also are socialized into standardized approaches to conflicts. When men are asked in our workshops "what do women do well in conflict?" they typically respond, "women use their emotions to get what they want." In discussion, it becomes clear that men feel that expressing emotions is a powerful tool that women use because men cannot "handle it when women cry." Similarly, men describe conflicts in aggressive, power-oriented terms. They often speak of "having it out," "decking the SOB," "not taking any s---." Furthermore, men are socialized into believing that the relational training that women receive (learning to attune to feelings and to the relational impacts of conflicts) gives the woman an "unfair advantage because they know what is going on." As a result, men are prone to push for "airing the issues" and "getting things on the table" in a manner that focuses attention on the content issues as compared to the relationship issues.

Men and women not only learn different overall strategies for doing conflict, such as avoidance, escalation, reduction, or maintenance, *they also learn to speak differently*. Eakins and Eakins (in press) report that women learn to do more expressive speaking than men. Expressive speech tells about the emotions of the speaker, his or her relationship to the other, and tends to be creative and tangential. Verbal expressiveness if often interpreted, in Berne's words (1964), as "stroking," or raising the status of another person, giving help, and providing attention to another person. This verbal stroking can be in the form of asking for opinions, asking for suggestions, for clarification, or of agreeing, reinforcing the statements of others, and complying with what another person wants you to do. Men often learn to depend on these expressions by women, and when they are not forthcoming, they think the woman is acting aggressively.

Men, on the other hand, often use task-oriented language. A study of mock jury deliberations revealed that while women contributed more positive (stroking) reactions to statements of others and showed more tension release, such as laughing more, men tended to describe the situation and make more suggestions for future action than did the women. They gave more opinions and "orientation talks." Men used more "let's get the job done" talk, while women used more expressions of support and solidarity (Strodtbeck and Mann 1956).

Men and women who choose to change their behavior, or who simply never have conformed to these stereotypic expectations, often are thought to be very peculiar. While "men in general" are thought to be good at task orientation, and "women in general" are thought to be good at the socioemotional orientation of communication in groups, not everyone fits this pattern. Men, for instance, who prefer to listen and support the ideas of women in the group are sometimes thought to be "passive" and withdrawn. Women who actively seek to reach decisions quickly and move the group along are labeled as "aggressive" and pushy. We suggest that you look at your own communicative behavior, especially in small groups, and see if you are satisfied with what you habitually do. Do you often come home from meetings saying "I had some good ideas but I knew nobody would listen" or "I don't know why I keep going to that group—they all expect me to lead it but I just don't care very much"? If you regularly find yourself frustrated in conflict situations because of feeling "out of place" according to your sex role, you might adopt some of the following suggestions:

1. Clarify your role when appropriate. For instance, you might say, "I have taken a supportive role for whatever the group is trying to come up with for a solution to our conflicts, but I am too involved in this conflict to be comfortable with that role, so I will be speaking up more."

2. Seek feedback when you think you are being ignored. Women often report the feeling that "When I try to get involved in the conflict, it's like a river just flows around me and continues on the other side after I talk." If this happens to you (either sex), you can ask questions after you finish. You can ask people to respond to your suggestion before they go on. You can assert that you think your statement is important and you do not want it ignored or overlooked.

3. You can point out when someone else is assigning you a role with which you are not comfortable at the time. You might say, for instance, "I get the feeling that you are expecting me to come up with some way out of this hassle. I don't know the way out. I'm

as angry and confused as you are. We're going to have to work together."

4. You can simply quit doing some of the communication behaviors with which you are not pleased at the time. Women can conciliate less when they don't feel like conciliating; men can stay quiet when they don't want to or can't think of problem-solving suggestions. Sometimes silence in a conflict situation forces other people with good ideas to express them, instead of depending on the habitual responses of others.

Men and women also react differently to competitive situations. In gamelike situations, when the sexes are pitted against each other, women tend to play more cooperatively against men than they do against women. Men play more competitively against women than they do other men—a strange finding in the light of the usual assumption that men are most aggressive and competitive against each other in sports. Women compete more against each other than they do against men. (Borgatta and Stimson 1963). Thus, the introduction of the opposite sex may tone down competitive behavior of women but spark this behavior in men. No wonder, then, that men and women have so much trouble working through conflicts with each other. Women are often startled by the intense competition that men exhibit—which may be more intense than men do with each other. Men may assume that women are not very competitive—when they are more competitive in single-sex groups. Of course, as some note, the fact that this research is done in a competitively structured game may pose some problems, since men may be presumed to be more accustomed to such situations. Practical suggestions coming from these findings, however, might be explored. In work situations where competition is important, male managers might do well to initially put women in small groups or single-sex groups in the beginning phases of their job orientation. Then the success they have might more easily be generalized across mixed-sex groups in the future. In noncompetitive situations, women can be rewarded for their supportive and expressive behavior while being encouraged to bring up ideas and be assertive. Men can be rewarded for their task orientation, while they are being asked careful questions about how they are responding emotionally to conflict situations. The sexes can help each other out, building on the strengths of each.

Another pattern of communication behavior that differs according to the sex of the person is *interruption behavior*. Have you had the experience of being told that you interrupt all the time and that you are rude? Or have you felt that you could never get a word in edgewise? One person can often drive others to distraction because he does not listen, or another can blow up when she thinks she is not being heard by the other people in the conflict. One person may sulk for days in righteous indignation over the overbearing manner of the other, while the other might assume that he has been considerate, has listened well, and has facilitated the conflict by giving helpful suggestions and keeping things "on the track." Some of these reactions may be tied to sex-related differences. Eakins and Eakins (in press) discuss interruption patterns of men and women and point out that men talk more in groups of people, and in part they attain this right to talk more by interrupting women and each other far more than women interrupt men (Kester 1972). Women also tend to let men interrupt—they do not "fight back" for their turns in conversations as much as men do. Zimmerman and West (1975) found that in same-sex conversations interruptions were distributed fairly evenly with no differences between men and women. But in male-female conversations, the patterns were very different. Ninety-eight to 100 percent of the interruptions were carried out by men. The transcripts of the conversations revealed no complaints from the women such as "You keep interrupting me" or "Let me finish."

Men to whom we have reported these results often are astonished, while women indicate that they knew something was happening. This does not assume, of course, that men are inherently rude and that women are polite—but that socialization is different, and people often attribute evil intent to the other side or assume that the other person had nothing to say. Again, as in role difficulties in groups, people can change their behavior if they want to. The female coauthor of this chapter entered into a pact with a female colleague on her faculty. They agreed to support each other when the other one was interrupted—to use phrases such as "Wait a minute, I want to hear what she has to say" or "Let her finish, please." After two meetings, several male colleagues remarked upon entering the meeting that they hoped they "weren't going to have to fight the women again" and hoped "you're in a better mood than last time." And, in one of our classes, Gary and Gayle were role-playing a conflict about who should be the next United States President, where Gayle frequently interrupted Gary. Gary, a usually articulate and outspoken member, was so astonished he could not even think of arguments. He said she was "attacking" and "destroying" him. Women who refuse to be interrupted, or who interrupt, will often incur hostility from males. And, men who sincerely try not to interrupt as much as they often have in the past are sometimes accused by girlfriends of "not being interested" or being "distracted." Old patterns die hard!

An important assumption, however, is that interruption patterns can be challenged and changed, and both people (or three, or ten) can gain a sense of respect for other parties by learning to listen carefully and actively.

Women feel more confident when they fight back for a turn, thus bearing less hostility toward the male with which they are having conflict, and men learn to slow down and listen, thus experiencing a higher quality decision made by the group and more satisfaction afterwards. Patterns can change.

Finally, we find in our observations that women use more accommodative conflict strategies, while men use competitive or exploitive ones. Men are more confortable with winning, while women are more comfortable with finding a fair outcome, acceptable to all. Neither of these strategies, as we discussed earlier in the chapter, is inherently "good." Sometimes the structure of a conflict is set up for winning and losing, and sometimes the structure is cooperative. The problem occurs when men and women get stuck in a role and cannot change when it is appropriate to change. For instance, in a conflict with parents and a teenage child over whether the child should drop out of school, the mother may find herself wanting everyone to be happy, when the hard reality is that they are, at the moment, locked into a win (stay in school)—lose (the child leaves school) setup. Rather than accommodation, a better choice would be to work to redefine the structure, as we will discuss in detail in Chapter 4. Men may find themselves saying after a conflict over money with their wife, "I got her to see my point of view," when they are locked into an interdependent system in which the wife can subvert any systen that she does not agree with. He would have been better off to drop the self-advantage approach and work toward a mutually accommodative solution.

We encourage men and women to explore their conflict roles, ask whether they are satisfied with them, and consider changing their habitual patterns when such change is appropriate. Friends, family, and co-workers can be an invaluable source of feedback for persons who are curious about their conflict styles—we encourage you to ask people who are important to you how you do conflict.

Relationship Styles of Conflict

The final section of this chapter deals with how individually oriented, sex-role oriented, and other personal differences in conflict style interact to form characteristic relationship styles of conflict. These individual styles blend to form a new relationship style, which is more than a simple addition of the two or more people. For instance, how do four people, two of whom like to avoid conflict when possible, one who is highly exploitative, and one who is conciliatory, choose to carry out their work-related conflicts? Obviously, no prediction is possible simply by listing characteristics of individuals. Each system is unique, and we find relationship approaches developing that are as creative and different as each situation. Each relationship takes on its own qualities.

A predominant style for doing conflict often changes with the change of conflict situations. Take the case of Annie, who is a competent professional woman respected by her peers. Annie, when in a conflict with her co-workers, will fully engage with them by usually compromising or collaborating. She "hangs in there" and makes her opinions known and is respected for her ability to think through the problem area. She is often reflective and goes home and thinks of ways to improve the situation, then returns and offers solutions. But when Annie goes camping with her parents, quite a different side of her is revealed. If her parents do things that bother her, she totally avoids the conflict. In fact, the longer she is with them the more she tends to disappear emotionally. She can be with her parents for days without fully engaging in open discussion. She has taken the role in the family as the silent one who is there but not heard. She accomplishes her goals by agreeing with what is discussed, then fading away and doing what she wants to anyway. Her conflict style changes dramatically from relationship to relationship.

Many of us are just like Annie, choosing one style in one situation and another for situations with different demands. And, when we are exposed to the context, such as family, work, or friends, on a frequent basis, the relationships themselves take on style of their own. One reason it is hard to be consistent in style across situations is because we learn patterns that allow us to adjust to the other person's, and then bring them forth when in their presence. This can be highly positive. If Annie were to become competitive in the presence of her parents, a major adjustment on their part would occur. Perhaps they all are satisfied with their present patterns. The problem comes, as always, when one person is not satisfied with the interaction.

One way to characterize predominate relationship styles is to discover any overt struggles over the conflict definition. Lederer and Jackson (1968) have described three basic types of relationships: (1) complementary, (2) symmetrical, and (3) parallel.

In a conflict occurring in a complementary relationship, the participants choose styles that complement one another. For instance, if one of the parties is competitive and aggressive, the other will accommodate. Such a patterning of responses maintains the ability of the relationship by one person adopting a style that does not compete openly with the other person's. In such cases, the conflict might be characterized by one person always asking for change in the other person, and the other accommodating to it. Another example of a complementary relational conflict pattern would be any form of open engagement by one person coupled with avoidance by the other.

Complementary relational patterns allow the participants to form definite images about the "personality" of the other party and to feel very sure about their own approach to conflict because the patterns often become solidly fixed in the relationship.

Symmetrical relationships are characterized by open striving for the same types of control in the relationship. For instance, if two co-workers both use the collaborative style in approaching conflict, then the similarity of their styles builds up a symmetrical system. Mac and Bill, for instance, both use similar ways to express themselves in a conflict between the two of them. Mac jostles and changes the topic and jokes, and so does Bill. Probably the easiest place to observe symmetrical relationships in operation is to watch two friends sharing experiences of the weekend. They often get into a pattern of each one relating a story, matched by the other. Symmetrical relationships, just like complementary ones, can work for the participants. In the case of symmetrical conflict styles, participants can come away from a conflict feeling like they have "held their own." And, participants who engage in symmetrical behaviors in conflicts can come away feeling a great deal of understanding for the other person's behavior since it is so much like their own.

Sometimes the open striving for the same types of control in symmetrical relationships can lead to unhealthy competition. For instance, mutual friends can easily adopt a symmetrical pattern that leads to "one-upsman-ship," where each person tries to better what the other has just contributed. The two friends then spend their time vying for control of the relationship rather than utilizing the symmetrical relationship as a way to share equally in the power. Some common variations on this theme are two boys boasting and counterboasting about their athletic ability, and the man and woman who first meet and get into the "Well, when I was in Europe, I . . ." competition. Even more familiar patterns are when two intimates each have the right to yell and scream at one another and do not produc-tively manage the conflict issues. The pattern is symmetrical and non-productive. All of the relational styles can be put to either productive or nonproductive use.

Parallel relationships develop when the participants develop flexible styles for relating and vary between establishing their power in symmetrical and complementary ways. In a parallel relationship, the individual styles do not become rigid or set—they change to meet the demands of the situation. Parallel relationships often offer the best chance for participants to grow and change. These three relationship styles can be applied as a beginning way to analyze satisfactory or unsatisfactory conflict relationships.

All on-going relationships develop styles of their own because parties to a conflict are interdependent—what each one does affects the other. In order to reduce the uncertainty about what will happen in the relationship, the participants tend to develop stabilized ways of conflicting. The uncertainty that is present in the beginning stages of all interpersonal relationships propels the participants to take steps to reduce it (Altman and Taylor 1973). To illustrate this, think of a relationship you now have with a close friend or someone you have worked with for a long period of time. Now, imagine an issue that you have recently had a conflict over or one that might be at issue in the near future. If you were to broach the issue with that person in your typical style, how might that other person respond? Would she or he yell, sulk, talk to you openly, or generally be receptive to your request for a change? Now, imagine that the very same issue arising between you and someone you have only known for one hour. If you were to start dealing with the conflict in the same way as you would with your friend, what would be the most likely response of the other person? It is hard to predict, because our ability to predict the behavior of the other person in a conflict is built up over a series of experiences. The relationship that you have with the new acquaintance has not yet developed a style of its own.

If you know that your friend and you have some regularized ways to handle conflict, whether it be symmetrical, complementary, or parallel, such knowledge lets you better predict the possible course of your conflicts. Relational styles, just like individual styles, bring some predictability into conflicts. Conflicts destroy relationships only when no answers are available for productively doing conflict.

Conflict Rituals

Once parties are involved in a conflict, they sometimes express their conflict based on the ritualistic styles that develop. If a mother and daughter develop a relationship style of shouting at one another, and you ask them to describe their conflicts, they will probably detail how the yelling match goes. Conflicts are composed of the issues, styles, power, goals, strategies, and tactics used by the participants, but often the persons involved only see the individual styles as characterizing the conflicts. While regularity in relational styles is useful, it can be carried too far. If the pattern becomes a ritual—a preset pattern of interlocking behaviors—then the rigidity can work against successful management of the conflict. For instance, a father and his daughter have a ritual that goes like this. She comes home and is upset with his limitations on her freedom (she is fifteen going on twenty). He intends to be inflexible about the hours he has set for her to be home from social occasions (he is forty-four going on eighty). About every three weeks, the girl comes home, starts talking about not "having any friends," and starts crying. The father, each time this occurs, responds by saying, "Oh, let her cry, it will blow over like it always does." He characterizes the conflict as the emotional outbursts of a teenager, and she characterizes the conflicts as the inflexible position of her father. This conflict, in fact, can be seen from many directions (such as analyzing the power moves that each participant makes), but the ritual gets acted out in a similar fashion each time. And the father and daughter continue to build up hostility over time.

Rituals for doing conflict develop most strongly in on-going relationships where the participants want some sense of order (even if it is chaotic). If the parties perceive themselves as very interdependent—two coworkers who share in the profits of the other or two intimates who invest emotionally in the other person—then rituals will develop as guides for their on-going interaction. As a result of the typical relationship styles that develop over time, people tend to develop beliefs about the ways they conflict. For instance, new couples like to focus on the lack of overt hostility as a sign of relational health. The "Heavenly Twins" (Lederer and Jackson 1968) when asked, "How is the relationship going?" respond with, "Great! We haven't even had a fight yet." The Heavenly Twins settle on the ritual of avoidance and convince themselves that since there are no open disagreements, everything is fine. They undoubtedly have other ways of managing their conflicts, but cling to the "no conflict" ritual as evidence that things are fine.

Another common ritual, especially for intimates, is the game of "Uproar." In "Uproar," the parties get into frequent battles. The fighting may serve the function of avoiding intimacy (Berne 1964) such that every time intimacy is appropriate, like before bed, someone picks a fight over a trivial matter. Or, if the intimates have been successful in building intimacy by fighting productively (Bach and Wyden 1968), then the battle continues for positive outcomes. In either event, participants can characterize the nature of their relationship based on how they, as a unit, conduct conflict. Fighters are often heard to say such things as, "We fight a lot, and really love each other" or "It may seem that we are unkind to each other, but we both understand that underneath all this acrimony is a real commitment to work things out. We find that by sharing our disagreements openly, we are then free to love openly too."

One ritual common in work settings is the ritual of "Yes Sir" where the subordinates give in on every issue involved in a conflict. In a typical case, the boss wants the worker to change some accepted pattern for doing things. The real estate salesperson transferred from commercial to residential sales, the faculty member assigned to teach different classes, and the cashier directed to change procedures for counting money at the end of the shift are all examples. The ritual gets set as the person with higher power gives an order, and the subordinate says "yes sir" while being distressed about the change. As a result, the underlying goes underground with the hostility, and total cooperation is not forthcoming. The superior then gets to believe that the subordinates are poor workers and issues more orders to which they reply, "yes sir."

Relationship rituals for doing conflict take innumerable forms. Just as individual styles vary and cannot all be characterized by a few simple classifications, an exhausting list of relationship styles would not be exhaustive. There are as many potential relational styles as there are relationships. We suggest that persons experiencing conflict look at their rituals and ask if they are productive for the goals of the relationship, whether it be work, family, artistic and creative, or teacher-student.

Productive and Destructive Styles

Most relationship styles can be destructive or productive. In the case of the dictator father and distressed daughter, the style itself was not necessarily destructive nor constructive. She might have enjoyed the father's setting limits. The destruction to the relationship came in the lack of trust displayed by both. Many people look at destructive styles as those where the conflict is out in the open and the participants vent hostile feelings. However, a relationship characterized by the inability or unwillingness of participants to confront conflicts openly can be even more destructive of the parties involved.

In conclusion, we offer several guides for determining if the conflict rituals operating in relationships are productive or destructive.

1. Are the parties stuck in a conflict style that seems to continue regardless of their efforts to change it? Often, destructive conflict can be identified when the participants have a feeling of being "out of control" of the relationship. When both parties say that they want to improve the relationship, yet their individual styles interlock in such a way that they both end up being miserable and unhappy, then the relationship rituals are not working for them. When the ritual gest so ingrained that the parties cannot have the freedom to change it (and want to), then the conflicts are likely to not be productive.

2. Are personal goals accomplished in the conflicts? If one of the parties finds that her or his goals are rarely accomplished, perhaps the relationship has been frozen in ways that are not productive. If the secretary finds that every time her boss curses at her, she backs down and withdraws on the issue, then she loses her ability to influence those decisions. Perpetually feeling powerless and helpless is a sign that your relationship rituals are not productive for you.

3. Do you find yourself trying to injure or wanting to harm the other person? If you find that in important relationships you come away from conflicts with a desire to "get" the other person, such a feeling can be a clue that somehow the relationship rituals have not been productive. The original goals in most conflicts are not to injure the other person—those vengeful feelings arise from feeling blocked from accomplishing your initial goals. For instance, if the participant in a small group wants to "clobber the leader over the head to make him shut-up" that is a sign that the leader's talkativeness is blocking some important goals of the participant. It may be that the self-esteem of the participant is suffering because he wants to make more contributions to the group, and the leader preempts him. In any event, hostile feelings toward another are a sign that the rituals you have worked out for the relationship are not working for you.

The more nearly that relationships can operate to fulfill the goals of the parties involved, the more healthy they will be. Destructive conflicts can be pinpointed by observing the relational blockages and using their existence as a guide to the health of the relationship. Both individuals and relationships can be characterized as having styles—the characteristic modes that emerge during the doing of conflict.

Summary

A good reason for determining your individual and relationship styles in conflict situations is that if you come to realize that your behavior is *stylistic,* that it is learned instead of inherent (since people aren't born with conflict styles), then *it can change.* In the next chapter, we will discuss power in interpersonal relationships. Change in conflict styles is only a first step toward productive conflict. A recognition of the power structure is also crucial.

Bibliography

Alberti, Robert E., and Emmons, Michael L. *Your Perfect Right: A Guide to Assertive Behavior.* San Luis Obispo, Ca.: Impact Press, 1974.

Altman, Irwin, and Taylor, Dalmas A. *Social Penetration: The Development of Interpersonal Relationships.* New York: Holt, Rinehart and Winston, Inc., 1973.

Bach, George R. and Wyden, Peter. *The Intimate Enemy.* New York: Avon Books, 1968.

Bardwick, Judith M. *Psychology of Women: A Study of Biocultural Conflicts.* New York: Harper & Row, Publishers, 1971.

Berne, Eric. *Games People Play.* New York: Grove Press, 1964.

Blake, R. R., and Mouton, J. S. *The Managerial Grid.* Houston, Tx.: Gulf Publishing Company, 1964.

Borgatta, E. F., and Stimson, J. "Sex Differences in Interaction Characteristics." *Journal of Social Psychology* 60(1963):89-100.

Eakins, Barbara Westbrook, and Eakins R. Gene. *Female-Male Communication.* Boston: Houghton Mifflin Company, in press.

Ellis, Don, and Fisher, B. Aubrey. "Phases of Conflict in Small Group Development: A Markow Analysis." *Human Communication Research* 1(1975):(3) 195-212.

Glick, Bruce, and Gross, Steven. "Marital Interaction and Marital Conflict: A Critical Evaluation of Current Research Strategies." *Journal of Marriage and the Family* 317(1975):505-512.

Hall, Jay. "Conflict Management Survey: A Survey of One's Characteristic Reaction to and Handling of Conflicts Between Himself and Others." Conroe, Tx.: Teleometrics International, 1969.

Harre, R. "Some Remarks on 'Rule' as a Scientific Concept." In *Understanding Other Persons,* edited by Theodore Mischel. Oxford: Basil Blackwell, 1974.

———, and Secord, P. F. *The Explanation of Social Behaviour.* Totowa, N.J.: Littlefield, Adams & Company, 1973.

Hart, Roderick P., and Burks, Don M. "Rhetorical Sensitivity and Social Interaction." *Speech Monographs* 39(2)(1972) 75-91.

Jamieson, D., and Thomas, K. "Power and Conflict in the Student-Teacher Relationship." *Journal of Applied Behavioral Science* 10(3)(1974):321-336.

Kester, Judy. Report in *Parade Magazine,* 7 May 1972.

Kilmann, Ralph, and Thomas, Kenneth. "Interpersonal Conflict-Handling Behavior as Reflections of Jungian Personality Dimensions." *Psychological Reports* 37 (1975):971-980.

———. "Developing a Forced-Choice Measure of Conflict-Handling Behavior: The 'Mode' Instrument." *Educational and Psychological Measurement,* in press.

Lawrence, P. R., and Lorsch, J. W. "Differentiation and Integration in Complex Organization." *Administrative Science Quarterly,* 12(1967);1-47.

Lederer, W. J., and Jackson, Don D. *Mirages of Marriage.* New York: W. W. Norton & Company, Inc., 1968.

Raush, Harold; Barry, W. A.; Hertel, R. K.; and Swain, M. A. *Communication, Conflict and Marriage.* San Francisco: Jossey-Bass, Inc., Publishers, 1974.

Rogers, L. Edna, and Farace, Richard. "Analysis of Relational Communication in Dyads." *Human Communication Research* 1(3)(1975):222-239.

Ruble, T. L., and Thomas, Kenneth. "Support for a Two Dimensional Model of Conflict Behavior." *Organizational Behavior and Human Performance* 16(1976):143-155.

Schuetz, Janice E. "A Contingent Model of Argumentation Based on a Game Theory Paradigm." Unpublished dissertation, University of Colorado, 1975.

Strodtbeck, Fred, and Mann, Richard. "Sex Role Differentiation in Jury Deliberations." *Sociometry* 19(1956):3-11.

Tedeschi, James T.; Schlenker, Barry R.; and Bonoma, Thomas V. *Conflict, Power and Games.* Chicago: Aldine Publishing Company, 1973.

Thomas, Kenneth, and Kilmann, Ralph. "The Social Desirability Variable in Organizational Research," *Academy of Management Journal,* 41(1975):413-420.

————. "Some Properties of Existing Conflict Behavior Instruments." Human Systems Development Study Center Working Paper," #73-11, Graduate School of Management, UCLA, 1973.

————. *Thomas-Kilmann Conflict Mode Instrument.* Tuxedo, N.Y.: Xicom, Inc.

Valentine, Kristen, and Fisher, B. Aubrey. "An Interaction Analysis of Verbal Innovative Deviance in Small Groups." *Speech Monographs,* 41(1974):413-420.

Villard, Kenneth, and Whipple, Leland J. *Beginnings in Relational Communication.* New York: John Wiley & Sons, Inc., 1976.

Wilmot, William W. *Dyadic Communication: A Transactional Perspective.* Reading, Mass.: Addison-Wesley Publishing Co., Inc., 1975.

Zimmerman, Don H., and West, Candace. "Sex Roles, Interruptions and Silence in Conversation." In *Language and Sex: Difference and Dominance,* edited by Barrie Thorne and Nancy Henley. Rowley, Mass.: Newbury House, Publishers, 1975.

Power in
Interpersonal Conflict

3

Just as the fundamental concept in physics is energy, one of the fundamental concepts in conflict theory is power. In interpersonal conflict situations especially, the power structures in the conflict are at the heart of any analysis. In fact, Duke (1976) says that "the central core of what we call conflict theory is not conflict at all, but rather *power*." This chapter will examine the role that interpersonal power plays in conflict situations and will probe the ways that people achieve and maintain power in conflict situations.

The Prevalence of Power

A natural interest of human beings is to elicit responses from others. We all try to exert some form of communicative influence—to move another person to help us accomplish our goals. This influence can have as its primary goal either independent, individual goals or goals that are interdependent and relationally oriented. Influence and attempts at gaining more power in a conflict do not have to be seen as negative—power is necessary to move a conflict along to some kind of productive management. If people have no influence over each other, they cannot participate in conflict together, since their communication would have no impact on the situation. With no influence, persons are not in a conflict at all, but are simply in a mutual monologue. Influence, therefore, is necessary. We will discuss attempts to gain power that enhance either individual goals or relationship goals. Further, we will also discuss cases where power attempts are made that directly harm the relationship or hinder individual goals. Power is central to the study of conflict and can be used for productive or destructive ends, but it is always present.

The centrality of power to understanding conflict can be seen in the following example. A college student is trying to add a course after the normal registration period has closed. The professor is letting the student know that the course is full of students and, therefore, "closed."

Student: Hey, are you the teacher of that introductory class that meets at 9:00 every day?

Professor:	Yes. Are you trying to add it?
Student:	Yes. You see, I have to graduate at the end of the next semester and this is the only elective that fits my schedule. If I don't get to add this course, then I won't graduate. This registration system is really archaic—and doesn't even work well for seniors like me. Can I add your course? I really need it!
Professor:	I just don't see how I can help you. The class is full and there are no empty chairs in the room.
Student:	Well, I would be willing to stand in the back of the room or just sit on the floor. I promise that I won't disturb your lecture. If you will let me add the class I'll be like a little mouse who never causes any trouble.
Professor:	Well, maybe you could come to class tomorrow and we can see if anyone is going to drop the course, and then you could take that space.

Each of the participants in this conflict is attempting to exercise communicative influence or control (Miller and Steinberg 1975). It is impossible to communicate without making some attempt to either exert influence or deny that you are exerting influence. In fact, the attempt to exercise influence or control is seen by some as one of the basic human needs. Schutz (1966) postulates that all people need a sense of inclusion, affection, and control to be satisfied and growing in their relationships. The ability to meaningfully influence important events around you is necessary for a sense of well-being and personal effectiveness. When we speak of power as being central to the study of conflict, we do not mean that people are always sneaky and try to get power illegitimately. As we have discussed, the productive exercise of your personal power is crucial to your self-concept. Without some abilities in the power arena of interpersonal relationships, you would soon feel worthless as a person. As you read this chapter, we suggest that you use your sources of feedback (friends, memories, personal writing, family members) to gain understanding about your habitual choices about the use of power. Try to gain a "power profile" of your own behavior—the way you really choose to communicate, not just the way you might want to be seen. Sometimes there is a difference! Remember that just as one cannot not *communicate, one does not have the option of not* using power. We only have options about whether our use of potential power will be destructive or productive for ourselves and others with whom we are in relationship.

Many people mistakenly believe that only dominating behaviors are ones that show an exercise of power. Sometimes the most powerful thing to do is to submit, go weak, and exercise power in a roundabout way. One of the more dramatic cases of how assumed or feigned obedience can lead to the exercise of power is given by Bettleheim (1960). He reports the case in World War II of a woman prisoner, formerly a dancer, who, just about to enter the gas chamber, was ordered by the commanding SS officer to dance. She "complied," and as she danced, approached him, seized his gun, and shot him. A less dramatic example of supposed low power is the typical case of the army private. He has been ordered to do KP duty; the only way he has of exercising power in the situation (without going to the brig) is to do as sloppy a job as he can and still get away with it. Similarly, in many couples, the silent one looks as if he or she has a low power situation, but may well have more interpersonal influence than the person doing most of the talking. Usually, the person looking as if he or she has the most power in a situation really does not. If you analyze the power structure, you will often find that the persons with the most influence do not look, at first glance, as if they have much. The relationship has developed a kind of compensation, especially in intimate relationships, so that one person does not appear to hold all the power.

Haley (1959) explains that whenever persons communicate, they also intuitively move to define their relationships. Most messages, verbal and nonverbal, have both content and relationship elements—the relationship element containing a message of definition of the way the people are going to relate to each other. Consider the following dialogue.

Jean	**Charles**
I'm really tired. I don't know whether I'm going to be able to take a drive or not.	
	Well, let me know pretty soon, because I want to get out in the country, and if you are too tired I'll give Rick a call.
I wanted to go. It's just that I didn't know I was going to have so much studying.	
	That's O.K. I wouldn't want you to go if you don't feel like it. Just let me know.
I'll try to wake myself up. I'll fix a cup of coffee. Do you want some?	
	No thanks. I'm going to go outside and get some sun.

In this dialogue, Jean's messages focus on the attempt to gain more influence over Charles' behavior and feelings. His statements primarily underscore that he is more interested in going driving than going driving *with Jean* (relational message), and that Jean's decision does not make much difference to him. Jean, intuitively realizing her low power situation, suggests a different joint activity (drinking a cup of coffee). Charles reasserts his high power position by turning her down. Of course these roles may well be temporary, but in this one bit of dialogue, Charles emerges as the person with the most power, since he allows Jean to have little influence on him. Messages always involve many complex meanings. One of their functions in any relationship is to juggle interpersonal influence.

Many of us have been subtly taught that power is negative with such phrases as "power corrupts." Therefore, we sometimes develop ways to convince ourselves and others that no control is being exercised. Haley (1959) lists the four most common attempts to *deny* exercising control. The person can (1) deny that *he or she* was responsible for communicating something; (2) deny that something *was* communicated; (3) deny that it was communicated *to the other person;* or (4) *deny the context* in which it was communicated. The person can deny that he or she is doing the communicating by claiming insanity, drug addiction, or that some outside force is controlling the communication. To say that you are not responsible for your communication (if others accept your definition) lets you exercise control while denying that you are. In its severe forms, this kind of communication episode creates double binds—the communication of two conflicting messages, paradoxical in that if one is followed, the other message automatically cannot be. Additionally, the person creating the double bind covers up the paradoxical nature of the message (Bateson 1972). For instance, the statement, "It's OK for you to take charge," can become a double bind if the person ostensibly giving away the power denies that power is actually kept securely in hand.

The simplest way to deny exercising control in a relationship is to say, "I did not say that," or to claim temporary amnesia. If the other party in the conflict will accept your definition of no responsibility, then you cannot be criticized for things that happen as a result of your message. Forms for denying that a message was produced are to speak in general terms or say that you are merely talking to yourself. For example, if a person is at home and a salesman rings the doorbell, the scenario might go like this.

Salesman: Hello, I'd like to take this opportun . . . .

Person: Oh, Yuk. Salespeople just ring my doorbell day and night. I wish people would leave me alone. All I get all day long is hassle, hassle, hassle. The entire world is into bugging me these days.

Salesman: I'm sorry, I . . . .

Person: Oh, I'm not talking about you. It's just that everyone bugs me day in and day out. I get no peace of mind. I wish the world would calm down and leave me alone.

Salesman: Maybe I can see you another time. I'm sorry I bothered you. . . .

The person who was bothered is exercising considerable control in the communication transaction, and also denying it by pretending that the remarks are not meant for that particular salesman. Another common way of denying that the comments were addressed to the other person is to claim that you were "just thinking out loud" and did not mean to imply anything toward the other person. For instance, a boss might say, muttering under his breath, "If I could count on people . . ." Then when a subordinate asks what is wrong, the boss could say, "What? Oh nothing—just a hard day."

The last way to deny communication control attempts is to deny that what has been said has been said *in this situation.* Saying, "I'm used to being treated unfairly by others; I probably always will be," denies the clear implication that the person present now is acting in a demeaning manner. All of the above examples are ways that people can deny exercising power in a relationship when in fact they really are. Whenever you communicate with another, what you say and do does exercise some communicative control by either going along with someone else's definition, struggling with them over the definition, or supplying it all yourself. Power exists in all interpersonal conflicts. Even when you would rather be seen as a person who does not exert power, you are exercising influence on *how the conflict relationship is going to be defined.*

A Relational View of Power

When people speak of power, they commonly act as if it is an attribute that people carry with them. For example, if you say, "Lynn is a powerful person," it sounds as if Lynn has some little package of power that she carries with her. But all power in interpersonal relations is a property of the social relationship rather than a quality of the individual. Lynn, for example, has power over her friends because she has resources that they value— when she asks people to do favors for her they usually do. But, if they did not value the things she had to offer (friendship, warmth, prestige, or other resources) then she would have no power over them. The boss, president, captain, or professor is given valued resources and "power" over others by a socially defined relationship, which only formalizes the bases upon which power attempts can be made.

Our orientation then, is that power is not some individualistic "thing" that people have, but is a product of the social relationship (Rogers 1974; Harsanyi 1962, Deutsch 1958; Dahl, 1957; Solomon 1960). Deutsch (1973, p. 15) states the case well:

> Power is a relational concept; it does not reside in the individual but rather in the relationship of the person to his environment. Thus, the power of an agent in a given situation is determined by the characteristics of the situation.

Rather than residing in people, "power is always interpersonal" (May 1972, p. 23). It is a product of the relationship between the parties involved. In the strictest sense, power is *given* from one party to another in a conflict.

We noted in Chapter 1 that parties to a conflict are interdependent and that they affect one another's outcomes. The following elements comprise our view of how power operates in interpersonal conflicts.

1. Parties are interdependent.

2. Parties have resources that another is dependent upon to reach their goals.

3. The ability to influence the goal attainment of the other is the *power* you have over him or her.

4. Each person in a conflict has some degree of power. Power is always a relative judgment:
    a. One party may have more power *compared to* the other party's power, and
    b. Power bases can shift during the course of conflict.

5. Persons in conflicts can make choices that define power either equally or unequally. Higher power persons can choose to share power by changing the structure of the power relationship.

6. Using power productively to achieve *both* individual and relational goals is a skill that can be learned. Most conflicts are not so rigidly structured that they cannot be changed. If one party insists that the power structure *cannot,* by definition, be changed, then that person is gaining something (whether that person has high or low power) from the present structure.

A precise analysis of the degree of power that parties can gain has been explored by Emerson (1962). He also saw power in relational terms and tried to specify why the amount of power one person has is directly tied to the nature of the relationship. In terms of two people, *A* and *B,* person *A* has power over B to the extent that B is dependent on A for goal attainment. Likewise, person B has power over person A to the extent that A is dependent on B. A simple formula expresses it like this:

$$P_{AB} = D_{BA}$$
(the power of A over B is equal to the dependence that B has on A), and
$$P_{BA} = D_{AB}$$
(the power of B over A is equal to the dependence that A has on B)

To illustrate this point, return to the example of the college student who is trying to add the course from the professor. To determine the power that the professor has over the student, we need to know: (1) What is the student's goal? (to add the class), and (2) How dependent is he on the professor to get the class? (very). To determine the power that the student has over the professor, we ask the same questions: (1) What is the professor's goal? (to have a full class and to appear to be "reasonable") and (2) How dependent is the professor on the student to accomplish goals? (slightly). Therefore, in this case, the professor has more power than the student does because the student is more dependent on the professor than the professor is on the student. Note, however, that *both* the professor and the student have some power, and the professor is more powerful only because she can mediate the goals that the student wants to achieve. If power is the ability to influence the other person's goal achievements, then both have power, although the professor has more *in that situation*.

One further refinement is necessary. You are dependent upon the other person to the degree of (1) importance of your goals that the other person can influence and (2) availability of other avenues for you to accomplish your goals. As Emerson states, "The dependence of Actor B upon Actor A is directly proportional to B's motivational investment in goals mediated by A, and inversely proportional to the availability of those goals to B outside of the A-B relation" (Emerson 1962, p. 31). In the case of the college student and the professor, the professor is less dependent on the student because there are other students available to fill the seats in her class and provide feedback to her.

You may have noticed that people have an intuitive understanding of how their dependence on another gives the other power over them. If, for example, a person gets involved in a conflict and is continually frustrated by the other's ability to control the resources (for example, your boss will not give you a raise), then one way to reduce the boss's power over you is to alter your goals. If after a few years in a new job a person is not valued by an organization and is not rewarded, a change of goals is likely. The disenchanted employee might remark, "It is not important to me what they pay me for this job. I'll just do the minimal amount of work and spend all my creative energy at my hobbies.'' By altering the importance of the goal, you reduce the power the other has over you. And the often-heard remark, ''There are other fish in the sea,'' when a person has been dropped in a love affair is just another way of saying that you have alternative sources for accomplishing your goals. (Or at least you hope you do, and want other people to think you do!)

We have power over people and they over us because our social relationship means that we are interdependent—we influence one another's ability to attain goals. Furthermore, the degree of power is a function of the comparison of dependence the two parties have on one another, and the degree of dependence is a product of how invested you are in the goals the other can mediate and how many other avenues are available for the attainment of those goals.

Bases of Power

The bases of power in each relationship depend, as we have noted, on what each person values and the nature of the relationship. In an attempt to specify the different types of power sources, French and Raven (1960) have listed five types of power.

Reward power occurs when person *B* is in a position to control the rewards that *A* will attain. Common examples are babies smiling at parents, supervisors determining salaries, and parents giving allowances to children for chores accomplished. Person *B* has something of value that person *A* wants. *Coercive* power is the reverse of reward power. *B* has some form of punishment that can be leveled against *A* if *A* does not do what *B* wants. In the simplest case, the parent's statement, ''Get to bed right now or I will spank you,'' is an exercise of coercive power. *Legitimate* power bases stem from *B*'s position in the social system that person *A* accepts. For example, if person *A* accepts the notion that the president of the social club has the right to initiate actions for the group, then the president has been given legitimate power. People often try to legitimize power by pointing out how they have been given power by someone higher. *Referent* power arises when person *A* identifies strongly with person *B*. For example, if your hero is a certain baseball star or movie personality, then that person has power to exercise influence on you because of your desire to appear like that person. Parents often use this form of power to motivate their children by saying, ''Big girls know how to dress themselves'' or ''If you want to grow up to be like Mom (or Dad) then eat your spinach.'' Finally, *expert* power occurs because person *A* has some special knowledge or expertise that is useful to others. The worker who is the only one who can operate the boiler at a large lumbermill has power because his expertise is badly needed. The medical doctor who has studied in order to understand diseases exercises power by the nature of the information offered. Expert power, just like the other types, is often used in concert with some other types. For instance, when a parent is trying to get a child to go to bed, he or she may call on any number of bases in order to attain set goals. The parent may claim to "know what is good for you because I've read books about the amount of sleep kids need" (expert power) while also exhorting the child to be like the parents (referent power). Also, the parent may conclude that even if the child does not want to go to bed, the parents are still boss (legitimate power and coercive power).

While these five bases of power are a good starting point, they are not a very complete description of the sources of power available in interpersonal conflicts. We suggest the addition of the word *currencies* to express the sources of power that people have in conflicts. Currencies are the resources that you have to "spend" in conflicts because they are valued by other people. When others value your currencies and see you as the avenue to attaining them, then you can exercise some degree of interpersonal power. Some of the major currencies that people can call upon during a conflict are: (1) intimacy currencies; (2) currencies arising out of interpersonal linkages; (3) currencies arising from position or status; and (4) currencies that are economic in nature.

You have *intimacy currencies* when you can offer warmth, affection, understanding, sexuality, or positive regard for others (or all of these). For example, if a father provides warmth and understanding to his teenage daughter who is going through a difficult time at school, his support is a currency for him in that relationship. Often, our culture trains us to develop some currencies at the expense of others. In many areas of contemporary American culture, for instance, women are seen as providing more warmth and affection than are men (Johnson 1976). If the mother in a family takes on the role of soothing hurt feelings, providing empathy and understanding to the children when they are buffeted by the world, and generally being the one who handles the relational needs of others, then her specialization at the task will sometimes make it difficult for others to trade on the same currency. We are all capable of using widely divergent currencies, but because of training and choice, we often develop one over the other. Intimacy currencies exist in both formal or informal relationships. Even in highly structured situations such as a very impersonal work environment, when the boss says "good job," the phrase is a form of intimacy. The distance between the people is lessened with the phrase. When a person who uses intimacy currencies a lot chooses to "trade" on them during a difficult conflict, he or she can either activate the currency by providing more warmth or by withdrawing it from others. Both offering and withdrawing warmth activate it as a currency in the relationship. When someone is "in a bad mood," they may be in a conflict and drawing on their intimacy currencies.

The second major type of currencies are those that revolve around *interpersonal linkages*. They are really an extended form of intimacy currencies that depend on your network of friends and supporters. People often obtain power based on whom they know and with whom they associate. For instance, if you have a good friend who has a mountain cabin that you can share with others, then you have attained some power (if your family wants to go to the cabin) because of your ability to obtain things through other people. It is interesting to see very young people trying to trade on their linkage currencies when they say such things as, "My Uncle Ben is a Park Ranger and he told me that. . ."

Interpersonal linkages help to attain power through coalition formation. Whenever you band together with another to gain some sense of strength (like two good friends might), then this coalition can be a form of power. The small boy who says, "You better not hit me, because if you do my older sister will beat you up," understands the potential value of coalitions. When others will come to our aid, our interpersonal power is usually strengthened. One of the most charming examples of an attempt to gain more power by coalition formation occurred with Jason, a four-year-old boy. He invented a friendly ghost, Karsha, who would come and help him in times of difficulty. After one particularly trying day with his younger sister (who was two years old), Jason recited to his father the virtues of Karsha. Karsha was "bigger than a mountain, a giant, who comes in the mornings and kills spiders with his hands. Karsha also makes electricity and has long hair. And, Karsha is mean to babies that bite little boys." In the Senoi culture, the value of coalitions to gain power is so recognized that children are taught to call upon friends and others in their dreams to help them overcome any threatening monsters that occur in the dreams (Garfield 1974).

One of the more unique examples of the use of interpersonal linkages occurred when a friend of ours was moving away from a town. She went to considerable effort to arrange it so her best friends all came to know one another and welcomed another friend to "the group" when he subsequently moved into town. As a result, she left town with an intact group composed of all her former associates who meet regularly. What better way to continue one's currency use after being gone?

Position and *status* are also common currencies. If you are in a position of leadership and can command resources, then that is likely to give you power. The President of the United States, regardless of whom he or she is, will always have some resources that will go along with the job. If you are in a leadership position, then you can help or block others in accomplishing their goals. Leadership and position, by its very nature, places one in a situation where others are dependent upon you—thus bringing a ready-made power relationship with it. Whatever the position you are in, secretary, leader, boss, or just being the figurehead, you will be in some position to control resources that others desire. For instance, if you are the president of a local environmental group, you will have some power because of the energy you expend trying to help the group accomplish its goals.

The final category of currencies are *economic* in nature. The economic currencies are control of money, gifts, and the like. Even the Master of Ceremonies of a game show on television assumes some power by being an intermediary between the contestants and some desired gifts. We know one fellow who tries very hard to be close and supportive with those around him and manifests it only in one way—to buy his friends things. He is trading on economic currencies in order to obtain the intimacy currencies from others. And, of course, whenever you give a gift to someone, you are exercising a currency of economics as well as intimacy and other kinds of messages. It is no surprise that people who give gifts to one another usually try to work out an agreement, probably implicitly, about the amount of money that can be spent to keep the power equal. If an inordinate amount of money is spent by one person, then typically the other person feels somewhat indebted. As Blau (1967, p. 108) says, "A person who gives others valuable gifts or renders them important services makes a claim for superior status by obligating them to himself." If people value your currencies, whether they are primarily economic, status, interpersonal linkages, or intimacy, you will have a basis of power.

Assessing Power

In order to productively engage in conflict, it is useful to know what your power is in that relationship. For instance, before you ask your boss for a raise, it is useful for you to be able to identify the power bases that you have available to accomplish your goals. Unfortunately, there is no magic formula available that you or anyone else can use to assess the relative amounts of power that you and the other conflict party have. Power is complex, with each party varying in sources of power and readiness to utilize the power. However, the following questions are a starting point in identifying the power you have in relation to the other party in a conflict.

1. *Who appears to be the most powerful?*
   The party who appears to run the show in a relationship often does not. The designated leader, for example, may not have as

much power as a member of the group who has more valuable currencies to offer. Similarly, in a marriage it may appear that the boisterous husband has more power, yet he is totally dependent upon his wife to support him emotionally so he can be gruff. Our analysis of power suggests that you observe the actual interactions between the conflicting parties and draw your conclusions based on the communicative patterns that emerge.

2. *Who accommodates whom the most?*

Many times, for instance, the "boss" is the servant. Everyone is familiar with the "nice guy" who always has a shoulder to cry on and "wouldn't hurt a fly." Often that person is imprisoned in the "myth of niceness" and really has little power to move, change, direct, confront, or displease associates for fear of losing the image of the "nice" boss (Bach and Goldberg 1974). If you observe who apologizes, smoothes things over, anticipates demands of the other person, and avoids doing anything to upset the other, that person is usually operating from a lower power position. The person may be accommodating because of discomfort with overtly exercising power. But for whatever reason, to continually adjust your own goals to the other without asking for some adjustment in return, indicates a lower power position.

3. *What are the patterns of power in the relationship?*

Instead of focusing on individual moves such as threats, it is more helpful to examine the relational patterns. You can focus on "interacts" rather than "acts" in a relationship (Fisher and Hawes 1971). From the interact perspective, you would ask what action by Jane is followed by what escalation or deescalation by Jack. How predictable is that pattern? Are there untested patterns of power in a relationship? Many times persons act as if no change were possible in the patterning of power. The observer can point out change possibilities by listening for key statements such as, "That's just the way it is" or "Oh, they would never do that—they wouldn't stand for it." The person may be saying, "I have not tested this out, and I'm not sure I want to, because it may be threatening to me." When marriage partners, for instance, assume no change is possible in relationships, that assumption may be saying more about the need of the one (usually low power party) not to challenge mutually established patterns. You can look at your own conflicts, and if you are always accepting the options that the other structures, you have less power. For instance, if your loved one says, "If you loved me you wouldn't leave me on the weekend," and you then accept that the only options are (1) to stay home and be "loving" or (2) to leave, then the other has more power. Whoever sets the pattern exercises more power.

4. *Who can best predict changes in the power relationship?*

One of the assumptions of Haley (1963) and others is that persons are not generally aware of the power they have. One cannot *not* use power, although one may consciously limit that power; but typically persons are relatively unaware of their sources of power and the sources of power of others. However, if one of the parties is demonstrably more aware of the power relationship than the other, such knowledge can be used as a currency. For instance, the one who is more relationally aware can better predict the behavior of the other in a conflict. Such relational knowledge, while not always openly used as a currency, can be a source of power.

5. *What decisions are a function of a complex ritualized pseudopower relationship?*

Many times decisions have been made far in advance, and the individual episodes are more an affirmation of the ritual nature of the relationship than a genuine exercise in decision-making. Korda (1975) suggests that politeness is often a mask for the reality that a decision has already been made, and emotions are not being engaged for the present encounter. Couples engage in complex decision-making processes whose outcomes can often be fairly accurately charted by observers ahead of time based on the unchallenged patterns. Whoever gains the most from the ritualized pattern has more power. For instance, if the ritual of decision-making ("the President makes all those decisions") precludes others from fully participating, the ritual reinforces an unequal power relationship. The entire process of institutionalized norms for making decisions merely reinforces existing power discrepancies. If one of two intimates always makes the financial decisions, then, at least in that area, the power balance becomes unequal and rigid.

6. *Who is invested in maintaining the power relationship at its present status, and why?*

Postman and Weingartner (1969) suggest that for any system, including interpersonal systems, the question should be asked, "Who is being protected by this system? Whom does it benefit?

Who would benefit from a change?'' Many times persons who say
they are doing things for others are invested in protecting their
own power and self-esteem by promoting no change in the relationship. If one of the parties uses a patronizing tone and the pro-
tective stance, then that party is probably being protected by the
present relationship.

7. *Where are the possibilities for change in the power structure?*

Where are the possibilities for bargaining? Has the close assess-
ment of power revealed an area of mutual interdependence previously unknown to the participants or the observer? Or have the
parties revealed that they are dissatisfied with things as they now
stand? If these ''change areas'' can be pinpointed, then the next
step, instituting the change in the power structure, can be made
more potentially productive and win-win. If you are one of the
parties in a conflict and you do not feel that any change is possible, it may be a sign that your currencies are not valued.

8. *Who exercises the right to label the conflict?*

The way a communication episode is labeled can greatly affect
its course. If one of the parties takes the prerogative of labeling
the communication—''There you go, trying to fight again''—then
the label can be used as a power tactic. If one of the rules of the
relationship is that conflict is to be ignored (such as is the case in
many areas—from business relationships to intimate ones), then to
label someone else's behavior as ''conflict'' or ''aggressive'' is a
tactic used to decrease the power of the other. High power persons can invoke two parallel strategies here. First, they can label
the behavior as ''conflict'' and draw the implication that ''conflict'' is bad (in other words, you may accomplish some of your
goals at their expense). Or, they may label your behavior as not a
''conflict'' and ignore your claims to be noticed. For instance,
during the Wounded Knee conflict in 1973, the government consistently downplayed the importance of the conflict while the AIM
Indians tried to continually escalate through the use of a counter-
balancing (Frost 1974). When the person in power says, ''We have
no conflict here,'' they may be saying, ''I have high power in this
situation and I want you to go away and pretend that you are not
upset and that you were wrong for trying to stir things up.''

9. *Who demonstrates the least interest?*

If one of the parties is in a position to be less interested in
maintaining the relationship, that position can be a source of

power for them. We noted earlier that a person's dependence on the goals mediated by the other determines the level of power that can be exercised. If one of the parties reduces his or her dependence on the other by attaining goals elsewhere, such as in outside love relationships, the power of the other is lessened. Waller and Hill (1951) noted that the "principle of least interest" means that the party who is less invested in the relationship for goal satisfaction has superior power over the other.

These questions can be used as indices of the nature of the power relationship between parties. Quite clearly, all parties have some degree of power over the others if they are in a conflict. But a careful evaluation of power makes it possible to plan change more effectively than simply assuming that power is obvious.

Sharing Power

Our overriding assumption in this chapter has been that it is useful to examine the nature of power, explore its bases, and understand one's own power compared to other parties' power. For some people, it is very disturbing to talk in open terms about exercising power in interpersonal conflicts. They are taught to believe that such things are best "left alone" and that interpersonal success is achieved by not taking such a "harsh" view of relationships. Many such people have been socialized to not seek power in open ways (Duke 1976). Commonly, such beliefs are followed by statements that if "everyone would be nice there would be no conflict." Carried to an extreme, it may be more satisfactory for such a person to consistently be in a low power position rather than to have to struggle for more impact in a given relationship. For some, having an unsatisfactory role is preferable because at least there is comfort in knowing what the role is.

Conflict participants have a better opportunity of making a long-range relationship work if there is some equity in the power relationship. The unrestrained use of raw power will often cycle back to damage the one who wields it. The autocratic father, the uncompromising boss, and the tyrannical teacher will all face some long-range negative consequences from hoarding their power. The "effective use of power involves restraint in its use in order that it can be retained . . ." (Duke 1976). Furthermore, if low power persons are continually subjected to harsh treatment or no goal attainment, they will likely produce some organized resistance to the other. In fact, as Bach and Wyden (1968) and May (1972) have noted, it is the powerless who become the most violent. When one reaches a stage that "nothing matters" (you can't attain your goals through accepted means), that is when violence is spawned. It is the person who feels powerless who turns to the last resort—aggression and violence. Paradoxically, it isn't power, but powerlessness, that corrupts (May 1972). Too much losing doesn't build character; it builds frustration and aggression.

A very typical example of how perceived unequal power builds aggression is the case of students and teachers. In one study when students were asked what options they considered using to resolve conflicts they had with more powerful teachers, they replied with items such as "use a .357 Magnum," "blow up his mailbox," "sabotage him," and "beat him up" (Wilmot 1976). Other studies dealing with teachers and students have demonstrated that if the teacher uses strong power over the student, then both the teacher and student disintegrate into coercive strategies to deal with one another (Jamison and Thomas 1974; Raven and Kruglanski 1968).

It is desirable in interpersonal relationships that will be ongoing, for a "balance of situational power" be used in the interpersonal peacemaking (Walton 1969). And, it has been shown that groups have a better chance of negotiating and adjudicating conflict when the participants have relatively equal power (Chesler and Lohman 1971). One of the crucial questions becomes, then, how does a low power person gain more power so the conflict can be conducted on a more productive basis? Chapter 6 on "Strategies and Tactics" will explore specific techniques that can be used by low power parties to increase their comparative power base. But, in general, low power parties can increase their power by decreasing their dependence on the other. Obviously, as noted earlier, you can reduce the importance of the goal that the other mediates, find other ways to accomplish the goal by developing new options, or you can retain your dependence in a given area and increase the other party's dependence in other areas.

Summary

Power is part and parcel of conflict. It lies at the heart of the choices that parties make during a conflict. It is relational in nature and arises because parties are interdependent and can mediate the goal attainments of one another. The overt recognition of power relations can open up new options for conflict behaviors.

Bibliography

Bach, George R., and Goldberg, Herb. *Creative Aggression: The Art of Assertive Living,* New York: Doubleday, 1974.

————, and Wyden, Peter. *The Intimate Enemy.* New York: Avon Books, 1968.

Bateson, Gregory. *Steps to an Ecology of the Mind.* New York: Ballantine Books, Inc., 1972.

Bettelheim, B. *The Informed Heart.* New York: The Free Press, 1960.

Blau, Peter M. *Exchange and Power in Social Life.* New York: John Wiley & Sons, 1964.

Chesler, M. A., and Lohman, J. E. "Changing Schools Through Student Advocacy." In *Organization Development in Schools,* edited by R. Schmuck and M. Miles, pp. 185-212. Palo Alto, Calif.: National Press Books, 1971.

Dahl, R. A. "The Concept of Power." *Behavioral Science* 2(1957):201-215.

Deutsch, Morton. "Trust and Suspicion." *Journal of Conflict Resolution* 2(1958):265-279.

Duke, James T. *Conflict and Power in Social Life.* Provo, Utah: Bringham Young University Press, 1976.

Emerson, R. M. "Power-Dependence Relations." *American Sociological Review* 27(1962):31-41.

Fisher, B. A., and Hawes, L. C. "An Interact System Model: Generating a Grounded Theory of Small Groups." *Quarterly Journal of Speech* 57(1971):444-453.

French, R. P., amd Raven, B. "The Bases of Social Power." In *Group Dynamics,* edited by Darwin Cartwright and Alvin Zander, pp. 601-623. New York: Harper & Row, Publishers, 1960.

Frost, Joyce Hocker. *The Implications of Conflict Theories for Rhetorical Criticism.* Unpublished dissertation, University of Texas, 1974.

Garfield, Patricia. *Creative Dreaming.* New York: Ballantine Books, Inc., 1974.

Haley, Jay. "An Interactional Description of Schizophrenia." *Psychiatry* 22(1959):321-332.

————. *The Power Tactics of Jesus Christ and Other Essays.* New York: Avon Books, 1969.

————. *Strategies of Psychotherapy.* New York: Grune and Stratton, 1963.

Harsanyi, John C. "Measurement of Social Power, Opportunity Costs, and the Theory of Two-Person Bargaining Games." *Behavioral Science* 7(1962):67-80.

————. "Measurement of Social Power in n-Person Reciprocal Power Situations." *Behavioral Science* 7(1962):81-90.

Jamieson, David W., and Thomas, Kenneth W. "Power and Conflict in the Student-Teacher Relationship." *Journal of Applied Behavioral Science* 10(1974):321-333.

Johnson, Paula. "Women and Power: Toward a Theory of Effectiveness." *Journal of Social Issues* 32(1976):99-110.

Korda, Michael. *Power! How to Get it, How to Use it!* New York: Random House, 1975.

May, Rollo. *Power and Innocence.* New York: Norton, 1972.

Miller, Gerald R., and Steinberg, Mark. *Between People: A New Analysis of Interpersonal Communication.* Chicago: Science Research Assoc., 1975.

Postman, Neil, and Weingartner, Charles. *Teaching as a Subversive Activity.* New York: Dell Publishing Company, 1969.

Raven, Bertram H., and Kruglanski, Arie W. "Conflict and Power," In *The Structure of Conflict* edited by Paul A. Swingle. New York: Academic Press, 1970.

Rogers, Mary F. "Instrumental and Infra-Resources: The Bases of Power." *American Journal of Sociology* 79(1974):1418-1433.

Schutz, William C. *The Interpersonal Underworld.* Palo Alto, Calif.: Science and Behavior Books, 1966.

Solomon, L. "The Influence of Some Types of Power Relationships and Game Strategies Upon the Development of Interpersonal Trust." *Journal of Abnormal and Social Psychology* 61(1960):223-230.

Waller, Willard & Hill, Reuben. *The Family.* New York: Dryden Press, 1951.

Walton, Richard E. *Interpersonal Peacemaking: Confrontations and Third-Party Consultation.* Reading, Mass.: Addison-Wesley Publishing Co., Inc., 1969.

Wilmot, William W. "The Influence of Personal Conflict Styles of Teachers on Student Attitudes Toward Conflict." Paper presented to Instructional Communication Division, International Communication Association Convention, Portland, Oregon, April 15, 1976.

Winter, David G. *The Power Motive.* New York: The Free Press, 1973.

The Structure
of Conflict

4

Whenever two parties are involved in a communication transaction, the actions of one influence the choices of the other. In a conflict situation, this interdependence of the parties is easily seen. If Jane and Gary are in a conflict over whether to go to a concert, and Gary says, "Either we attend the concert or we don't go out anymore," then his action has set some boundaries on Jane's responses. She can either go, not go, or she can attempt to define the choices differently. She may, for example, ask Gary why he feels so strongly about the concert, then use that information to open up more options for both of them. Whichever option she selects, the *choices of each party influence the available choices of the other.* The choices of the parties, coupled with the rewards that follow given choices, comprise the *structure* of the conflict. When Gary tried to limit Jane to two options, he was attempting to impose his structure on the conflict. Likewise, Jane's response was an attempt to alter the structure by adding more options.

One of the key elements to more fully understanding conflict is a recognition that each conflict has a structure. The choices, perceptions, and payoffs of the parties are what constitute the structure in each conflict. For example, if a person believes that the world is a competitive, win-lose place, then these beliefs will be reflected in the structure of choices that person gives to others. Within a given situation, the actions of both parties influence the structure.

In this chapter we will present the following ideas:

1. The structure of a conflict is composed of (a) the choices available to the parties and (b) the rewards (payoffs) they receive from selecting a given choice.

2. Structure arises from the perceptions and actions of *both* parties—it is the joint product of the interaction of the parties.

3. Each choice a party makes either reinforces the existing structure or is an attempt to redefine the structure.

To more fully explain the central role of structure in conflicts, two related types of "games" will be examined in detail. First, experimental game theory will be discussed as an introduction to a system in which structure is clearly specified. Second, "real life," or nonlaboratory, games, in which parties attempt to impose structure on a relationship will be viewed. Within these game situations, the effects of one party imposing and the other accepting a certain structure are apparent.

Game Theory Fundamentals

Basic Assumptions and Terms

We have all participated in games of one sort or another. Playing baseball, bowling, or even losing money in pinball machines are activities involving people in games of skill. Besides games of skill, there are (as every Las Vegas fanatic knows) games of chance. Playing the odds on horses or "Russian Roulette" with a loaded pistol are both variations on the same theme of chance. Some of the most fascinating games, however, are games of *strategy*.[1] In ticktacktoe, the strategies or choices are very simple. But in a game of chess, the strategies become extremely complex. Both are games of strategy because the *results of each player's moves are dependent on the other player's moves*. Game theory is exclusively concerned with games of strategy where the best course of action for a participant "depends on what he expects the other participant to do" (Schelling 1960, pp. 9-10). In all types of strategic games, your rewards for playing depend on how well you outwit your opponent (Rapoport 1960). Each strategy is a conditional choice, conditional upon the choices made by the other players (Rapoport 1970). In checkers, for instance, your decision to try and make a checker a "king" so it can move both directions on the board depends on your present standing in the game and your estimates of what your opponent is likely to do. Within the laboratory situation, participants are typically placed in strategic games where they vie for points with each move. As a result, the participants (called *actors* and *players* in game theory) follow well-defined interests—they try to maximize their gains.

Since we are primarily interested in interdependent conflict processes, the structure of laboratory games offers insights for those learning conflict management skills. Unlike informal conflicts, laboratory games have *overt* rules that specify whose move it is, what the choices are for each player, and what signifies the game's termination. In checkers, for example, the rules limit the players to one move at a time—first *A* moves, then *B*, then *A* again. Further, the players are limited to moving onto one square at a time unless they are jumping the opponent's pieces. Finally, the game is declared over when one player has won by capturing all the opponent's checkers.

---

1. Strategic games are based on the assumption that players make *rational* moves, that is, behavior based on a "conscious calculation of advantages, a calculation that is in turn based on an explicit and internally consistent value system" (Schelling 1960, p. 6).

In addition to performing a conscious calculation of possible strategies, a *rational* player is "one who maximizes his gains and minimizes his loses given the rules of the game and the alternatives open to other players" (Steinfatt and Miller 1974, p. 19). Of course, the assumption means that the players (1) know the possible outcomes of the game (for example, winning or losing in checkers), (2) understand the rules of the game, (3) make intentional choices as a result of the conscious calculation of advantages that go with different choices available (Frost 1974), and (4) are interested in the *payoff*. The payoff for most games of strategy such as checkers is simply winning or losing. Experimental game theory builds upon these assumptions and then examines the strategic decisions that participants make in order to maximize their gains (Shubik, et al. 1974).

The strategic games studied by game theory are not all the same. The two basic types are (1) constant-sum games and (2) nonconstant-sum games. In *constant-sum* games, the "interests of the players are diametrically opposed, for any payoff received by one necessarily reduces the payoff to the others" (Steinfatt and Miller 1974, p. 17). In checkers, chess, polo, baseball, canasta, and thousands of other games, one party wins while the other party loses. The games are called constant-sum because the sum of all wins and losses from each move are the same. If *A* and *B* are two persons playing table tennis, at the conclusion of each game, the winner gets one point, the loser nothing. It is labeled a constant-sum game because the algebraic sum of winnings is always one.[2]

Games in which the interests of the participants are only partially opposed are labeled nonconstant-sum games. An example of a nonconstant-sum game is the well-known Prisoner's Dilemma. The game centers on the following situation. Two criminal suspects have been captured by the police for a crime. The police separate them and instruct each that two choices exist: confess or remain silent. If only one prisoner confesses, he or she will be set free and given a reward while the other prisoner will receive a heavy sentence. If both confess, they will both go to jail with light sentences. And, if both remain silent the police will have no case, and they will both go free. Figure 2 represents the *payoff matrix* for each prisoner's choices.

Each prisoner is faced with a dilemma. If one confesses and the other does not, the first goes free. But if the first confesses and the other prisoner does too, they both go to jail. If one remains silent and so does the other

---

2. A special subcategory of constant-sum games is labeled zero-sum. In zero-sum games, if one person gains $+1$ and the other -1, for example, the sum of all wins and losses for each move is zero. All other constant-sum games where the sum of winnings and losings is not zero are called nonzero sum games. Technically, the terms constant-sum and nonconstant-sum refer to the payoffs for each move, not for the end result of the game (winning and losing).

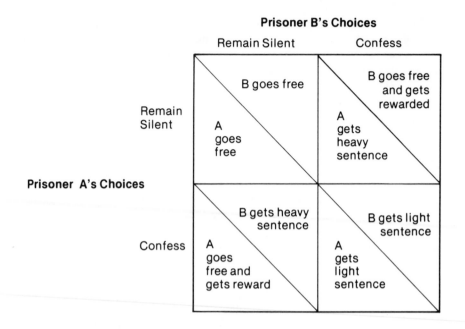

Figure 2. Prisoner's Dilemma payoff matrix.

one, then they both go free. But, if one remains silent trusting the other to do so too, the trusting prisoner will get a heavy sentence.

In experimental theory, the payoffs are always listed in numerical terms, so let's take Figure 2 and simply put numbers in to represent the payoffs.[3] The payoffs to the prisoners from their possible choices are as follows:

    2 = going free and getting a reward
    1 = going free
  − 1 = light sentence
  − 2 = heavy sentence

Figure 3 displays in numerical terms the situation in which the prisoners find themselves.

---

3. The terms "payoffs" and "utilities" have special meaning in game theory literature. While payoffs are the numbers the parties receive, utilities are the parties "subjective valuations" of payoffs (Schelling 1960, p. 287). While it may appear that a father is not acting rationally by letting his son win in a game between the two, his utilities for "losing"—being emotionally close to the boy, establishing rapport, etc.—far outweigh for him the "winning" of the game. Even though the designation between payoffs and utilities is crucial for game theoreticians, in this book, when in later chapters we refer to "payoffs" in relationships, we will be assuming the subjective valuations of the parties. In interpersonal situations the payoffs to the parties are the rewards they receive, which are determined by their "utilities," or personal valuing processes.

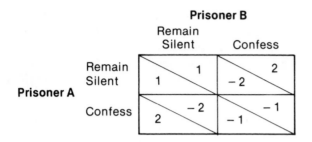

Figure 3. Prisoner's Dilemma numerical payoff matrix.

Notice that the numbers in Figure 3 correspond to the payoffs listed in Figure 2. The situation is identical, but the payoffs are listed numerically. The possible payoffs from the choices of players (or prisoners) *A* and *B* are:

Choices	Payoffs
A confesses	*A* gets − 1
B confesses	*B* gets − 1
A confesses	*A* gets + 2
B is silent	*B* gets − 2
A is silent	*A* gets − 2
B confesses	*B* gets + 2
A is silent	*A* gets + 1
B is silent	*B* gets + 1

This simplified example has equipped you to read the payoff matrix, which is similar to payoff matrices traditionally found in game theory studies. In this case, a nonconstant-sum game was used as an example. Obviously, nonconstant- and constant-sum games of these varieties are games of strategy—payoffs to the participants are a joint product of both parties' choices.

Most conflict situations, like the prisoner's dilemma, reflect *mixed-motive* situations. The situation is mixed because each participant is in an ambivalent relationship with the other. The relationship is a mixture of "mutual dependence and conflict, of partnership and competition" (Schelling 1960, p. 89). As a result, the strategies adopted by the participants reflect their interdependence on the other participant's choice. These games, therefore, have value for persons studying *relational* conflict. Each

---

4. This payoff schedule appears at first glance to differ from the classic one reiterated by Rapport (1967). It is, however, identical in form. It is the same matrix condition but the choices are simply inverted.

prisoner in the Prisoner's Dilemma is in a quandry because of uncertainty about the partner's choices. Furthermore, if you play the Prisoner's Dilemma game for a number of trials, your choices may change depending on what your partner chooses. In such a case, you are adopting a *mixed strategy.* Your choices are dependent upon the previous choices made in the game by your continuing guesses about the choices the other participant will be likely to select.

In the typical experimental game, the parties make many moves. After each move, the players receive points, and the game proceeds to the next move. After a series of rounds, the cumulative points for the players are scored, and the points are compared.

Structure of Games

The structure of a game is composed of (1) the number of choices for players and (2) the payoffs that the participants will receive for their choices, which are made in a framework of specified rules. For example, you already saw the basic structure of the Prisoner's Dilemma in Figure 2. The payoffs can be increased, yet the structure remains the same because the number of choices and comparisons between choices are basically the same. Figure 4 illustrates six different payoff schedules for the Prisoner's Dilemma game.

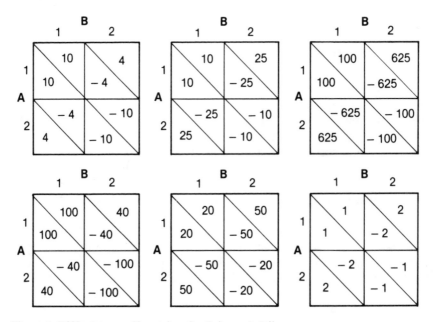

Figure 4. Different payoff matrices for Prisoner's Dilemma.

Note that the basic structure is similar in all the cases. Regardless which payoff matrix one is involved with in a particular game, the underlying dilemma is basically the same: should the participants try to "go for broke" and choose #1 taking the chance that the other will too? Or, should a participant select #2 so both he or she and the other party will get positive points, risking that the other will not try for choice #1 and get an early lead in points?

A change in the *structure of a game* can alter the conflict that the parties are in. The matrix for "Chicken," while using the same number of choices as Prisoner's Dilemma, reflects a very different type of conflict because of a change in payoffs resulting from the choices. The high school variety of Chicken, reminiscent of the 1950s, is two teenagers driving their cars at high speed directly at one another. The driver who swerves to avoid a head-on collision is "Chicken" and loses the contest. A sample payoff matrix for Chicken is in Figure 5.

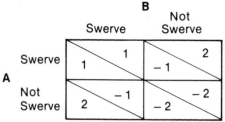

Figure 5. Payoff matrix for Chicken.

If each participant swerves at the last minute, neither has lost more face than the other, both live, and each gets minimal points. But if only one player "chickens out" and the other does not, the "chicken" gets a − 1 and the "nonchicken" gets + 2. Finally, if no one swerves, they will both be maimed or killed in the head-on crash, definitely a − 2 for each (at least)! The game of Chicken has parallels to the international scene (Swingle 1970). When nations structure their relations so that the only way they can threaten an opponent is to open themselves up to tremendous risk, they have set up a game of Chicken. A nation that responds to another "if you don't stop that, I'll set off a nuclear bomb that will destroy us all" is structuring the conflict in the international game similar to that in Chicken.[5]

One of the contributions of game theory to our interpersonal conflict study is that it provides a mechanism for understanding structure in other

---

5. A husband who says "If you look at another man, I'll leave you," or a professor who says "If you don't all have the assignment read, I'll give you a ten-page essay test" (which the professor then has to grade) are both situations like the Chicken game.

conflicts by identifying choices and their resultant payoff schedules. One can tell by looking at the choices and the payoff matrix of the game of Chicken for example, what the situation is for the participants.[6] The payoff matrices coupled with the rules for the game specify the relationship between the participants—especially in terms of cooperation and competition. And, *because the structure of the situation is isolated,* the terms basic to understanding the conflict are clearly stated. The complex process of conflict is specified in terms of elements capable of being studied. Game theory is not the same as conflict theory, but contributes to a wide study of conflict primarily because of the clarity of the structuring process.

Beyond Game Theory

Communication

The most serious limitation of game theory is that it often underrates the importance of communication in conflict.[7] One of the problems is that communication between participants is seen as incidental to their choices in a game. In a game you have (1) behavioral moves and (2) talk—the two are taken to be separate. But in an interpersonal conflict outside a game experiment, the talk often constitutes the most important moves. If two men are in a bar and begin hurling insults at one another, their talk serves to (1) structure the payoff matrices and (2) produce payoffs. If man *A*, in front of his friends, can call man *B* a coward, he will receive payoffs. Furthermore, the talking establishes what the payoffs will be. By calling the other a coward, he restricts the choices of man *B* to (1) respond, escalate, and receive prestige payoffs, or (2) retreat and be laughed at. In interpersonal conflicts *communication is an integral part of the process.* Communication behaviors serve to (1) define the conflict, (2) structure the payoff matrices, (3) accrue payoffs from the matrices, (4) coordinate participant moves, (5) influence the direction the conflict takes (deescalate, avoid, maintain, or escalate), and (6) provide avenues of possible management of the conflict.

Choice and Uncertainty

One of the comforting things about some experimental games is that both participants can directly observe the structure of the conflict. As a partici-

---

6. For a detailed look at the possibilities of 2 × 2 games (two players each with two choices), *see* Rapoprt and Guyer (1966).
7. There are numerous limitations to game theory, many of which are not crucial to understanding structure. For more comprehensive treatments *see* Pruitt, 1967; Gergen, 1969; and Wilmot, 1975b.

pant in a game conflict situation you can observe the choices and the payoffs that you and the other participants will receive. In some games, however, the structure is hidden from the parties.

In nonlaboratory conflicts, the role of choice is also central. Choice involves obtaining information about the environment so that one can select alternatives (Ackoff and Emery 1972). In real-life conflicts, people experience more uncertainty than in laboratory situations. When you behave toward another there is always a degree of uncertainty regarding:

1. The other party's perception of your behavior? (does the other party misinterpret you?)

2. Your perception of the other party's behavior? (do you misinterpret the other party?)

3. What payoffs will you receive from your choices? (if you choose to shout and scream, will you get your way?)

4. What payoffs will the other party get from choices made?

5. How is the conflict structured? Did you unnecessarily cast the two of you into a win-lose situation where you had to "save face" in order to "win" (like the game of Chicken mentioned earlier)?

These and other uncertainties are present in interpersonal conflict situations. While experimental games are often games of pure strategy, real-life conflicts have elements of games of strategy, games of skill (one's perceptiveness in determining payoffs), and games of chance. In a conflict, the *selection of your own choice leads to uncertain outcomes. You make moves without full awareness of the structure of the conflict.* Take the case of a man whose four-year-old son has a habit of demanding the father's full attention when the father is talking on the telephone. The boy pesters and demands attention precisely when dad is unwilling to give it. The son feels neglected, and the father feels hassled. In the midst of the conflict the father says, "just a minute Jason," and it works fine. The next time the father is on the phone, however, the "just a minute Jason" only increases the boy's demands for attention. The father's choice (to try and stall the boy) works one time and not the next. And, even the time honored "shut up" is no guaranteed choice. The father's choices lead to uncertain outcomes, since another choice-making person is participating in the structure.

In nonlaboratory conflicts, dramatic increases in uncertainty about structure take place because of the *number of choices* available to each participant. While in the simplest game, one selects from choice one or choice two, in nonexperimental conflict, the choices are usually virtually unlimited.

And, "the wider the choice, the larger the set of alternatives open to use, the more uncertain we are as to how to proceed . . ." (Frick 1968, p. 182).[8] A quick look at a real life conflict, and just a few of the choices available to *one* of the participants, will serve to show that at any given point in time the participants have a countless number of options. Sue and Sam are a romantic couple. Sam went drinking last Friday instead of going to a movie with Sue and did not call her to let her know he would not be going with her to the movie. She sat and waited two hours for him to arrive, and he never did appear. Here are just a few of her choices in reacting to his no-show for the show:

1. ignore Sam

2. call Sam up

3. talk to a friend and have the friend tell Sam how upset Sue is

4. pretend it did not happen

5. escalate the conflict by threatening Sam with breaking off the relationship

6. write Sam a letter and write him off

7. cry

8. forgive Sam and wonder what she did to drive him to drink

9. blame it all on Sam's friends who "led him astray"

These are just a few of the many choices Sue has in responding. In addition, whatever Sue's first response is to him, he has numerous options too. The difficult thing is that for both Sue and Sam, the *consequences of their choices* are not easily determined. Sue can be thinking that if she chooses #5 and threatens to break off the relationship that Sam will be contrite, will shower her with love and affection, and promise to not be so thoughtless again. But if Sam chooses instead to attack and says, "The reason I had to get drunk is because you have made my life miserable," all of her calculations have been unhelpful. In such interpersonal conflicts, payoffs from one's choices are often uncertain.

In conflict situations each participant, wanting to know what the payoffs will be from one's choices, has to be "sensitive to the possible reactions of others to his own conduct" (Shibutani 1968, p. 333). You have to estimate

---

8. As Rapoport (1967) notes, in the most basic game, a 2 × 2, there are 78 nonequivalent payoffs possible. An extension to two players with three choices each brings nearly two billion possible unique payoff arrangements. Imagine the structural complexity when two parties each have fifty choices!

what the other's perception of the situation will be. When you are at a high degree of uncertainty regarding the other's perception of the situation, the *risk* from your choices is high. The high school boy who wants to date a girl finds it hard "to guess how much he would like himself if he were the girl that he wants to date" (Schelling 1960, p. 117).[9]

Each participant's estimates of the choices the other has and the payoffs the other will receive from each choice (depending of course on your choices) lead to some complex conflicts. Some of the game theory literature suggests that instructions to participants to cooperate predispose players to cooperate precisely because each player knows the other player heard the instructions and will probably cooperate (Braver and Barnett 1974). But how does one, in the absence of "rules" laid down by an experimenter, predict what options the other will have to choose from in a conflict situation? Basically, you (1) can ask the other party, (2) observe past behavior in like situations, (3) assume that you are in the other's place and predict what your choice would be, or (4) guess about uncertain societal rules of behavior in such circumstances without knowing whether the other party will follow the rules. None of these is a totally reliable guide. Maybe Sam predicts that Sue will react to his Friday night partying by blaming it on herself. But this particular Friday she talked to a friend who helped her see that Sam was responsible for his own actions. So, when Sam calls her, she breaks off the relationship. Her past behavior was no guarantee of her present response.

Payoffs are jointly determined based on the interdependent actions of both participants. When we *misread* another's payoffs (think that a choice is more or less desirable to another than it is), then the basic structure of the conflict is misread (Lumsden 1973). Sue may think Sam is trying to make her "one down" in the relationship and shows it by his independent decision to drink. But, one reason Sam went drinking is because he was afraid that Sue would decide at the last minute to cancel their evening together. So, to drown his misery of possible rejection, he drank. Payoffs can even be misread when two participants know one another and care for another. Take the case of the couple who got caught in the altruistic trap. He says, "I want to do whatever you want to do tonight." If she responds with a similar approach, and neither can state a preference, then they will probably go nowhere. Schelling (1960, p. 87) captures the complexity of trying to account for the other's choices, which is akin to a communication spiral (Wilmot 1975a).

---

9. And he feels euphoric if he has underestimated her liking of him. Many happy romantic interludes occur when both underestimate how attracted the other is and then they discover that the attraction is mutual.

The best choice for either depends on what he expects the other to do knowing that the other is similarly guided, so that each is aware that each must try to guess what the second guesses the first will guess the second to guess and so on, in the familiar spiral of reciprocal expectations.

And if one or more of the participants is unclear about desired payoffs, the system gets even more complex. Two people who are trying to decide whether to get married may easily experience the following conflict. He has asked her to get married. She may respond with, "I love you but I do not want to have either you or me committed to one person." He, after several trying weeks, decides to begin seeing both her and another woman. After his first date with the second young woman, the first woman gets very upset with him. She makes it very plain that she has been emotionally hurt by his actions. In short, he was not quite as committed to her as she wanted him to be. So, while she is expressing her hurt to him, she says, "but, I don't want to ask you to be committed only to me because I don't want to feel that I have to be committed to you." Her unclarity about what payoffs she receives introduces even more complexity into the system. He has to deal with:

1. what do I want?

2. what does she want? (she says one thing and acts another)

3. what I want is partly dependent on what she wants

4. what I want is partly dependent on what she wants to want (no commitment), which contradicts what she wants as revealed by her behavior

5. and, what she wants plus what she wants to want are partly dependent on what she thinks I want. But, if I can't rely on consistent responses from her, that changes what I want, because what I want is partly dependent on what she wants, but she . . .

And, he realizes that her statement, "I don't want to be or have you committed" reveals just how much she really cares for him.[10]

The process of estimating payoffs is a tricky business! Some conflict participants realize that one very "rational" behavior in a conflict is to disguise what your payoffs are so the other cannot predict your choices. When the man says, "if you do that again, I'll never speak to you again as long as I live" and his wife replies "is that a threat or a promise?" she has thrown him off balance. His estimate of how she will react to his choice is challenged by her response. A participant can also throw off the other's

---

10. A paradoxical thanks to John Cote, another devotee of R. D. Laing and his *Knots*.

prediction about his payoffs by pretending ignorance of the first person's action or by pretending to be irrational. Children often avoid the "warning glance from a parent, knowing that if they perceive it the parent is obligated to punish noncompliance" (Schelling 1960, p. 149). This tactic is often called "disqualification" of communication. If your ignorance, or feigned ignorance, about the results of choices is believed by the other person, it can work to your advantage. The interpretation of another's behavior involves estimating what choices that person has. If the other person confuses us about the available choices, we cannot predict the behavior.

In nonexperimental conflict, the difficulty in estimating choices and consequent payoffs makes prediction a risky business. It may well be that one of the reasons people dislike conflict is because of all the doubt and uncertainty present in the communication system. Many choose a "low hassle" strategy to avoid the difficult choices occurring in an uncertain situation. A student in one of our classes, for instance, receives money every month from his parents, banks it without spending a cent, and intends to give it to them when he graduates. He wants independence, but is afraid to confront them with a desire for change, because he is uncertain of their responses. So they continue in the existing relationship.

Real-Life Games

Establishing the Structures

Have you had the experience of finding yourself in a communication situation that seemed to have a "hidden message?" Perhaps normal conversation was occurring, but you had the nagging feeling that somewhere, someone had predetermined what was going on. A student came up to one of us after a particularly unsuccessful media-lecture in a large class—everything had gone wrong, the timing had been off, and the experience was one of those you would rather forget. He said, "I'd like to know who was responsible for that disaster last Tuesday." The instructor responded, "Well, a lot of people worked on it, but you seem to have something else on your mind. What do you want to tell me about your reaction?" The student looked nonplussed for a moment, then proceeded to describe his dissatisfaction with the hour. In the terminology of Eric Berne, who wrote the popular *Games People Play* (1964), the "game" was stopped. The outcome—open listening—was clearly not what the student originally had in mind. He wanted to gripe. Getting permission to gripe changed the structure of the experience.

In this section, we will discuss games and gamelike communication experiences that occur in everyday lives. Berne defines games as "ongoing series of complementary ulterior transactions progressing toward a well-defined, predictable outcome" (1964, p. 48). In other words, in a game interaction, people "go along" with the setup situation (complementary communication), not changing the basic structure of the game. The formula for any game could be described as: the con (or hooker) = the gimmick (hidden motive) = response (of the other person), which then becomes *switched* (the hidden outcome emerges) which results in *confusion* about how to respond further, which finally results in the *payoff,* the point of the game in the first place. The payoff may be that one party gets "one up" on the other, or that people find ways to spend their time together, or that a person confirms an opinion about oneself or someone else (such as "I'm no good and never do anything right"). Games vary in importance and intensity, with some being relatively harmless time-structuring devices and some resulting in what Berne calls "third-degree" outcomes, such as suicide, murder, divorce, or pathological despair. The distinguishing characteristics of *games* used in the connotation of Transactional Analysis, from which we derive this discussion, is (1) their ulterior quality and (2) the payoff. Thus not all social communication is gamelike. Even when communication seems overly ritualized, or conflicts are always fought in the same way, the interaction may not be a game.

While structure in daily conflicts is sometimes difficult to isolate precisely, we often have enough information to make estimates of the structure and its impact. The role of such structure is central to our understanding of conflict. The party setting the options for the other party has power over the other party. Whoever has the most influence on (1) defining the available choices and (2) setting the payoffs for the available options has higher power (Apfelbaum 1974). Influencing the structure of a conflict, therefore, is synonymous with control over the other party. This influence is a crucial power move available to players.

Some of the best examples of this control attempt come from the Transactional Analysis literature. Many of the games played appear in some form in interpersonal conflicts. Some examples of these games are listed in Figure 6.

Take the case of the "Now I've Got You, You S.O.B." (NIGYSOB) game. This game is designed to limit the options of the other so that player is trapped, thereby proving that he or she is full of faults, and giving the initial player "revenge power" over the other. For instance, take the case of two business colleagues who both have a chance for a prestigious promotion. Their friendship is important to them. They make a pact (the con) saying it's OK in the rules of their friendship to compete for the job; and no matter who wins, they will still be friends and support each other. The pact

Name of the Game	Payoff
"If it weren't for you" "See what you made me do"	blaming others for one's own behavior
"I'm only trying to help you"	to see oneself as a "savior"—whether the person wants to be saved or not
"Blemish"	picking out faults of others so you feel "one up"
"Rapo"	setting up a seduction attempt, then putting someone else down for falling for it
"Now I've got you, you Son of a Bitch"	maneuvering someone into a position where you have surprise high-power
"Kick me"; "Stupid"	proving you can never do anything right, therefore you aren't responsible for your actions—they are predetermined
"Poor me"	getting others to help you enjoy misery
"Harried"	copping out and getting permission to not be responsible for what you do

Figure 6. Common conflict games.

is a con because party *A* thinks he will win anyway, and does not think through how he will feel if party *B* wins. Party *B* gets the promotion, after some competitive tactics. Party *A* switches by saying, "A true friend wouldn't have treated me that way. Our friendship will never be the same." Because the relationship was important, the guilt motive becomes important and the winning party is "had," and party *A* can say, in essence, "Now I've got you, you son of a bitch." The hidden payoff was punishment for the loser to exercise over the winner.

In all conflict situations, whether it is overtly obvious or not, each party's moves influence the structure of the conflict. When the father says, "Carina, if you throw your milk on the floor once more, I'll spank you," he is trying to set the choices (spill or don't spill) and the payoffs (spank or don't spank). In a broad sense, every time one communicates, the nature of the participants' relationship is defined; no behavior stands in isolation. Every move or choice reverberates throughout the system and either reinforces or alters the structure of the conflict. Even going along with a game reinforces the structure.

A final example of a "game" or attempt at controlling the structure of the transaction needs to be noted because of the difficulty parties have in restructuring it. The "double bind" is a particularly destructive structuring. The payoff to this game is structuring the experience to find fault with another, and in its extreme forms it is believed to be a contributor to schizophrenia (Bateson 1972). In a typically cited case, a mother defines her conflict with a child such that the child cannot clearly interpret her communication. On the verbal level she may say, "Come here so Mom can give you love," and if he comes close she says, "You only did that because I told you to. You don't really love me." If he ignores the verbal command, she also punishes him. Further, the situation is usually one where he cannot escape, thus the "binding" becomes real. The mother (1) sets out limited options, (2) punishes him for either choice and this is accompanied by (3) the impossibility of him leaving the situation. The child cannot *not* choose.

Whenever one of the conflict participants systematically tries to totally control the structure of the conflict, such behavior is not productive since one participant is trying to hold *all* the power in the relationship and persons who are in an extremely low power role typically become passive, overly cooperative, or devious. This structuring may well be against the goals of a long-term relationship. Attempts at total structural control come in many guises—ranging from hysterical sobbing, to shouting, to extreme avoidance of the conflict. For example, if two friends are in a conflict over how close they are to become (one wants to be a closer friend, the other likes the friendship the way it is), and the person favoring the status quo completely denies the existence of a conflict, the avoidance strategy is working to *reinforce* the present structure. Anything a participant does or does not do either reinforces the structure or attempts to alter it.

Altering the Structure

The structure of a conflict is the joint product of both parties' actions. Therefore, if a structure is being set by one party the second has to cooperate with it or it will not be established. When you are in a conflict and the other participant is trying to structure it, you have several choices available. In fact, the entire process of managing conflict can be seen as establishing different choices and/or payoffs for the choices. Unlike players of laboratory games, real-world players have a "unique opportunity to define the nature of the conflict they are engaged in" (Gallo 1972).

The easiest advice to give is to say that both parties should have an equal say in structuring the choices and payoffs. Advocates of Parent Effectiveness Training (Gordon 1970) tell parents to let kids fully participate in selecting options. This depends on where you both (or all) want the relationship to go. But if you are a child or anyone else who is on the receiving end of a structural definition that the other party wants to impose, what do you do? Basically, you attempt to alter the structure by (1) refusing to play the game, or (2) refusing to provide the expected payoff. For instance, if the other party's payoff involves putting you down, then you can respond by changing the subject or telling a joke. Whatever the chosen course of action, it should directly impact on the structure of the game. If you reply within the context of the game, it will usually be "in ways which produce great personal harm to both sides" (Meininger 1973, p. 128). Other attempts at restructuring will be discussed in Chapter 6, "Strategies and Tactics," where suggestions for increasing one's power are offered.

One word of pessimism. People often have a difficult time recognizing the structure of a conflict. One study demonstrated that when asked to specify the *structure* of a conflict, subjects still reported on *behaviors* of the parties (Shubik, Wolf, and Poon, 1974). It may be that people need training so they can draw conclusions about choices and payoffs in addition to the behaviors that are a response to them. Or, it may just be that structure is difficult to see in conflicts because the available choices are often not clear, and neither are the payoffs. In most conflict situations, the degree of uncertainty may be so high as to preclude a precise accounting of the structure. But the more fully parties can understand the structuring process, the better able they will be to attain their own and mutual goals in a conflict.

All parties in a conflict share responsibility for its development, and can usually have an impact on its structure. If participants are not pleased with the choices they have, they need to either work for more choices or alter the payoffs for current ones.

Summary

All communication events, whether they are games or not, have structure. In this chapter we have discussed games as a special kind of communication interaction because within games the structure of the relationship is most easily seen. In the rest of the book, we will discuss the restructuring of other communication episodes so they may be more productive for the participants involved. But awareness of structure enhances even the most informal communication in which persons engage.

Bibliography

Ackoff, Russell, and Emery, Fred. *On Purposeful Systems.* Chicago: Aldine Publishing Co., 1972.

Apfelbaum, Erika. "On Conflicts and Bargaining." In *Advances in Experimental Social Psychology 7,* edited by Leonard Berkowitz, pp. 103-156. New York: Academic Press, Inc., 1974.

Bateson, Gregory. *Steps to an Ecology of Mind.* New York: Ballantine Books, Inc., 1972.

Berne, Eric. *Games People Play.* New York: Grove Press, Inc., 1964.

Bostrom, Robert N. "Game Theory in Communication Research." *The Journal of Communication,* 18 December 1968, pp. 369-388.

Braver, Sanford, and Barnett, Bruce. "Perception of Opponent's Motives and Cooperation in a Mixed-Motive Game." *Journal of Conflict Resolution,* December 1974, pp. 686-699.

Fink, Clinton P. "Some Conceptual Difficulties in the Theory of Social Conflict." *Journal of Conflict Resolution,* December 1968, pp. 412-460.

Frick, F. C. "The Application of Information Theory in the Behavioral Sciences." In *Modern Systems Research for the Behavioral Scientist,* edited by Walter Buckley, pp. 182-185. New York: Aldine Publishing Co., 1968.

Frohlich, Norman. "Self-Interest or Altruism, What Difference?" *Journal of Conflict Resolution,* March 1974, pp. 57-73.

Frost, Joyce Hocker. "The Implications of Conflict Theories for Rhetorical Criticism." Unpublished dissertation, University of Texas, 1974.

Gallo, Philip S. "Prisoner's of Our Own Dilemma." In *Cooperation and Competition: Readings on Mixed-Motive Games,* edited by Lawrence S. Wrightsman, John O'Connor, and Norma J. Baker, pp. 43-49. Belmont: Brooks/Cole Publishing Co., 1972.

Garner, Katherine, and Deutsch, Morton. "Cooperative Behavior in Dyads. *Journal of Conflict Resolution,* December 1974, pp. 634-645.

Gergen, Kenneth J. *The Psychology of Behavior Exchange.* Reading, Mass.: Addison-Wesley Publishing Co., Inc., 1969.

Gordon, Thomas. *Parent Effectiveness Training.* New York: Peter H. Wyden, 1970.

Luce, R. Duncan, and Raiffa, Howard. *Games and Decisions.* New York: John Wiley & Sons, Inc., 1957.

Lumsden, Malvern. "The Cyprus Conflict as a Prisoner's Dilemma Game." *Journal of Conflict Resolution,* March 1973, pp. 7-32.

Meininger, Jut. *Success With Transactional Analysis.* New York: Gossett & Dunlap, Inc., 1973.

Miller, Gerald R., and Simons, Herbert W., eds. *Perspectives on Communication in Social Conflict.* Englewood Cliffs, N.J.: Prentice-Hall, Inc., 1974.

Pruitt, Dean G. "Reward Structure and Cooperation: The Decomposed Prisoner's Dilemma Game." *Journal of Personality and Social Psychology* 7 1(1967):21-27.

Rapoport, Anatol. "Conflict Resolution in the Light of Game Theory and Beyond." In *The Structure of Conflict,* edited by Paul Swingle, pp. 1-43. New York: Academic Press, Inc., 1970.

————. "Critiques of Game Theory." In *Modern Systems Research for the Behavioral Scientist,* edited by Walter Buckley, pp. 474-489. Chicago: Aldine Publishing Co., 1968.

————. "Exploiter Comments." *Journal of Conflict Resolution,* June 1973, pp. 317-319.

————. "Exploiter, Leader, Hero, and Martyr: The Four Archetypes of the 2 × 2 Game." *Behavioral Science,* 12(1967):81-84.

————. *Fights, Games, and Debates.* Ann Arbor, Mich.: University of Michigan Press, 1960.

————, and Guyer, M. A. "A Taxonomy of 2 × 2 Games." *General Systems* 2(1966):203-214.

————, and Orwant, Carol. "Experimental Games: A Review." *Behavioral Science.* 7(1962):1-37.

Schelling, Thomas C. "The Strategy of Conflict." Cambridge, Mass.: Harvard University Press, 1960.

Shibutani, Tamotsu. "A Cybernetic Approach to Motivation." In *Modern Systems Research for the Behavioral Sciences,* edited by Walter Buckley. Chicago: Aldine Publishing Co., 1968.

Shubik, Martin; Wolf, Gerrit; and Poon, Byron. "Perception of Payoff Structure and Opponent's Behavior in Related Matrix Games." *Journal of Conflict Resolution,* December 1974, pp. 646-655.

Siebold, David R., and Steinfatt, Thomas M. "Game Theory and the Study of Human Communication." Paper presented to the Speech Communication Association Convention, December 27-31, 1974, Chicago, Ill.

Steinfatt, Thomas M., and Miller, Gerald R. "Communication in Game Theorectic Models of Conflict." In *Perspectives on Communication in Social Conflict,* edited by Miller and Simons, pp. 14-75. Englewood Cliffs, N.J.: Prentice-Hall, Inc., 1974.

———; Seibold, David R.; and Frye, Jerry K. "Communication in Game Similiated Conflicts: Two Experiments." *Speech Monographs* 41(1974):24-35.

Swenson, Clifford H., Jr. *An Introduction to Interpersonal Relations.* Glenview, Ill.: Scott, Foresman & Co., 1973.

Swingle, Paul. "Dangerous Games." In *The Structure of Conflict*, edited by Swingle, pp. 235-276. New York: Academic Press, Inc., 1970.

Terhune, K. W. "Motive, Situation, and Interpersonal Conflict Within Prisoner's Dilemma." *Journal of Personality and Social Psychology* 8(1968):3, part 2, pp. 1-24.

Vinacke, W. E. "Variables in Experimental Games: Toward a Field Theory." *Psychological Bulletin* 71(1969):293-318.

Von Neumann, John, and Morgenstern, Oskar. *Theory of Games and Economic Behavior.* Printeton, N.J.: Princeton University Press, 1944.

Watzlawick, Paul; Beavin, Janet H.; and Jackson, Don D. *Pragmatics of Human Communication.* New Hork: W. W. Norton & Co., 1967.

Wilmot, William W. *Dyadic Communication: A Transactional Perspective,* Reading, Mass.: Addison-Wesley Publishing Co., Inc., 1975a.

———. "Beyond Game Theory: A Real Life Approach." Paper presented to Western Speech Communication Association Convention, Seattle, Washington, November 25, 1975b.

Analyzing Issues and Setting Goals

5

In Chapter 2 we discussed personal styles of doing conflict and focused almost entirely on the individual's contribution to a conflict relationship. In Chapter 3 we examined the role of power in conflicts; and in Chapter 4 we used a game theory approach to help identify the structure of conflict interactions. In this chapter, we will deal with the questions, "Where do I/we want to go? What are our goals?" The emphasis in this chapter is on how people can understand the realities of their differing goals and thereby improve the chances of a conflict being productive. People are more likely to get what they want (separately and together) when they can identify what they want than when their points of conflict and their goals remain undefined and vague. Goals can be more clearly identified than they usually are in conflicts.

Conflict is a struggle over goals that are perceived to be incompatible. The goals may actually be incompatible if all parties try to achieve them, or they may be reachable without conflict if they are redefined. When goals are incompatible, a "hard" statement should be faced—people cannot get everything they want in a conflict if their opponents get everything they want. Persons in relationship can work to change perceptions of incompatible goals, but this involves a conscious choice. We do not easily give up goals we cherish.

We often hear people in conflict situations state goals similar to the following:

I just want to resolve this fairly for everyone.

I only want to protect my rights.

We both want to enhance our relationship with each other.

I want to solve this dispute over who gets the job so we don't have to keep fighting and not getting work done.

These statements all have "rightness" and a sense of justice imbedded in them in the minds of the speaker. They are good beginning statements, but they aren't precise enough to make up a statement of goals that is useful for guiding decisions about the use of power, strategies, and tactics. For instance, the first speaker has not indicated how involved he or she is in the

85

conflict. How committed is that person to resolving the conflict? What is he or she willing to give up? What is "fair" in the mind of that speaker? A goal statement, arrived at openly in a group or dyad, should take into account at least these questions if it is to be precise enough to guide action. Goal analysis is a complex process that is necessary before satisfactory growth and change can take place in conflict interactions. Only by examining goals can you be fully aware that you are engaged in conflict, then assess the conflict as it progresses, and know when the conflict has been successfully managed.

Three Kinds of Goals

Goals and objectives are synonymous with "something desirable; something to be achieved; a target to strive for or to aim at." Notice in the definition of goals and objectives that not only does a person identify a *desired end state,* but one also commits oneself to some *action designed to make that state come about.* Goals imply activity—they are not static, faraway dreams or wishes. Often, however, goals are fuzzy "wishful thinking" statements in which no one takes responsibility for any action. One political decision-making group with whom we worked spent a weekend working out their conflicts. Over the course of the three days together, we kept track of all the goal statements and decisions they made. We counted 143 goal statements or decisions. Only sixteen, however, contained an "action plan" for reaching the goal.

Prospective Goals

One pattern is prevalent in groups and in personal relationships. Even when people say what they want, they neglect the "how do we get there?" part of the statement. This comes about because goals are seen often as a statement to be made ahead of time—before the communication transaction occurs. This prior view of goals is labeled a *prospective* view by Hawes and Smith (1973). Most of the attention given to goal analysis takes this prospective approach. Mager (1972), in his popular manual on goal setting, gives the following useful suggestions:

1. Write down the goal using whatever words best describe the intent.

2. Write down the performances that would cause you to agree the goal has been achieved. . . .

3. Sort out the list, deleting duplications and unwanted entries on the list.

4. Then write a complete statement for each performance, describing the nature, quality, or amount you will consider acceptable.

5. Test the statements with the question, "If someone achieved or demonstrated each of these performances, would I be willing to say he has achieved the goal?" When you can answer yes, the analysis is finished.

All of the above procedures work well for figuring out what you want. For instance, a woman might say before an important personnel meeting, "I want that promotion more than Katy does, so I'm going to do everything I can, including direct competition with her, to get it." This is a clear prospective goal. But we disagree with Mager that with a statement of prospective goals, the analysis is finished.

Transactive Goals

Often people do not become aware of how much goals change during a conflict. We have all had the experience of changing what we want during talks with others. We call this process a *transactive* view of goal development—the goals change as a result of the communication transaction. This only takes place if participants are open to change and listen to the desires of others. Thus, an overemphasis on prospective goal development can limit a group to a set of goals in which they no longer believe.

Recently a school board member was trying to decide how to handle the fact that she strongly opposed closed, or "executive," sessions of the board while her colleagues on the board were in favor of them because of expediency. She discussed the incipient conflict with friends ahead of time, rehearsing what she was going to do (prospective goals). Then she acted on some of those behaviors during the next board meeting and did not follow exactly what she had thought she would. She compromised to agree with her colleagues that some meetings, in limited circumstances, were acceptable. This change process is an example of transactive goal development.

Retrospective Goals

The final perspective on goals is discussed by Schutz (1967) and Weick (1969). They advocate the point of view that goals are primarily *retrospective*—they only make sense after the behavior in a conflict takes place. Since we do not know the size and implications of a conflict until we look back on it, goals serve an explanatory, not a predicting, function. A board member we mentioned earlier reported to us, "I knew they were furious about my forcing the issue of open meetings at the School Board—that's why I avoided them in the hall—to give them a chance to cool off." The person *retrospectively* explains behavior that may have been confusing while the transaction took place.

Toulmin (1958), writing on decision-making, suggests that most people spend a large part of their time and energy *justifying* past behavior or decisions they have made. Argument assumes a *retrospective* quality, with people needing to explain to themselves and others why they made the choices they did. This process often happens with intimates. They may have a very intense conflict over whether the woman should accept a job offer that would mean that the man would have to move with her to another city. Before they discuss the issue they may say, "Let's decide what's best for both of us together" (prospective goal). During the conflict, they discuss everything from preferences about the part of the country to live in to availability of further schooling (transactive goals become important). Then after the conflict, the woman might say retrospectively, "I wanted to see if you really meant that my career is important to you."

Transactive goal development has received far less attention than have either prospective or retrospective goals. Because transactive goals arise during conflict episodes, they will be stressed in the remainder of this chapter. This relational approach to goal definition is consistent with a definition of conflict emphasizing interdependence: "Conflict is an expressed struggle between at least two interdependent parties, who perceive incompatible goals, scarce rewards, and interference from the other party in achieving their goals. They are in a position of opposition in conjunction with cooperation."

In order to deal effectively with transactive goals, people in conflict must learn to negotiate productively. Johnson and Johnson (1975, pp. 178-79) characterize a negotiation relationship as having at least five elements: (1) at least two persons, (2) cooperative and competitive elements, (3) interdependence, (4) working toward reasonable settlement (chance of being accepted by the other), and (5) being dependent on the other for information about a possible agreement. They also assert that the goals in any conflict interaction are (1) reaching agreement and (2) improving the basic cooperative interdependence among the members (1975, p. 176). These descriptions of the conflict relationship emphasize the transactional nature of the development of goals—one cannot know all the goals either beforehand or afterwards unless one is in interdependent communication with the other conflict participants. Bargaining over incompatible goals, therefore, needs to take into account the changing goals of the participants and the communication behaviors that help in negotiating goals productively.

The following dialogue exemplifies how new goals are advanced as a conflict progresses. Note that the two parties see themselves as interdependent, and they value their relationship as well as solving the immediate problem of finding the lost object. They have both content and relationship goals in the conflict. In the dialogue, one woman calls another to request the return of some jewelry she has loaned.

Statement of Parties	**Analysis**
First phone call:	
Amy: "You know that silver star pendant I loaned you—I guess you didn't return it with the rest of the jewelry, because I can't find it."	#1 Prospective goal: *get the pendant back from Janice.*
Janice: "I don't have it. I remember that I didn't borrow it because I knew it was valuable to you. You must have misplaced it somewhere. But I'll look."	#2 Prospective goal: *incompatible with #1. Janice can't give it back and refuses responsibility for its disappearance.*
Second phone call:	Prospective goal #1:
Amy: "I still can't find it—I'm getting panicky. I'll hold while you go look. Please check everywhere it might be."	*(still maintains) nonrecognition of Janice's position. Escalates previous goal statement.*
Janice: "This is really difficult. You are upset about the necklace, and I don't know what I can do since I honestly don't think I have it. But what really concerns me is that you are upset, and upset at me. That's new for us. You mean a lot to me and this hurts."	Transactive goal #3: *introduces new goal possibility; "affirming the relationship in spite of problems."*
Amy: "I know. I really don't want to put it all on you. I'm glad you understand, though. You know, John gave me that necklace."	Agrees with transactive goal #3: *agrees to discuss "affirming the relationship" as a new, additional goal.*
Janice: "Well, what can we do to get this solved? I feel awful."	Transactive goal #3: *acceptance of mutual goal—work together toward new goal #4—find the necklace without damaging the relationship (new transactive goal).*
Amy: "I'll hang up and we'll both go look everywhere and then report back."	Transactive goal #5: *agrees on mutual plan of action advanced.*
Janice: "OK. And then we'll come up with something if we don't find it right away. Cross your fingers."	Transactive goal #6: *advances new goal—"expectation of future negotiation of goals" while reinforcing #5.*

As we have seen all too often, prospective goals sometimes get in the way of a creative redefinition of goals. As Hesse (1948, p. 113) says in *Siddhartha,* "When someone is seeking . . . it happens quite easily that he only sees the thing that he is seeking, that he is unable to find anything, unable to absorb anything, because he has a goal, because he is obsessed with his goal."

Advantages of Goal Clarity

We often hear people say something like this when discussing goals: "I don't want to be a manipulative person. If I figure out goals ahead of time, I'm behaving like a used-car salesman instead of a friend. I want to avoid that pushy approach." Phillips and Metzger, in their book *Intimate Communication* (1976), address this problem very creatively. They assert that all effective communication is *rhetorical,* or goal directed. In purely expressive communication, people talk about their feelings randonly and are often dismayed when, after a lot of self-disclosure and sharing, the other people involved do not react in the way hoped for by the first person. In a rhetorical orientation to communication, people direct their energies toward creating relationships that fit their individual and relational goals. They further assert that people cannot avoid being goal-directed part of the time, so they can benefit from their conflict interactions by consciously taking responsibility for clarifying their goals and, when appropriate, sharing these goals with others.

An example of this kind of goal sharing occurred recently in our department. The chairperson complained that the faculty was not paying enough attention to university politics. He made several statements over a period of a week or so urging more attendance at meetings, more discussion of long-term budget and curriculum plans, and voluntary participation in activities around campus. Since all this happened at the beginning of a quarter when the rest of the faculty were feeling busy, pushed, hassled by bureaucracy, and underappreciated, the response in the faculty was negative. A genuine conflict began brewing. Finally the chairperson said, "Since keeping us involved in the university is my job, I feel really down when nobody supports what I'm doing. I need some feedback on what you think so I'm not just floundering around." Because he changed his goal statement from, "Why don't you people work more?" to "I need support for what I'm doing," the conflict was reduced and productively managed.

When our goals are clarified, we have a better chance of attaining them. First, it is important to clarify prospective goals so we feel clear in our interactions. Sometimes a conflict seems so large and shadowy that we do not recognize progress when it occurs. A caucus of citizens interested in slowing growth in their city might face perpetual frustration if they advocated "no growth" in all areas. If they decide on pushing (1) a 3 percent housing growth rate, (2) citizen review of all shopping centers, and (3) election of one of their spokespersons to city council, then they have set up goals that might be reached. Just as important, they will be able to feel a sense of success when and if they reach their goals. They also will need to revise their goals in the light of their experience (transactively) and continue to reclarify what they want.

If your goals are clear, *then they can be altered more easily*. In an intimate relationship, if you see your goal as "being loved," it is so general that attaining it is difficult. But, if you specify that by "being loved" you mean that you want someone to spend time with you, you can determine that the expectation needs some slight modification. As a result, you can change goals so that your chance of attaining them is increased.

Another advantage of clarifying your goals is that you can *begin to more fully understand that others have goals too*. Therefore, if the other party is avoiding you, you can say, "she is avoiding me in order to secure some space for herself, which she needs to recuperate from her job." Such a view is more productive and opens more options for change than to merely conclude, "she avoids me." Goal analysis lets one see behavior as tied into goals that others desire instead of behavior being seen as an end in itself. Furthermore, as the other party (or yourself) changes tactics, the behavioral change can be seen as another attempt for them to achieve their goals. Take the case of one of our students who was very upset over a grade he received on an assignment. In class just after the assignment was handed back he said, "that entire assignment was really dumb." His tactic was open disparagement of the teacher. Later, in a private conference, he confided that to get a C meant he could not get the job he wanted upon graduation. And, after the teacher refused to change the grade because he saw the paper as a general mish-mash of words, the student again became aggressive. Then, when the teacher suggested that he redo the assignment without penalty, the student became very cooperative. The student's tactics changed dramatically: from disparagement, to disclosure, to aggression, to cooperation. Yet, he was still the same person. An understanding of his goals helps one see past his behavior and not immediately classify him as a pessimistic, disparaging sort of person. The tactical changes can be seen in the context of the goals they try to facilitate, rather than ends in themselves.

When goals are clarified it is possible to avoid locking in your definition of a relationship; therefore it can change. Tactics are sometimes confused with the definition of the relationship. For instance, two coworkers may say, "Oh, Marion and I always fight. We never agree on anything." This description may be quite accurate, but a better description would be, "Marion always wants help. She likes to work together on plans. I like to work by myself." By defining the incompatible goals instead of the tactics ("fighting"), the possibility for negotiating those goals is set up, even if that possibility only exists in one person's mind.

When goals are clarified, you can keep track of whether your behavior has changed (tactics) or your goals have changed. For example, sometimes groups start avoiding each other. A manager may look at two groups who have been openly competing over a long-range plan and decide that "people have worked out their differences." Actually, the combatants may have just "gone underground" and are temporarily using avoidance while they think up other competitive tactics. A check on whether goals have changed would give the manager a clearer view of what is happening in the organization.

The final reason for clarification of goals is that *we often get what we ask for.* How many times have you planned and schemed for days, only to find that the person in power was perfectly willing to give you what you want? A friend we know once was miserable because her children would not give her any free time on the weekends. She began to believe they did not respect her needs. Finally she said in tears one Thursday night, "If I don't have some time alone, I"ll go crazy." The teenagers were glad to make plans to give her time with no responsibilities. She simply never had asked.

In our view, destructive goals (setting out to injure or destroy the other party either physically or psychologically) occur because (1) we are interdependent with others, (2) this interdependence can place the other in a position to interfere with our goals, and (3) we react to the frustration by then choosing to wage destructive action against the other. One student of ours expressed it well. When she was asked "what do you do when someone says something that hurts your feelings?" she replied, "I just counterattack by going for the jugular vein. If they are going to hurt me, then I'll get them too." The student's goal in the interpersonal situation is to have her self-esteem supported by the other. When the other doesn't support her, the student "counterattacks." Destructive goals are chosen out of frustration, when some other goal does not appear possible. In really heated conflicts, it is common for both parties to be locked into a spiral of attack and justification. They justify their own actions because of "what the other person did to me." The foreman of the logging work crew says, "these lazy guys just do not want to work, so I won't pay them overtime," while the workers say, "the company doesn't want us to make any money so to hell with them, we will work at our own pace." Frustration over not attaining goals (even though they may be unclear) leads to the formulation of destructive goals.

Unfortunately, many people become so accustomed to not achieving their goals for power and self-esteem that they adopt a repetitive destructive stance toward others. The frustration over not accomplishing goals becomes internalized and frozen into an outlook that the goal of relationships is to "get the other guy." In more extreme forms, it is a case of fanaticism, which consists in redoubling your efforts when you have forgotten your aim. In destructive conflict, the attitudes of the parties change from "concern over the initial issues to concern over not yielding" (Swingle 1970, p. ix).

If destructive goals arise out of frustration over blockage of other goals, then a careful clarifying of goals can often arrest the march of hostility that accompanies a shift to destructive goals. When you feel like you want to destroy or danage the other person, a good question to ask is, "what is it that I want that he or she is interfering with?" Then, you may be able to avoid getting locked into destructive goals.

The Difference Between Goals and Issues

We find confusion both in peoples' conversations and in communication literature over goals and issues. They are often treated as if they are the same thing. The following distinction, however, may be useful. *Goals are end points of planned behavior* resulting from a clash of issues. *Issues are points in a conflict at which one side affirms and the other side(s) denies.* In an issue clash, the sharpest disagreements are dramatically pinpointed. Try listing the points of conflict in two columns to clarify differing points of view. For example:

School Superintendent	Title IX Coordinator
No one will tell me how much money to spend on girls' athletics.	*The law says that equal money must be spent for boys' and girls' athletics.*
Contact sports are dangerous for mixed groups.	*Some contact sports are not any more dangerous to mixed groups than single-sex groups.*

People have a better chance of managing their conflicts when goals are developed from the analysis of appropriate issue clashes. Frequently, however, goals are developed almost randomly instead of coming from already defined issue clashes. For instance, the superintendent quoted above may develop a goal of minimizing cooperation with all sex discrimination guidelines instead of identifying the issues that are most disagreeable to him. And the coordinator may develop a goal of "goading" the superintendent instead of a less destructive goal of cooperation where possible. Or a couple may decide that they want to spend more time at home (prospective goals). Over the past few weeks, they have been arguing over how much time they spend with friends. The husband wants to spend more time working on his "do-it-yourself" projects, while the wife wants to spend more time playing tennis with their friends. So they decide to stay home more—without deciding whether the at-home time is to be primarily "together" time or "separate" time. Then the wife gets angry when the husband wants to be out in his workroom, because she assumed that if they are going to stay home, they would compensate for the reduced recreation time by spending more time together. The husband assumed that staying home meant he could work more on his projects. Talking about the issue of "together vs. separate" time might have led to a more appropriate goal than simply staying at home. Goal development is more realistic when it follows a discussion of the issues that are bothering the parties involved in a conflict.

Determining What You Want

The process of goal analysis does not have to be a cut and dried experience of writing and then comparing goals, meeting and writing them down on a flip chart and then numbering them, or other formal processes. These methods can work in groups when there is a lot of diversity, but other methods are also helpful. The process of goal development does not begin when people say, "Let's figure out our goals." It goes on constantly, and attention to the almost intuitive process of goal development can be fascinating and instructive for families, work groups, and intimates. All of us constantly create messages for ourselves and other people with whom we are interdependent—goal development can start with understanding the energy that already goes to the push to get what we want.

One way of beginning to figure out what we do *not* want is to look askance at goals that have the following characteristics.

1. *Goals that are too old and need revising.* Couples often continue to give half-hearted energy to goals developed when they got married instead of revising them as the relationship matures. They try to find new ways to make these old goals work instead of revising the goals. For instance, one couple moved around a lot when they were first married, and they developed a "you and me against the world" philosophy, which was quite appropriate for the constant situation of being new in town. Later, as their careers matured and they became more settled, they felt that something was wrong with their relationship since they did not have "goals" anymore.

Instead of feeling that it was time to move, they could have explored other ways to get the same closeness they experienced early in the relationship.

Formally defined, prospective goals may be relied upon too much instead of letting transactive goals emerge with the passing of time. Then the prospective goals may become "old" and not useful as guides for planning for an organization or for an individual's behavior. The staff of a small community agency with which we worked felt frustrated—they expressed the feeling that they were not meeting their goals. Yet they were signing up new volunteers each day, placing them in agencies, keeping in touch with them, and assessing their work. Early in the volunteer agency's development, however, a goal had been written into several job descriptions. The specific goal causing discomfort was that of providing information about their function to various civic and community groups by sending someone on the staff to speak at meetings. The staff kept trying to get someone to take over this function, engendering much hostility with each other since no one wanted to. Finally they determined that the public relations goal had been formalized when they did not have enough volunteers— now that they had more than they could handle, the goal was out of date and needed revision.

2. *"Should" goals are often not actually valued by the participants in a group or a friendship.* Mager and Pipe's (1970) book on performance objectives is subtitled "You Really Oughta Wanta." It outlines some of the problems of thinking that people are really committed to goals that someone else, such as management, parents, teachers, administrators, set—thinking that subordinates "oughta" want to achieve the goals. Nothing is drearier than feeling a continuous sense of failure because of not achieving what one "should" do. Perhaps the goals should be renegotiated instead of redoubling efforts that only serve to make us feel guilty when we do not meet them. Often these goals are stated in broad, humanistic terms, such as, "We want to reach out to those less fortunate than we are" or "We will become better organized." These goals could be broken down into more realistic segments and then might be attainable. A church with which we are familiar hired a new minister. One of the primary things stressed in the interview was the need to grow, attract young people, and be attractive to college students and professional people. The church had remained small for a number of years, with a very stable population of people, primarily retired, who had moved to the city from

small farming communities. Gradually, as the new minister began to bring in new, younger members, and as the new members began to ask for changes in priorities in budget and services, the "should" nature of the prospective goal became apparent. The older people were upset that they were losing control of the one place where they felt comfortable and at home. They were disturbed by the unconventional beliefs and practices of the younger members. They longed, naturally enough, for "the good old days." Gradually the congregation was able to evolve trans-active goals of accommodation and mutual support and respect— after the "should" character of the initial goal statement was debunked.

3. *Goals of which people have to be constantly reminded* probably are not serving the function they were originally intended to serve. Offices that put mottoes on the wall or publish memos reminding people that they are not following the goals that they set together probably should redo their goals. At a workshop for faculty of a junior high, the attention level was quite low, snide comments were being made, and people kept asking about the coffee break time. Finally it came out that the principal had set the agenda for the workshop over the objections of the planning committee, and the group was supposedly working on "goals" for their coming school year, when actually they were simply coping with the individual goals of the principal. No wonder they were bored!

An imaginative way to begin to figure out what you really do want is to observe yourself, your work group, your family, you, and your intimates as if you were an outside participant observer doing research on yourself. Some of the same kinds of questions asked by people doing research aimed at discovering the underlying reality of the participants in a social system are also useful for your own purposes. In participant observation research, the researcher does not begin with categories that he or she thinks will appear in the communication of the participants being watched. Categories of meaning emerge only after watching patterns develop in the behavior of the persons being studied (Rushing 1975). Questions to help in discovering the meaning already being attached to communication behavior might be like the following: (1) When do we work together well? (2) Where is the energy going in this group or dyad? At what times are we most excited and alive? (3) When do we feel successful? (4) Which goals get common agreement from almost everyone involved with their attainment? (5) What are we willing to pay for? Which purchases seem not like a chore but a pleasure? (6) Which activities make us feel as if we are doing what we ought to do without feeling guilty when we do not?

A friend of ours decided last year to initiate a lawsuit as a result of some discriminatory action taken against him in his job. He had been in conflict with his employer for over a year, but the conflict was stalemated. He found it excessively difficult to find a lawyer, find the relevant files, keep track of what had been said in meetings, and pay the bills for the legal action. Then he left town and let the matter lie dormant for some months. Finally, when questioned by close friends, he decided that what he really wanted to do was concentrate energy on seeing that similar conditions did not emerge in the future. A researcher would have heard his verbal statement, "I am involved in an important lawsuit," and watched his behavior that was directed everywhere but at a lawsuit, and concluded, "He wants to want to carry on the lawsuit, but no significant energy is going in that direction. Maybe he wants to do something else more now." Observation of your own and your conflict group's behavior will give you clues about your activities and goals you really do value as opposed to goals you might think you should value. This does not mean, of course, that people should only do things they are already excited about—but the underlying meaning of present activities might suggest future productive goals.

Developing Productive Goals

We are interested in isolating skills that enhance productive goal development. Perhaps by looking at some common goals that people choose (although usually not consciously), we may work toward more productive choices about future conflict managing devices. Usually goals that are based on revenge ("I'll show them . . .") are useful occasionally to get an individual motivated to change, but grow old after a while. Even more tragically, people get involved in goals that further outcomes that are exactly opposite of what they really want. People feeling suicidal cut themselves off from support systems. When we are afraid of being rejected we cut ourselves off from the people who might reject us . . . and from whom we desperately need love and acceptance. When we are afraid of failure, we refuse to try to achieve. When we are afraid of being too dependent, we go to the other extreme and try to become totally independent. Goals that put us outside the social and communication system with which we are necessarily interdependent are usually destructive. We need to learn to "do" conflict in the system instead of rejecting the people in the system. As long as we must reject to become free, we are never truly free. A young boy we know had a conflict with two of his playmates. The only solution he knew was to go home—but then he would feel lonely and left out. Adults fall into the same pattern—we leave, avoid, reject before others reject us—only to find that the conflict is not resolved by our leaving; we simply internalize the conflict and have to deal with it by ourselves.

The following suggestions come from observations of groups and couples over a five-year period. They are not rules in a formal sense, but they are communication behaviors that seem to help people in conflicts set meaningful goals so they can work toward management of their present conflicts. You can probably come up with others of your own—but give these a try the next time you feel yourself getting stuck or thinking that the situation is so unclear you cannot get anywhere. They may sound overly altruistic, but our experience has been that good faith negotiation behaviors are at least as important in interpersonal conflicts as they are in labor-management and other more formalized negotiations. We believe that negotiation is a productive activity. To some the word implies deceit, tension, and hostility— but learning goal setting and negotiation skills can make people feel more comfortable with each other, can help them work effectively together, and can give people options for staying together instead of avoiding or leaving each other.

In the next chapter, we will discuss more specifically the strategies and tactics of successful negotiation. In this list, we focus on the goal setting, clarifying and redefining process in negotiation.

1. *Try to make many choices available* to the parties involved. People tend to become defensive when they are being controlled by having no options available to them. In destructive conflict behavior, options are closed instead of opened. Mutual rewards are not desired, and deception and outlandish promises are often employed (Miller and Steinberg 1975, p. 134). When a father asserts that his teenage daughter will enjoy going to the family reunion once she gets there and will not miss the rock concert, he is attempting to control her options unrealistically. She may indeed enjoy the gathering, but she will remember the control. One of our colleagues is a master at opening options for other people. An exceptionally clear thinker, Wayne works to describe all the available choices he sees in a conflict. Even when a group vote against the option that he wants, Wayne serves the function of showing respect for differing points of view and of making sure no one felt coerced. He acts out the concept he has written about—that people in arguments can adopt an open style of argument respecting others instead of coercing or deceiving them (Brockriede 1972).

2. In productive conflict behavior, one tries to treat other persons as *persons* and not as *things* only. They treat the conflict as an *interpersonal* experience rather than a *noninterpersonal* experience. *Interpersonal* communication bases its predictions of others' behavior on psychological, personal data derived from the in-

dividual instead of from cultural or sociological data (Miller and Steinberg 1975, p. 22). For instance, take the case of a student and professor arguing about a grade. The professor has much of the power in the conflict situation, (though not all). The professor is a white male, and the student is a Chicano male. If the professor thinks, "Most of the Mexican-Americans I've known or heard of are lazy—I'll bet this guy is just trying to get an easy grade out of me," and then proceeds to act on this prediction of the other person's motives, then the professor is communicating (and conflicting) *noninterpersonally*. If he listens to what the student is saying and makes a judgment about his motivations based on what he heard then and there, he is communicating *interpersonally*. He makes his choices based on an appreciation of the other's role instead of just thinking that the person is a "thing" blocking his goals.

3. One discriminates as to *when and where control is to be exercised* in a productive conflict situation. People who always try to exercise power, especially coercively, as conflict "gangsters," who cannot or do not discriminate among situations—they always want power over the other person. Stating, as we did above, that you cannot avoid using power and participating in conflict does not mean that you always must choose to try to maximize your *own* choices to the exclusion of the furthering of the choices of the other person. Everyone is familiar with the kind of person who always has to be "one up" on another person. They try to get the last word, manipulate every situation to their advantage (and to the detriment of others), and generally end up with a low level of trust being generated, even if they are very powerful and "win" often.

4. You further productive conflict behavior when you take responsibility for *accuracy of communication*. In many conflicts, accuracy cannot be checked "objectively" by an outsider. For instance, in the following situation, only the man involved knows what is accurate information for him.

Wife: Honey, what's wrong? You look down tonight.

Husband: Nothing's wrong. I'm just tired.

Wife: I know. You're angry at me because I said I'd pick you up on time so you could get to the game by 6:00, and I was a little late. I told you I was sorry.

Husband: Just forget it. Nothing's wrong. What's on TV?

Perhaps nothing was troubling the man. Probably, however, he was indeed irritated, but refused to discuss it. When people "stockpile" or "gunnysack" (Bach and Wyden 1968) their grievances, they let the grievances keep piling up. By doing this, they are still engaging in conflict, but are giving incomplete or inaccurate information to the other person in the conflict. The possibilities are better for conflicts being carried out productively when people take responsibility for their own choices instead of choosing to not see their role in the conflict.

5. *Goals should be placed in terms that are "do-able"* (Phillips and Metzger 1976). When goals are do-able, you can tell whether they are being achieved or not and adjust accordingly. In the case of a job, a do-able goal would be to increase my sales by 40 percent over last year as opposed to saying "I want to improve." In an intimate relationship, a do-able goal would be "to compliment him for the good things he does for me" contrasted to "being nicer." It seems that the establishment of do-able goals in private relationships is more difficult than in the public sector because the terms used to describe interpersonal relations are often ephemeral (Phillips and Metzger 1976). The more clarity and specificity we can have in goals, the better chance we will have of achieving them.

6. Most conflicts incorporate both *content and relationship goals.* Participants want certain beliefs advanced, certain behavior changed, tasks performed, and promises made, but they also want to define the conflict relationship differently. For instance, a city manager and city council may have a conflict over whether to fire the city attorney or not. Issues such as time on the job, competence, policies he or she supports, productivity in the department, and ability to perform the tasks required are primarily, although not totally, *content* issues. But the most heat may be raised by the *relationship* issue of who has the right to hire and fire—the city manager or the city council—and content issues may become secondary to the relationship issue, in this case *power,* that the two sides are in conflict over. Productive goal analysis incorporates both kinds of issues and does not devalue either one; usually the relationship issue is ignored by one side or the other as a power ploy. Remember that the dual goals in most conflicts are to (1) reach agreement and (2) enhance the relationship for future communication. Both are equally important.

7. *Include emotional data as well as more "objective" data* when goals are formulated. People, as we have said in Chapter 2,

always have reasons for what they do, even though their reasons may not be your reasons. Therefore, discounting some reasons because they are "only emotional" is not productive for the relationship. Talk about your own feelings and encourage others, even your opponents, to talk about their feelings. If this is not done, the agreements reached about the goals desired in the conflict are likely to be shallow and carry little power with the participants.

8. *Try to avoid polarizing* into separate groups too early, or polarizing your position too early in the goal negotiations. There is nothing inherently wrong about polarizing, but the practice does not work very well. If groups get identified as totally aligned with one point of view and refuse to listen to other points of view, they will have less chance for compromise if compromise is necessary.

9. *Decide which goals are actually incompatible at the moment and which ones only seem to be incompatible.* Some incompatibilities never change—people feel so strongly about their side of the issue that they are unchangeable. Sometimes these conflicting goals can be sidestepped or tabled for another time and the goals that are negotiable can be dealt with. Try to discourage the attitude of, "If you do not agree with me about this important issue, then you cannot agree with me about anything."

10. *Avoid reaching easy agreement on goals by persuing by premature voting,* by giving away your power to some authority, or by using chance measures (flipping coins) when the seriousness of the conflict suggests more careful attention to the negotiation. Often a group has to redo a conflict because the resolution reached the first time around was totally unrealistic or did not take into account the deep feelings of the participants involved. Recently a native American tribe in Montana tried to decide where to build a tribal complex. Long-standing rivalry came into play, and when the first vote was taken, the losing side accused the other side of trickery and refused to go along with the decision. Since the cooperation of all was essential, the process had to be repeated. They had not negotiated enough before voting.

11. If you seem to be stuck and no one can agree on anything, *discuss the extent to which you are related as groups or as individuals* in the group. Sometimes reminding each other of your interdependence serves the function of breaking down excessive stubbornness that gets in the way of advancement of new goals. Remind others that if everyone could get exactly what he or she wanted, you would not be in conflict; it would already be happily

resolved. Groups that do not need each other and individuals who are not interdependent seldom are involved in conflict, since the activity of conflict is so stressful and uncomfortable to many people.

12. *Start the negotiation session* (even an informal one) *with the points of agreement,* no matter how vague, instead of the points of disagreement. This helps give people common goals and some sense of the interdependence they share.

13. *In personal conflicts,* it is usually a good idea to avoid making stands and then giving in as a ploy. People catch on to the ruse, and your credibility is then lowered.

14. *Avoid stating goals in terms of winning and losing.* Talk in terms of what is best for the common good. If a win-lose orientation seems inevitable, before final decisions are made, assess again the degree of interdependence of the participants. What is "lost" in the future by "winning" now?

15. *State empathetic feelings when you have them.* Show understanding of the other point of view when you feel it even if you make it clear that you disagree with the other side. Your understanding enhances the productive nature of the negotiations and does not decrease your chances of getting what you want.

16. *Suggest outside assistance* when you feel this might be necessary and acceptable by other parties in the conflict. Sometimes participants in a conflict are too close to the situation to suggest any more productive avenues. This is the time to ask help from an appropriate third party. This process will be discussed in detail in Chapter 7.

Summary

In conclusion, we reemphasize that goal development is crucial to the successful management of any conflict. Goals that get set in concrete are too heavy, and goals that are as ephemeral as the air are useless. Realistic, well-negotiated goals move people closer to the possibility of successful conflict management.

Bibliography

Bach, George, and Wyden, Peter. *The Intimate Enemy: How to Fight Fair in Love and Marriage.* New York: Avon Books, 1968.

Brockriede, Wayne. "Arguers as Lovers." *Philosophy and Rhetoric.* Winter 1972, pp. 1-11.

Hawes, Leonard, and Smith, David H. "A Critique of Assumptions Underlying the Study of Communication in Conflict." *Quarterly Journal of Speech* 59(1973):423-435.

Hesse, Hermann. *Siddhartha.* New York: New Directions Publishing Corp., 1951.

Johnson, David W., and Johnson, Frank P. *Joining Together: Group Theory and Group Skills.* Englewood Cliffs, N.J.: Prentice-Hall, Inc., 1975.

Mager, Robert, and Pipe, Peter. *Analyzing Performance Problems:* or *You Really Oughta Wanna.* Belmont, Calif.: Fearon Publishers, Inc., 1970.

———. *Goal Analysis.* Belmont, Calif.: Fearon Publishers, Inc., 1972.

Miller, Gerald R., and Steinberg, Mark. *Between People: A New Analysis of Interpersonal Communication.* Palo Alto, Calif.: Science Research Associates, 1975.

Phillips, Gerald, and Metzger, Nancy. *Intimate Communication.* Boston, Mass.: Allyn & Bacon, Inc., 1976.

Rieke, Richard D., and Sillars, Malcolm O. *Argumentation and the Decision Making Process.* New York: John Wiley & Sons, Inc., 1975.

Rushing, Janice. *Participant Observation: A Neglected Method of Small Group Research.* Paper presented at Western Speech Communication Association, Newport Beach, California, November 1974.

Schutz, Alfred. *The Phenomenology of the Social World.* Translated by George Walsh and Frederick Lehnert. Evanston, Ill.: Northwestern University Press, 1967.

Toulmin, Stephen. *The Uses of Argument.* Cambridge, Mass.: Cambridge University Press, 1958.

Weick, Karl E. *The Social Psychology of Organizing.* Reading, Mass.: Addison-Wesley Publishing Co., Inc., 1969.

Strategies and Tactics

6

Teenage son: My dad is really shaky about my borrowing the car. I hope I can get it for Saturday night.

Friend: Listen, my dad used to be the same way because he was afraid I'd get drunk and wreck his new 280Z.

Teenage son: Hey, that's what my dad is afraid of too. He's always harping about "teenage drunken drivers" and "DWI cases" clogging up the courts.

Friend: When you talk to him, tell him that you don't want to wreck his car because then you would be without any wheels. And, tell him that you won't drink while you use his car.

Characteristics of Strategies and Tactics

Basic Conflict Directions

The individuals in the preceding example are demonstrating the early stages of what is commonly called "strategizing." People make strategic plans in order to push this conflict in the direction they want it to go.

Conflicting individuals and units have four primary choices about the *direction* the conflict they are in will take. They may (1) *avoid,* (2) *maintain* at the present level, (3) *reduce,* or (4) *escalate* it. Often, people are not aware that once in a conflict any strategic choice they make will have an impact on the direction the conflict takes. Some make the choice of direction openly and are fully aware of it. For instance, when someone says, "He really went too far that time. I'm going to blow the lid off of this," a desire to escalate the conflict is observable. Other times, however, parties make choices that move the conflict in one of the four directions without being aware of the impact of the choice. When a conflict party says "I know you are upset, but I refuse to argue with you again," the choice of "not making a choice" is avoidance. Regardless of what a participant chooses to do, if there is an expressed struggle over perceived incompatible goals with another interdependent party, then any tactical choice tends to move the conflict in one of the four directions.

A *strategic* choice in a conflict is a "planned method of conducting operations" (Phillips and Metzger 1976, p. 134) where a conflict participant attempts to move the conflict in one of the four basic directions of escalation, deescalation, maintenance, or avoidance. A strategy in a conflict is similar to strategies in any situation where one tries to accomplish goals where the other interdependent party can interfere. For instance, in football, basketball, and other competitive games, strategy sessions involve planning coordinated series of moves to accomplish the goal. People choose strategies based on where they want to go (goal), the direction they want to travel to get there (strategic direction), and the available tactics (tactical options). The strategy in a conflict provides the link between the goals and the tactics. *Strategies are the large, general game plans in conflicts, and tactics are the moves made to advance the conflict in the strategic direction that the participants informally and implicitly work out among themselves.*

An example of the use of strategic thinking comes from a student we know. In a small group class the students were required to work closely and produce a group report. In one of the more active groups, one of the members began airing the notion that she felt left out. As a result, the person who led the group into most of its task accomplishment became threatened and a conflict between the woman and the leader went on for an hour. Later, when the woman was asked to join the group to work on the final writing of the report, she began to avoid members of the group. She chose a strategic direction of avoidance. Then, one other female member of the group became concerned and frustrated at the first woman's lack of involvement with the group. In discussing what to do she said, "I don't know whether to keep calling her up and offering to help her with her part of the report (strategically deescalating) or to just leave her a note telling her to forget it (strategic avoidance). The crucial decision for the woman was over the strategic direction in which she should move the conflict.

Often the choice of a strategic direction is made without being fully aware of the available options. For example, one of our friends recently resigned her job, having been very unhappy with the working conditions. For awhile, she discussed the possible resignation with friends. She said she "really had no choice—I have to get out of here." With discussion, she realized she had several choices. She could (1) resign, an option that would avoid, then reduce the conflict. She could have (2) confronted the supervisor with her grievances, an option that would have escalated, and then, possibly, reduced the conflict. She could have (3) stayed for a definite period, a choice to live with and maintain the conflict at present levels. She chose finally the resignation option and felt happy about it because everything had been considered. She no longer felt "cornered."

Finally, conflict participants can *change* the direction a conflict is going by a careful reconsideration of goals, strategy, and tactics. Many close friends and lovers find themselves in conflicts that seem to keep escalating until there is a conscious effort to reduce or deescalate. When one of the parties says something like, "We are both getting more and more hostile and are trying to prove the other wrong. Let's back up and see what it is we really want," an attempt is being made to change the direction of the conflict. If the other person is like minded, the direction can be altered. Just as goals are transactional and change during the interaction, so are the directions that each party is advancing in the conflict. Every choice of a tactic supports an implicit, underlying choice of an overall strategy or direction of a conflict.

Strategies That Define Relationships

One final example of overall strategic game plans is provided by Brockriede's (1972) three-phase paradigm of arguers as rapists, seducers, and lovers. Not only do conflict participants support an overall direction in conflicts (avoidance, reduction, maintenance, and escalation), they also choose strategies based on how the relationships are defined in the conflict. In the "rapist" style (this paradigm is not meant to imply just sexual behavior, but all kinds of communication behavior), participants "function through power, through an ability to apply psychic and physical sanctions, through rewards and especially punishments, through commands and threats" (Brockriede 1972, p. 2). The conflict or argument is often escalated since participants are interested in coercion instead of gaining assent as a result of a carefully reasoned argument. The intent of those using the rapist style is to manipulate and violate the personhood of the "victims" or parties in the conflict. People often react with anger and even violence, thus escalating the conflict, when it becomes obvious that the "cards are stacked" or that one person has structured the conflict so that it is very likely that he or she will win—in a win-lose sense.

In some situations, the structure of the conflict is set up for the participants to encourage the escalation/rapist strategy. In the courtroom, legislative hearings, political debates, and forensic tournaments (Brockriede 1972, p. 3) the structure of the conflict encourages the coercion, or rapist, strategy.

When one person has chosen, however unconsciously, the rapist definition of a conflict strategy, one of the parties functions as a victim, even though most people would say they most certainly do not want to be victimized. Often, the person who feels out of power and victimized escalates to a point, then gives up, thinking, "There's nothing I can do to win anyway." In effect, the participants have cooperated in the escalation direction. Once we saw a very angry person try to take over the microphone and the floor in a church convention. He shouted loudly, disrupted the proceedings, and was finally given five minutes to state his case. He did so, supporting with vehemence the pullout of his church group from a large national group, which he perceived as being too liberal. He chose the rapist style to escalate the direction of the conflict—soon he and the chairman were yelling back and forth at each other, and tensions were rising. Finally, the man threw the microphone down, stormed out, yelling, "I couldn't even get a hearing." Then he held a news conference out in the foyer denouncing the leadership of the group. Although the man chose to become an "innocent victim" of the power group, he also strategically escalated so he would have a hearing in the local press. It was to his advantage to be perceived as the victim after escalating.

An overall direction of avoidance of the conflict issues is provided by the paradigm of "seduction" (Brockriede 1972, p. 4). In the seduction style, the low power person using seduction tries to charm or trick the other conflict party into going along with what he or she desires. Argument tactics from classical reasoning that support this avoidance strategy are such tactics as "ignoring the question, begging the question, the red-herring appeal, and appeals to ignorance or to prejudice" (Brockriede 1972, p. 4). The clash between issues is not direct, the issues are circumvented in what sometimes turns out to be a deceptive, charming, or even "cutesy" way. It is not important to the seducer to appeal to the other party's sense of free choice. She or he wants what is wanted no matter what, but is not willing (or perhaps able) to ask for it directly.

For instance, Liz recently asked friends of hers to help her find a job for the summer. She appeared very weak, took little initiative, and became stuck in a low-energy period in her life. She dropped in on her friends often, politely asking for "any suggestions" they might have for finding a job, but was evasive and confused when friends suggested that she needed help from an employment service. It appeared that she was trying to "seduce" her friends into taking responsibility for her, but needed, for her own self-concept's sake, to avoid any direct clash over the issues her friends found important. Finally, her choice of the avoidance strategy gained her great disservice since her friends got tired of trying to help her. So they started avoiding her.

In the "lover" style of argument conflict relationships are bilateral and equal. "The lover-arguer cares enough about what he is arguing about to feel the tensions of risking his self, but he cares enough about his coarguers to avoid the fanaticism that might induce him to commit rape or seduction" (Brockriede 1972, p. 5). The "lover" style of argument and conflict might be used for any of the conflict strategies—choice of this style influences the direction, whether it be avoidance, maintenance, reduction, or deescalation, and influences the choices of tactics available to the persons in conflict. It is this style, applied to any strategy, that we recommend. In our opinion, the lover style (whether it be with bosses, families, students, friends, or lovers) provides the best possibility for productive conflict precisely because it requires adaptation to the interests of the other.

In sum, strategic decisions are made in all conflicts that tend to advance the conflict in one of the four basic directions of escalation, deescalation, maintenance, or avoidance. Since all participants do some degree of strategizing, they tend to exert influence on the conflict.

The Process of Strategic Planning in Conflicts

Although strategic plans occur spontaneously and continuously, we do not mean to imply that they are always purposefully mapped out or closely examined ahead of time. Like transactional goals, strategies emerge during the conflict episode. Unfortunately, the words "strategy" and "tactic" carry negative meanings for many people. For example, in interpersonal situations, one way to damage someone's credibility is to call him "strategic" (Gibb 1961). People who are given that label are seen as manipulative, aloof, uncaring, and illegitimately powerful. We do not use the term "strategy" or even "tactics" to suggest that people should be more manipulative or deceitful. We believe that confict participants invoke strategies and tactics in order to accomplish their goals. Strategies and tactics are simply terms that can be used to describe the process of selecting options. Planning courses of action is a very natural and necessary human activity and is central to every conflict situation. The purpose of this chapter is to descriptively examine communication choices that conflict participants make, chart the effects they have in given conflicts, and examine tactics for instances of appropriate and inappropriate use.

Choose Strategies and Tactics Based on Goals

Participants in a conflict have notions about (1) their own goals, (2) the other's goals, (3) their options, (4) the other's options, and (5) possible consequences that will result from the tactical options chosen. Even though participants often do not progress through these steps one at a time or announce their thinking processes to the other participant, both research and anecdotal reports demonstrate the existence of tactical considerations. The game theory research cited in Chapter 4 demonstrates that in structured conflicts participants make choices, estimate choices of others, and strive to attain goals by using tactics. Classroom and training use of a modified prisoner's dilemma game demonstrates that participants typically try to either (1) win the most points or (2) win a "moral" victory by playing in such a way as to attain their personal goals. Tactical choices for winning the game include persuading the other team to make an error, offering rewards to the other team to lose, skillful negotiation, sending false information to the other team, and even lying. And, when a team is trying to claim a moral victory (by showing how they are "above" competition and winning), typical tactics involve playing as if strategy does not matter, giving the other team incomplete information, and deriding the other team's ethical principles (Wilmot and Frost 1977). Just as in games where one competes for points, conflict participants in real life make decisions about tactical options and make choices. One study (Wilmot 1976) asked college students to recall conflicts they had had with teachers. In all cases (most of the conflicts were over grades), the students reported that they had made a choice based on what effect that choice would produce. Additionally, when asked, "What options did you consider and reject?" the students all gave answers. Some thought of tactics like "telling his departmental chairperson," and others considered "punching out his lights." Luckily for the teachers, not all tactical options were used. One hapless teacher, however, flunked his nephew and, according to the nephew's report, "got a bloody nose, compliments of me."

When participants are involved in a conflict, they are inextricably tied together. Just as in the prisoner's dilemma game, real-life choices yield payoffs according to the choice that the other also makes. Bob and Joe were roommates who did not get along, so Bob began making moves to torment Joe. When Bob began verbally abusing Joe, Joe's response was to move out. But, had Joe responded by offering compromise, asking Bob what he wanted, or other options, then the payoff to Bob would have been different. This interdependence propels conflict participants to both (1) have their own preferences and (2) select a preference based on how they think the other will react.

The making of choices in a conflict is often assumed. Consider, for example, the case of two people involved in a conflict where tactical choices can be traced. As Laing et al. (1966) have noted, communication participants each have a perspective, meta-perspective, and meta-meta-perspective on selected issues relevant to their relationship. The perspective is what you think of *X,* in this case, what options you see yourself as having. Meta-perspectives involve estimates of the other's perspectives. And each meta-meta-perspective involves guesses about what the other *thinks you are thinking.* In illustration, reflect upon a young man and a young woman who are trying to determine whether to continue their relationship or not. They have been dating for three months, are pretty serious about one another, but the man is not as committed as the woman and wants to "let her down easily." He has been pushing for spending less time together, more individual freedom, and a gradual phaseout of the relationship. She wants to move the relationship to a firmer ground, make a public commitment about their relationship, and eventually marry. Up to this point in time, they have been having a few arguments but no major conflicts. However, Gayle now wants to have John accompany her home to meet her parents. They have had a short discussion, and Gayle has said, "I'd like you to meet my parents. How about us driving up during vacation?" He has responded,

"Well, I'll have to think about that. I was planning on staying here and ski-ing with Paul." The following sequence of steps could illustrate the tactical process that each might mentally rehearse before they meet again the following day.

Gayle	John

Prospective Goals

Have John travel home to meet my parents.

Avoid any further entanglements; (not meet her parents).

Strategic Directions

Deescalate or maintain the conflict so John will visit my parents.

Escalate the conflict, if necessary, so I can keep from visiting her parents.

Tactical Choices

A. Assumptions underlying tactical choicemaking:

Perspective
I want him to meet my parents.

Perspective
I don't want to meet her parents. I want to ski.

Meta-perspective
He wants to meet my parents, but might also like to ski.

Meta-perspective
She wants me to meet her parents at all costs.

Meta-meta-perspective
He thinks I want him to meet my parents regardless of the other choices.

Meta-meta-perspective
She thinks I want to meet her parents, and that I want to ski.

B. Consideration of tactical options:

1. *I could let him know that he can ski around home. If I do, though, he will claim that it isn't as good as staying here and skiing Snow Bowl.*

1. *If I tell her that I want to ski, she will probably suggest that I ski with her parents. If so, I'll just tell her that I've been wanting to ski Snow Bowl with Paul for two years.*

2. *If I get mad and make him feel guilty, he will just stop listening.*

2. *I could tell her that I don't want to be so involved and meeting her parents is an uncomfortable thing.*

3. *If I go to Paul and ask him to speak to John, it would help, unless Paul really wants him to stay here. So, I'll have to per-suade Paul that it is more impor-tant that John go.*

3. *I could ask Paul to tell her that the skiing is really important, so she won't try to make me leave.*

4. *I could have my parents call him and invite him to stay while talk-ing about skiing.*

4. *I could just avoid her for two days and then say "my plans are all made."*

Notice that each person thinks of (1) his or her own preference, (2) what that choice will likely produce in the other, and (3) an estimate of the probability of success. Then, each person chooses the option that is most likely to help accomplish desired goals. In our example, Gayle decides that her best bet is to persuade Paul to talk to John. John, meanwhile, is going to choose option #1 and concentrate his arguments on skiing. As they get together, the conflict unfolds as follows:

Gayle: Well John, I have to make my travel plans. Will you be going with me to meet my parents?

John: Gayle, you know that I've wanted to ski Snow Bowl with Paul. Now you've talked to him and try to get him to back out. It really makes me mad. Why don't you just leave my friends alone?

Gayle: Well, I just wanted to . . . .

John: I don't care, you are interfering with my life. I was trying to decide about skiing and the trip home with you, then you go and try to get my friends to make up my mind for me. Why do you have to push so hard for things you want?

Gayle: Well, I thought that Paul would just help you.

John: That does it! You wanted a decision and you will get it. I'm going to stay here and ski and not visit your parents.

Obviously, Gayle's choice for an approach was not effective, because she could not predict that John would escalate the conflict. As it turned out, John and Gayle broke up right after she returned from her vacation and he from his ski trip.

Notice at this point that the tactical options all focus on *content* issues, while *relationship* issues probably loom as being more important in each person's mind. For instance, the "shall we be close or shall we be farther apart?" relationship consideration outweighs the importance of skiing. The symbolic meaning of the trip home is far more important than other content considerations.

As this example illustrates, parties do think through options, thus, necessarily incorporating a judgment of how the other will react. However, it is often difficult to predict exactly what the tactical choices of the other person will be. Even the best tactician in the world is incapable of precisely predicting the outcome of the tactical choices that parties make. Predictions are difficult to make because each party is placed into this position.

1. I have my preferences.

2. The other has her preferences.

3. My choice will depend, in part, on what choice I think she will make.

4. Her choice will depend, in part, on what she thinks my choice will be.

5. And, her choice hinges on my choice which hinges on her choice which depends on mine which. . . .

Refer to the skiing example one more time. Note that Gayle had made an incorrect judgment regarding John's potential options. The misjudgment happened primarily because she incorrectly assessed their interdependence.

Gather the Available Information

The difficulty predicting what others will do often surprises us. We find ourselves saying something like "I was completely overwhelmed. The last thing I expected was for Mary to resign. And now here we are at the middle of budget preparation time and we have to find a new person." A person bursts into tears unexpectedly or suddenly becomes defensive and bitter, and we are surprised. One of the many reasons we are surprised by the communication behavior of others is that we do not use the information available to us through productive observation techniques. People send messages, often unintentionally, all the time, but often we are "blown away" by behavior that might have been predictable if we had observed with care and insight. Yarbrough (1977) gives several suggestions for carrying out productive experiential observations. Levels of observation should remain distinct. We often confuse (1) behaviors we can actually observe and (2) our interpretations of behaviors we observe (Haney 1973). In a husband-wife conflict, the wife might exclaim, "I know you're angry at me. You never understand when I want to spend some time alone. I work hard, too, you know!" This statement is an *interpretation*. If she were reporting behavior she could observe, she might say, "You're so quiet. Ever since I said I didn't want to go out tonight and wanted to read by myself, you haven't spoken to me." This is an *observation*. The husband then has more leeway to interpret for himself what his behavior means. Staying away from "mind-rapes" ("I know exactly what you're thinking") moves any potential conflict toward the possibility of being carried out in a productive manner. To encourage observation instead of interpretation, describe what you sense, feel, see, hear, touch, smell instead of what your interpretations of these observations are. The most important principle of accurate observation is to focus on what *is* happening instead of what *should be happening* (Yarbrough 1977). Instead of saying, "You shouldn't be angry just because I want to spend some time alone," say "You look angry. Are you?" (The person says "yes.") When did that feeling first occur?" Then the respondent has a chance to tell you more about what the feelings really are, and that statement will be full of information you need to make cooperative tactical choices. You need to know the degree of anger, when the anger pattern started, what he is feeling, and what he wants you to do before a productive strategy with supporting tactical choices can be developed. Of course, most of this thinking is done very quickly, not in a ponderous, step-by-step fashion. But it has been our experience that people are able to develop this cooperative strategic skill with understanding and experience.

Another major block to good observation is the projection or attribution of your own feelings to another. The feelings you are most likely to project onto another person are the ones with which you are most uncomfortable. Jung (1968) terms this projection our "shadow" selves—the repressed, out-of-awareness selves with which we are not very familiar because they are threatening in some way. This projection happens often. When you say, "I think it's tense in here," a more appropriate statement might be, "I am feeling very tense." At a recent faculty meeting one of us made a plea for finding an office for a new faculty member who was housed on the floor above the rest of the faculty members. The statement was made, "It's hard to relate to someone who's on the next floor—he gets left out." The faculty member in the out-of-the-way office then said, "I like it up there. I have privacy." It then became obvious that a more accurate statement would have been, "I have trouble relating to you up there. I miss your presence." The projection (almost literally like a projection on a screen away from the camera) then could have been dealt with as a personal feeling instead of a supposed group feeling.

Another block to good observation is needing to always be right in your perceptions. If a person seems to you to be acting in a defensive manner, try to take that observation and make it specific instead of labeling the person "defensive" and then fighting to maintain the accuracy of that perception. When you give your data for the perception, "You seem concerned that I'm trying to make a decision without you— that's not what I want to do," instead of saying, "You sure get defensive when I talk about what I want to spend my money from my raise on!" you are presenting your perception as an observation that needs to be checked out, not as an article of faith.

Other blocks to helpful observation are judging and scorning the feelings and actions of others, trying too soon to help the person "get over" negative feelings by explaining why he or she has them or communicating that you have the person all figured out or diagnosed, which typically sets people up for a win-lose power struggle over whose interpretation is right (Yarbrough 1977). When observation is used in an open manner, a large amount of new data become available to people who are in conflicts. Sadly, these data are often unavailable because of our need to be *right*. Many people in conflicts argue to convince themselves and others that they are right, leave the scene convinced they are right, and then have little understanding of the strategic and tactical choices the other persons are probably going to make.

Conflict participants are always in a state of some uncertainty. Even though we cannot teach you to predict all choices, we can help in understanding the process. As noted above, each tactical choice involves understanding your individual and relational goals and predicting the probable response of the other person(s) to your tactical choices.

Tactical Choices

Avoidance Tactics

One of the most common strategies for coping with conflict or potential conflict is avoidance. When we ask people to comment on how they handle conflicts, the large majority say something like, "I try not to let them happen," "I try to concentrate on the good things we have," or "I hate for people to yell at each other so I change the subject." All of these devices are communicative tactics that utilize the strategy of avoidance. Avoidance has an undeserved bad name among those interested in conflict management— especially conflict facilitators who have a psychological or therapeutic orientation. Avoidance is typically practiced in the first stages of relationship development. When intimates first get together, they usually accentuate the happy, loving, positive features of their new unity; thus when they look back on their relationship, they often remember "not having to fight so much" with longing since that phase reminds of the excitement of new love. But as couples, workers, families, and friends build up a reservoir of rewards, they are able to employ other tactics in conflicts. Both avoidance and escalation can lead to either destructive or productive conflict. When avoidance is overused, however, and there is never any escalation, there is a static quality to the interactions (Rausch 1974, p. 208), and growth is not as likely as when tactics are used more creatively. Avoidance is neither positive or negative in and of itself. It would be ludicrous to say, "One should always confront conflict" or "One should always avoid conflict." As we have discussed, the goals of the conflict episode and the relationship are the most important considerations—tactical choices depend on the goals being pursued by the participants.

Avoidance is often an appropriate, useful tactic. When persons can gain nothing by confronting, when power is drastically unequal, or when people want to stay far apart instead of coming closer together, avoidance is often an appropriate strategic direction. Some of the following tactics will help you avoid eminent conflict when it is in your own (or the other parties') best interest to do so. We will also discuss *misuses* of these avoidance tactics. Conflict management will grow smoother for you if you develop a wide repertoire of these tactics and if you are able to recognize their misuse.

Postponement

Bach and Wyden, in *The Intimate Enemy* (1968), suggest that setting a time for a later conflict is a productive avoidance tactic. They suggest "fighting by appointment." While often there is no choice, we do agree with this suggestion. The tactic is used this way. Gloria is upset. She wants to talk to her husband Sam late at night. Sam has an appointment at eight o'clock in the morning.

Gloria: I am so upset that I can't sleep. What ever possessed you to talk about our summer plans to the Carters at the party? You know we've been trying to get free of doing things with them. You said last week. . . .

Sam: Can't we talk about this in the morning?

Gloria: It's fine for you to say that. You don't have to deal with Judy when she calls tomorrow to decide where we'll take our families for a joint vacation. *I* have to talk to her and tell her we changed our minds.

Sam: I'm sorry I brought it up. But I'm sleepy and I don't want to talk about it.

At this point, the avoidance tactic Sam is using—"Maybe if I close my eyes all this hassle will go away"—is certainly not productive. His twin goals, (1) to get some sleep and (2) to avoid further antagonizing his wife, are not likely to be met. By this time Gloria is probably angry not only about his lack of discretion at the party but his refusal to talk to her about it. An example of a productive postponement tactic follows.

Sam: Gloria, I know you're upset. I also feel foolish. But I am exhausted and I really don't want to deal with all the issues now. When Judy calls tomorrow, tell her we haven't had a chance to talk yet and you'll call her back. Then when I come home from work tomorrow we'll discuss the whole thing.

Gloria: You always say that, and it never gets talked about.

Sam: This time it will. We'll sit down before dinner, banish the kids, and the two of us will talk. I know you're upset.

Gloria: OK, if we really will. I know it's hard to talk in public like that. They presume so much. . . .

Postponement as a tactic works best when several conditions are present. First of all, emotional content of the conflict needs to be acknowledged while referring other issues to a later time. Sam said, "I know you're upset," acknowledging the depth of Gloria's feelings. She would not have been likely to go along with the postponement if he had said, "It's stupid for you to be upset. We'll work it out later." After the emotional content is acknowledged, all parties have to agree on a time that is soon and realistic. If Sam had said, "We'll talk about it sometime soon," that would not have been precise enough. The other party has to believe that the postponer really means to bring up the issue later. Postponement does not work well as a tactic if the other people involved think they are being put off, never to return to the issue. Statements such as a vague "we'll have to work on that sometime" or "let's all try harder to get along" are often giveaways that the person making the statement has no intention of voluntarily coming back to the conflict at issue.

Another time when it is usually not appropriate to postpone is when all parties have energy and a desire to work out the conflict right then. Postponement without good reason, just to let people "cool off," might waste a valuable resource—emotional investment in a particular conflict. When the time and energy are available for working out an issue, it is better dealt with immediately.

Controlling the Process

We were recently told by a divorced couple about their bargaining session where they set the size of childcare payments. They conducted the bargaining without legal help. Both indicated that they did not "start" negotiating until they spent thirty minutes arguing over how to proceed. One party wanted to air emotional responses during their talk, while the other party wanted to outlaw any personal comments and concentrate on the actual money required to raise children by looking at old checkbooks and other records. Neither realized that this "prenegotiation" session was a crucial tactical effort at controlling the process in which important decisions would be made. In this case, both parties wanted to specify that anything other than their own preferred area of discussion was out of order. This attempt was (in this case) an unsuccessful try at avoiding future conflict and gaining personal advantage by controlling the process. As we have discussed, the person who sets up the rules gains power in a conflict.

On the other hand, setting a joint agenda ahead of time when both or all parties agree to do so can be a highly productive avoidance tactic. Many of the issues are negotiated while deciding what to discuss—power is assessed, coalitions are speculated upon, strength of involvement is estimated. A leader can facilitate mutual agenda setting by saying something like, "What shall we discuss tomorrow at staff meeting?'' or ''Before we leave I want to settle upon the topics to be covered by this committee.''

Resorting to Formal Rules

In the above example, the parties involved tried to impose informal rules of their own choice on the situation. Often, formal rules such as Robert's Rules of Order, majority rule, seniority, rank, or other formal rule structures are used to make a decision, avoid immediate conflict, and hopefully, reach resolution of the conflict. Many times, as we all know, these tactics are useful and reasonable avoidance/resolution tactics. Other times, however, the importance of the minority is overlooked. Calling for a vote is easy; premature voting without taking account of the consequences for those who lose simply postpones the conflict until later. Especially in situations such as groups of close friends and coworkers, voting is often invoked inappropriately. Cheap resolution is attained. The power issue in the conflict is not solved since the power is brought in from elsewhere instead of being worked out among the participants in the conflict (Filley 1975).

Another variation of the ''resorting to rules'' avoidance tactic is used by leaders of organizations, conferences, persons chairing meetings, or superiors in a staff meeting. This tactic might be called the ''arbitrary break'' tactic. A colleague of ours told of a conference she attended in Great Britain on the subject of conflict among British Commonwealth subjects who emigrated to England. Just as the discussion got involved with racial issues, a gentleman from the West Indies spoke out strongly against racial prejudice in England. The chairman pounded the gavel and announced that he was terribly sorry but that the conference must break for afternoon tea! Evidently, the chairman used arbitrary tea breaks to intervene and change the direction of any potential conflict. The conference ended in bitter frustration for the participants. Other examples of arbitrary breaks might be lunch breaks coming early, cutting off speakers after a certain time even though the audience wants them to continue, calling for further study, tabling a motion, or any other tactic that purchases temporary avoidance at the expense of a desired thorough discussion of a problem. Of course, all of the above tactics might be used productively if the people involved are not ready to make a decision, if violence seems to be forthcoming, or if more information would help resolve the conflict and a break helps secure that information.

Changing the Physical Environment

Many times when we lead conflict simulation games such as ''Starpower'' and ''Power Play,'' we hear participants discussing moving to another room to avoid contact with the other groups—the physical contact with competing groups is conflict-provoking. Often we notice people moving closer to another person with whom they sense potential conflict in an attempt to move into the close personal space region so that conflict might be less likely. And, of course, the ultimate physical avoidance tactic is simply to leave the scene—not always a cowardly copout. When you are terribly outnumbered, physically threatened, tricked into being present for a conflict in which you do not wish to participate, or do not wish to even maintain physical presence for some ethical reason, then walking out can be effective. This tactic is overused, especially by people who hope that their action will bring the other people racing after them, begging them to come back. However, when you genuinely desire not to be present and are willing to take the consequences for the action—leave! A friend of ours was accused once of personal prejudice toward an employee in the organization for which he worked. His negative rating had caused the employee to be fired. The employee called and asked for a meeting to discuss the reasons, and the employer agreed. At the time of the meeting, however, the disgruntled employee came into the manager's office with seven friends and associates, including the union representative. The manager refused to discuss the matter without *his* boss present, told them his objections, and left—probably a wise temporary avoidance tactic.

Tacit Coordination

Sometimes observers of a conflict have the feeling that much communication is either going on privately, or that an awful lot has been decided upon ahead of time since even parties who are opposed to each other are cooperating—even to the point of being extremely polite to opposing parties. Sometimes the end point of a bargaining session, hiring session, salary negotiating session, or policy question is indeed fixed. Much of the time, however, the cooperation going on is tacit, or "understood." Full communication about the actual conflict is impossible or undesirable, yet there is a certain amount of unspoken understanding present. Schelling (1960) has developed several games in which the object is to predict what the other person will do in a specified situation so that players can thus choose the best move. When there are common interests in coming to the same conclusion and avoiding a win-lose conflict situation, parties may work together even when they cannot or will not communicate freely. Mental, tacit understanding influences the partners' moves. Avoidance of conflict also occurs when people try to predict the votes of others ahead of time to determine "which way the wind blows" or when people try to time requests of others to occur when the other party is most likely to give in to the request. Students learn to avoid conflict in exam week by showing tacit understanding of professors' preoccupation with grading exams and making clear that requests for regarding or renegotiating a grade, for instance, are meant for some later time. Another common tacit conflict avoidance move is for parties disputing over money or other tangible scarce resources to *split the difference* between the high and the low offers—unless there is good reason not to accept such an offer. Americans usually expect the other party to be a good sport and split the difference.

Another tacit avoidance tactic is developed from the idea of "fairness." Schelling suggests that the moral force of "fairness" is much more powerful than we might think. One party may not want to violate trust, for example, not because violation of trust is not desirable, but because the public or other reference groups expect fair behavior—thus reinforcing in a powerful way the tendency toward fairness and equity (Schelling 1960). In a classroom situation, for instance, a student may ask the teacher in front of other students for a postponement of the test scheduled for that day, explaining that the library lost the reserve reading material that was to be covered and many of the students had not had a chance to read the material. The teacher is almost compelled to avoid conflict by agreeing, since the moral force of fairness pushed for that move, toward postponement. If the teacher said, "You are responsible for doing the reading. The test is today—take it today or not at all," the repercussions for such an unfair move would likely be strong, provoking intense conflict.

Precueing

Conflict can be productively avoided by giving enough information about yourself prior to a conflict so that other persons know what to expect about you. Goffman (1959) says that "Information about the individual helps to define the situation, enabling others to know in advance what he will expect of them and what they may expect of him." Congruent behavior (verbal and nonverbal communication representing the emotions a person feels at a given time) helps to "precue" others about your probable response to a move by another party. One can precue nonverbally by not trying to hide distress in an intimate conflict or by other nonverbal behaviors that demonstrate the true state of feeling at the time of the potential conflict. Quiet attention can show the others that you are serious and involved in the issue at hand.

Gunnysacking and Dumptrucking

These strange sounding tactics, coined by Bach and Wyden in *The Intimate Enemy* (1968), are actually a combination of avoidance and escalation. When one person in an interpersonal system hides gripes, keeps count of grievances, holds grudges, suppresses potential conflicts, then "empties the gunnysack" or "dumptrucks" on the other person, a destructive avoidance tactic has been used. Often the conflict inside the person has grown to such a state that the person doing the "dumping" actually wants to hurt the other person instead of working out the conflict. It becomes a hit-and-run maneuver, with the recipient of all the angry words standing bewildered wondering, "What got into him/her?" These hiding tactics are the opposite of productive postponement. Extreme cases result in resignations, divorces, shouting matches, irreparably damaged relationships, and bitter misunderstandings.

Sometimes the person doing the dumping is trying to act upon the desire to be open and honest, but open and honest communication presupposes that the person doing the initiating wants to hear what the other person has to say in response. The gunnysacker is not interested in any response; the goal is to get rid of hard feelings by giving them all to someone else. The tactic is often used by people who try to tell you that "it's all for your own good."

Coercive Tactics

Coercion is often used primarily to escalate a conflict, but "strong-arm tactics" are also used to avoid conflict, at least temporarily. We are always surprised when managers or students work on case studies involving a complex organizational conflict in which a manager does not want to work with another manager who has just been hired. Many times the productive solution that a group comes up with has to do with simply having the boss tell the employees to get along with each other and shape up. This kind of suppression is only a temporary peacemaking tactic. The underlying causes for the dislike of the two employees for each other have not been dealt with. As we discussed in Chapter 5, there are always at least two goals in the resolution of any conflict: (1) to reach agreement and (2) to enhance the relationship for future conflict management. When a third party uses coercion, invoking outside punishments (such as loss of the job) to reach agreement and avoid future conflict, only half of the relational task has been dealt with. The same kind of coercive tactic is also used destructively in many family situations. Parents resort in desperation to coercion (I'm bigger than you, that's why!") instead of gaining willing adherence to their rules, and children reach forced agreement, but the relationship is certainly not enhanced for future conflict management. The avoidance of conflict is temporary. As Ruesch (1957, p. 265) says, "The manipulative attitude is particularly pernicious when parents consistently approach their children in this manner without interposing periods of primarily enlightening communication. (Such a practice) forces the child to develop inappropriate replies which are geared to cope with coercion rather than with information." Growing up consistently with people who use coercion as a conflict tactic teaches people that they cannot expect reasonableness to work, that people cannot reach agreement anyway, and that they should either grow up so they can use coercion too or just avoid conflict altogether.

Miller and Steinberg (1975) speak of "power gangsters" who learn that coercion sometimes works to get what they want. They then learn to overuse the tactic, finally getting "hooked" on the power itself instead of looking for productive management devices appropriate for the situation and the people involved in the situation. The use of superior power in itself is not always negative, but learning to rely on the power differential to manage conflict locks people into a limited repertoire of management tactics.

A final coercive tactic often used for avoidance of conflict is the *side payment* (Filly 1975), *payola,* or bribe offered to someone to keep them quiet and out of potential conflict. Many times even good friends use this tactic—it is not limited to Godfather-type operations where someone is "made an offer he can't refuse." Until recent years, women in organizations were often given much attention for socioemotional role-taking such as making coffee, planning employee picnics, heading the United Fund Drive, and leading the newcomer orientation sessions. These activities gave the women visibility, and women involved often did not realize until they were entrenched into the roles that they were not being involved in policymaking and high level decision-making. They were in a system that avoided conflict through bribes. Remember that many bribes are emotional in nature, not the kind that are illegal. In intimate relationships, people often work out a complex "emotional blackmail" system in which one party tacitly agrees not to push a certain issue if the other party will reciprocate by avoiding a different painful issue. The "deal" (although never overtly discussed) might be, "I'll not push for more time from you if you keep me happy by giving me money and social prestige."

Linguistic Manipulation

Linguistic manipulation, or labeling, is also an avoidance tactic. The tactic relies upon redefining the conflict people are in or upon attaching a label to oneself or another person that is likely to promote avoidance of the conflict for some reason. For instance in a conflict simulation game, a player once said, after he figured out the rules of the game, "Let's create our own lesson plan." What the man actually was asking for was for the participants to take over the running of the game, change it to one involving less conflict, and replace the designated leaders with new ones. The words "lesson plan" are innocuous sounding words that create an entirely different impression than if the disgruntled player had said, "Hey! Let's have a revolution and throw these overaggressive manipulative bastards out!" The adherence he gained might not have come so easily if he had *labeled* his suggestion as a revolution instead of a change in lesson plans. Linguistic manipulation also can be used by parties who want to convince the other participants that there is no conflict at all. We are all familiar with the person who says, "We aren't really in conflict, we just have a minor difference about procedures." If the person were using language to escalate instead of avoid conflict, he or she might say, "We seem to have no agreement whatsoever about our procedures." Relabeling does not have to be used in a dishonest way, however. Taking the opportunity to say something a different way is often sufficient for avoiding what is beginning to be a pointless, ill-defined conflict that is better off avoided.

Refusal to Recognize the Conflict

Refusing to recognize that a conflict exists is kin to the tactic discussed above of relabeling and redefining. We have all probably experienced the utter frustration of having another person with whom we sense there is indeed genuine conflict refuse to acknowledge that conflict might be occurring. This sensation is much like trying to fight a cloud—nothing we can say makes any difference. Refusal to recognize the existence of a conflict is sometimes a productive, power-shifting ploy for persons in high power positions who would have to give up some of their autonomy to make decisions if they entered the negotiation process. Often, however, the nonrecognition of conflict is a painful, disconfirming experience. When one person is unsure of his or her ability to handle conflict in touchy, important areas, the chosen tactic may be nonrecognition, which may be better than having to face the issue and use skills of communication with which the threatened party does not feel comfortable. One of us witnessed a couple at dinner who were caught in this regressive communication spiral. The wife was upset and tense. She appeared to be near tears, answering in monosyllables and looking down at her plate. The husband was seemingly unaware of her distress as he joked and talked to other guests. He made a slightly cutting remark about the wife, and she burst into tears and became embarrassed since company was present. The husband shrugged and said, "I didn't know she was in a bad mood." The wife had been trying to nonverbally precue the husband that something was wrong, but because of their particular relational pattern, he needed not to see what was happening. In his desire to avoid a conflict, a larger one was created.

Fogging

The final avoidance tactic we will discuss is *fogging*. This tactic has been popularized by assertiveness training books in the last few years. It is a tactic we find useful when one is in a low power situation or does not want to engage in conflict because the involvement level is too low. It works like this. Bob tells Jenny with some disgust, "You can't ever make up your mind about what you want to do. You take forever." Jenny, not wanting to provoke a conflict at that moment, or perhaps not wanting to fight because she is not involved enough with Bob, says, "I *do* take a long time." Instead of replying to the underlying criticism and request or demand for change ("Dammit, hurry up and make up your mind!"), she *fogs* by agreeing with part of the criticism but choosing to ignore the rest of it. This tactic can be crazy-making if overused, and we are not suggesting that it is always productive. It is, however, an option for use when you feel you are being dragged into a conflict that is not one you want to invest yourself in at the time. For further reading on this tactic, see Phelps and Austin (1975) and Smith (1975).

Escalation Tactics

In an escalating conflict, involvement increases, issues are sharply defined, the number of issues usually increases, and parties polarize. Escalation tactics function to increase the intensity of a conflict by highlighting the interdependence of the parties and simultaneously putting pressure on the other to capitulate. At their core, all the escalation methods involve an attempt to place more pressure on the *other* to change, instead of changing the structure of the relationship. One of the fascinating aspects of escalatory tactics is that they involve (1) asserting more force on the other to change by threatening to act or acting *independently* of the other's wishes while (2) relying on relational *interdependence* as a condition to help bring the other "into line." In most conflicts where escalation is occurring, tactics appear in clusters—people often threaten, confront the other, and polarize all at the same time. We will discuss each tactic separately, however, in order to specify its nature.

Too many of us, when we see someone using a tactic of escalation, automatically assume that the party wants to end the relationship. Just as avoidance can be invoked to either strengthen or weaken a relationship, escalation can serve many purposes. If someone escalates a conflict by shouting at you, "You are *always* bugging me, lay off!" they might be trying to (1) strengthen the relationship by telling you (awkwardly) that you are important to them, (2) wanting to merely exercise more independence from you than in the past, (3) wanting you to fight back to prove your love, or (4) wanting to destroy the relationship. Apfelbaum (1974) makes a strong argument that many tactics are designed to get a response from the other, since the estimate of the responsiveness of the other is a key to planning your own course of action. As we proceed through the discussion of escalatory tactics, we will demonstrate how each tactic can be used for divergent purposes.

Labeling

Whenever one tries to escalate a conflict by the choice of words used, the tactic of labeling is occurring. The two major types of labeling are (1) naming the other person or party and (2) labeling the conflict or the relationship. We have all seen examples of labeling the other party. Consider the following two roommates.

Sally: Sarah, don't you think you should clean your side of the room? I've asked you four times this week.

Sarah: Sally, you sure are on my back a lot about the room. I told you I'd clean it when I had a chance.

Sally: That's just it, you *never* have a chance. You just don't want to do your share.

Sarah: Look, Sally, if you weren't such a nag, I'd do it right now.

Sally: Yes, and if you weren't such a slob, I wouldn't have to keep reminding you.

Clearly, the roommates are both bent on escalating the intensity of the conflict by the name-calling. We have all seen young boys and girls call others names as a way to torment each other. And the feeble reply of "sticks and stones will break my bones, but names will never hurt me," is an attempt to deny the impact of the names. In conflicts, people escalate by labeling the other party as if the enemy were a person even when it is not. For instance, a minority political group will often label the government as "fascist," "communist," "reactionary," or some equally undesirable label in order to escalate the conflict. And, the ruling party will work at naming the opposition too. An escalatory label used by a party performs two functions. First, it provides a shorthand way of describing how you see the other's motives and, it provides more fuel to the escalatory direction. Labeling both expresses the escalation and produces more escalation. Unfortunately, if the label serves the function of incensing the other, the escalation will breed escalation. Many people have experienced situations where parties stand and hurl insults back and forth until violence occurs or someone leaves in rage.

Labeling of the other party can serve productive ends as well, especially if the chosen label provides for just enough escalation for the conflict episode to be engaged, closely but not uncontrollably. This might happen with two men who are close friends and are playing foosball. One of the players goes to great effort to defeat his friend. If his behavior is a real surprise to the less competitive friend, the friend might reasonably say, "Carl, you are a competitive son-of-a-gun. You wanted to win at almost all costs." This limited escalation performs the function of alerting the friend that a conflict has been engaged and that the behavior was not desirable. Obviously, if the label of another, within the context of a given relationship, provides for some restrained escalation of the conflict, it serves a productive purpose. Many people who have a close relationship use their knowledge of name-calling as a fun device. Two best friends can call one another "egghead" and "fishface" without any relational deterioration. But if a man says, "OK, bossy," to his wife, she might well pick up an underlying desire on his part to discuss her behavior that is bothering him. The label provides the trigger to get the (hopefully) productive conflict going.

The second major type of labeling is when a conflict participant provides a label for the conflict. While only slightly distinct from supplying a label for the other party, these sets of labels reveal how the person sees the structure of the conflict. More extreme examples occur when a person "over crucializes" the relational strain. For instance, if a supervisor labels her employee's suggestions for improvement by saying, "What we have here is a win-lose conflict where they are trying to undermine our authority," she is escalating the situation. Any form of polarization serves the function of escalating the conflict. If a husband says to his wife, "Say, what's for dinner tonight?" and she responds, "I'm not going to tell you because if I do we'll just fight again," her label for the probable relationship definition will likely have an escalating effect.

Labeling has tremendous impact on how persons classify their relationship. If you place yourself in the position of describing the relational history, you can set the stage for a long-term escalation. For instance, if an intimate says, "Willis and I fight constantly. All we do is have one serious conflict after another," the labeling of the relationship makes it difficult to see it as a joint venture. It sounds more like mutual war that will forever recur.

One can also productively escalate by relational labeling. The tactic is especially appropriate when you need to alter the other party's perception of the conflict. If an employee and supervisor cannot seem to resolve a question of salary raise, the employee can escalate by labeling the prolonged discussions as a "serious conflict." Similarly, if two intimates are in a situation where one is upset and the other is avoiding, the distressed party can increase chances for a hearing by suggesting that the other "does not think we have a relational problem, but we do."

Issue Expansion

Issue expansion is the second major type of escalatory tactic. It is the opposite of fractionation (breaking a conflict down into component parts) and occurs when a person purposefully balloons the issues (Raush, Barry, Hertel, and Swain 1974). Issue expansion can be particularly effective in bringing up relational concerns by using the content issues as the first step. The tactic allows the other to see how significant the content is in relation to your self-esteem. The following incident happened in the kitchen of a married couple.

She:	Honey, be sure to put the coffee on.
He:	It is on the table already.
She:	But the new mugs aren't out. I'll exchange these for the new ones. Say, how are the hamburgers doing? Did you put plenty of Worchestershire sauce on them.?
He:	Dammit, you don't think I can do anything right? You complain about the meals. This morning you said you didn't like my clothes. You don't like any of my tastes.

The issue expansion happened when he moved the discussion from the specific items into his feeling that he could not do anything right. And, it served the function of signaling to her that his self-esteem regarding cooking and clothes was hanging by a thin thread.

Issue expansion, by bringing up related topics (clothes), makes it clear to the other party that more is at stake than just the content issue of coffee and hamburgers. A sensitive observer of the interaction will also note that issue expansion allows the person who is upset to send messages regarding the relational aspects of the conflict. In essence, he is saying, "I feel inferior to you on these matters. My feelings of inferiority are underlying all of the specific responses that I give to you."

Of course, issue expansion can be unproductive as well. If left unchecked or if responded to in a like manner, it can lead the participants into unproductive charges and countercharges. If the party is not attuned to the underlying relational issues, the conflict can be derailed for extended periods of time.

Coalition Formation

Coalition formation is another tactic that serves to move the conflict in escalatory directions. Whenever a party appeals to others to join the cause and assist him or her in attaining a goal, a coalition has been formed. The prime function that coalition formation serves is to increase the power of that party (Caplow 1968; Gamson 1961). Coalitions are so prevalent and well understood that all one has to do is listen to what conflict participants say about coalition formation in order to realize their potential for escalation. Small children talk about "ganging up on me" and corporation officers talk about the "opposition joining hands to defeat us." Similarly, whenever a power group is discussing "dividing and conquering" they are talking about how to effectively break up a coalition that is forming.

Coalition formation is escalatory because it (1) highlights the disparity of power between the conflict participants and (2) demonstrates an attempt to shift the power balance. Whether a small child is saying "my big brother is going to beat you up" or a political leader is discussing "cooperation between us so that we can overpower the opposition," the fact that coalition formation is a power move is apparent to all.

Coalitions are of varying types, ranging from conservative (those that preserve the basic structure of the conflict but give the low power parties more power) to revolutionary (Caplow 1968). A revolutionary coalition is formed when two less powerful individuals or groups pool their power and thereby overcome the most singly powerful person or group. This process can be exemplified by the case of three vice-presidents of an organization, in which person A has superior power to either person B or person C. However, the joint combination of B and C is larger than A. When a conflict occurs so that other modes of management are not working, the vice-presidents may get to the point of forcing a power showdown. The formation of the BC coalition, therefore, is inherently revolutionary because it will upset the prescribed order of things and be in a position to determine policy.

When coalitions do not affect the overall power balance, they seldom form. If, in the case above, person A still would have superior power over B and C even if B and C formed a coalition, it would not be to B and C's advantage to form a coalition (Caplow 1968).

Not only do coalitions tend to form in overt, power-play situations as a way to gain more influence, they tend to also form whenever there are three parties to a conflict. It seems to be almost a natural product of the desire to form close relationships that three entities align themselves into a dyad plus one. At any point in a conflict, the participants tend to form into a group of two in contrast to the singular person. If a third party enters into the relationship of two friends in order to help manage the conflict, it will be extremely difficult for the third friend to not form into a closer bond with one of the parties compared to the other. One of the most natural tendencies of any triad is to subdivide into a dyadic coalition plus one (Caplow 1968; Wilmot 1975). It is not accidental that marriages and other intimate relationships are usually formed by two people coming together and forming a coalition.

Coalitions form naturally and serve to escalate conflicts when they arise. If you are trying to maintain your superior power position, therefore, it is sometimes expedient to prohibit the forming of coalitions by the less powerful members. Ruling political parties in many countries make their first new "law of the land" prohibitions against public gatherings and meetings where coalitions can be formed. Managers make sure meetings include everyone in decision-making so the need for coalitions will decrease.

Threats

For many, escalation is synonymous with threats. Threats, which come in many forms, all have a common underlying element that makes them effective in escalating a conflict. All threats move the conflict to a position where one or more of the parties are willing to inflict punishment or harm on the other in order to achieve their goal. Furthermore, they focus the attention of the conflict upon what each party has to lose rather than emphasizing cooperative elements and thus escalate the conflict (Swingle 1970). As Frost (1974) has noted, threats are one of the most basic devices used in conflict, especially implied threats. Tedeschi (1970, 1972) has outlined the distinctions between threats, promises, warnings, and mendations. Figure 7 shows how the devices are related to one another.

	Source Controls The Outcome	Source Does Not Control The Outcome
Negative Sanction	Threat	Warning
Positive Sanction	Promise	Recommendation[1]

Figure 7. Tactical devices related to threats.

If the source (the other party) is in a position to control the outcome you will experience, the application of a negative sanction is a threat. For instance, the parent who says, "Clean up your plate or I'll spank you," the employer who cajoles, "Get with the program and work harder or you will be laid off," and the lover who shouts, "If you do that once more, I'll leave and never come back," are all in the position to invoke the negative sanction they control. Warnings, however, are invoked by a source who is not personally in control of the sanctions that he or she is warning you about. The friend who says, "If you don't stop treating your father so badly, he will cut you out of his will" is issuing you a warning—a negative sanction that he does not control. Similarly, the source who promises you rewards, but someone else controls the goodies, can make a "recommendation" to you, but not a promise.

A threat, which is a middle ground between an argument and the use of brute force, can be used productively in conflict situations. Threats are not necessarily unproductive or harmful to either the conflict participants or

---

1. Tedeschi calls these "mendations," but we prefer "recommendations" because the word makes more intuitive sense to us.

their relationship. For instance, one of the most productive uses of threats is to give a clear message to the other conflict participant that you feel strongly about the conflict and that you are commmitted to your goals. The girl friend who says, "If you ever say those things about me again, I'll leave you," makes it abundantly clear to her partner that she is committed to not being belittled. Being willing to risk relational harmony for the sake of goal attainment helps the other party assess your seriousness. Walton (1969) also notes that the use of stress in a conflict by a third party can produce the maximum climate for the management of the conflict. When a parent, for example, has two warring children on his hands and says, "If you two don't learn how to get along with one another, you won't play together any more," he produces some motivation for the siblings to learn how to deal with their difficulties.

Often, threats are productive tactics precisely because they are so effective in generating change in the other party. The often-quoted example of the "silent treatment," when one party will not exchange verbally but gives off nonverbal cues of disapproval is a nonverbal threat. The offending party who receives the "silent treatment" is aware that some effort must be expended to keep the relationship on productive grounds.

Threats are often used productively in conjunction with other tactics. For instance, negotiations commonly begin with threats and, as the bargaining process continues, move to other tactics. The negative reactions that threats bring can be used to help build a sense of relief when they are discontinued. A high level of threat followed by a low level of threat gives the parties a sense that improvement is necessary and that it can be accomplished in a climate that is improving (Walton 1969).

Threats cannot be used productively (or even destructively) unless the person being threatened believes that the threat is credible. A threat is credible only if (1) the other party is in a position to administer the punishment, (2) the other party appears willing to invoke the punishment, and (3) the punishment is something to be avoided. When the other party is not in a position to administer the threat, then an attempt threat becomes a warning. If your work associates (who do not control your salary) say to you, "If you continue coming to work at odd hours, you'll never get a raise," they are not using a threat, but a warning. Similarly, if your friends say, "You had better quit trying to get your Dad to buy you expensive gifts, or he will get mad and not give you anything," then it is not a credible threat. The threat is credible only if the person making the threat is capable of invoking the negative sanction.

Often the other party is *able* to administer a threat, but not *willing* to use it. A coworker who threatens to tell the boss that someone's work is not up to par cannot issue a credible threat if the boss dislikes "squealers." Similarly, in intimate relationships, one intimate will often say, "If you want to make your summer plans alone, go ahead. But if you do, then don't expect to find me here when you come back." Such a threat (relational suicide) is effective only if the person who makes the threat is really willing to lose the other person over this one issue. It is the *perception* that the other party is willing to use the threat that makes it effective. As a result, intimates and others often never test out the willingness of the party to invoke the threat and live under the control of the other person for years. Poker players all know that a "bluff" is being able to maneuver the other party into thinking that you are willing to bet all your life's winnings on this single draw of cards. The only successful bluff is one that the other party believes is true (Frost 1974).

A special case of threat is a blackmail attempt used as a tactic to accomplish preset goals. In blackmail, the victim is relatively powerless and passive. Furthermore, it is assumed that the victim is rational, that he or she can weigh the risks associated with not going along with the blackmailer's demands (Frost 1974). Just as in other kinds of threats, the blackmailer must assure the victim that he *will* invoke the sanctions, not just that he *might* (Schelling 1960). The effectiveness of the blackmail attempt rests on an assumption that the victim wants to avoid the punishment and that the blackmailer can convince the victim of the unfavorable power structure. Blackmailers' seizures of hostages often demonstrate that while the hostages and their friends fear for their lives (thus giving the blackmailer power), outside forces such as the police can also track down a blackmailer and punish him later. So, even if the blackmailer gets his wishes, superior force may be called against him during the commission of his blackmail or later. Harsanyi (1962) labels the one-sided thinking of the blackmailer as the "Blackmailer's Fallacy." If the blackmailer reasons that he can cause $1,000 worth of damage to a victim, then he should be able to extract a ransom worth any amount up to $1,000 because the victim will still be better off paying. But, as Harsanyi notes, similar reasoning could also apply from the other point of view. The victim (or the victim's friends) could argue that the blackmailer should accept any ransom greater than zero since the blackmailer would be better off than if no agreement were reached. The key, however, is that the blackmailer has control of all the significant power, and often the power balance shifts once the threat is carried out or the ransom received. The blackmailer's power is derived from holding destructive forces in check while threatening to use them.

Finally, threats are effective only if the threatened negative sanction is something the party wants to avoid. In the case of attempted relational suicide where the intimate threatened to leave if the other made summer plans alone, that action may be precisely what the person planning the separate summer wants. It is not uncommon for intimates to set the other up to destroy the relationship by continually engaging in conflicting behaviors. So, before you issue your next threat to a close friend or family member, keep in mind that your threat is effective only if he or she does not want the "undesirable" end result. Similar scenarios happen in all levels of relationships. One faculty member we know was offered a job at a competing university and when he went to his chairman and threatened to leave unless his salary was raised, the chairman replied, "Gee, I hope you enjoy the climate down South."

One of the standard teachings to young children is to "be nice. Don't tell Sam that you will punch him in the nose if he touches your truck. You shouldn't be mean to your friends!" Threats are often suppressed by adults almost as fast as they spring from children's lips because threats are often unproductive and not appropriate. We learn that threats are a lot like power—most of us like using them more than we like having them used against us.

The use of coercion usually brings dissatisfaction for the coerced. Jamieson and Thomas (1974), after reviewing a number of studies, found that when classroom teachers used coercion on students with whom they had conflicts, the students were very dissatisfied with the results. They also found that coercion is the most-used tactic by teachers in conflict situations, and as a result, students are distrustful of the process of doing conflict. As we noted in the chapter on power, persons who are constantly in low power positions feel either apathetic or hostile. Therefore, the use of threats (which magnify the power discrepancy between the parties) tends to promote relational dissatisfaction and distrust. In effect, threats and coercion "rub in" the power difference.

Threats can also escalate a conflict beyond the limits where participants can productively handle it. Two friends may begin with friendly threats to test the degree of commitment to one another and find out that as the threat level continues, serious relational concerns increase. Pretty soon, they are threatening one another with a breaking off of the relationship. Many a conflict participant has come away from a conflict with a feeling of, "I wish I hadn't said that." Such reactions are the result of using threats to counter other threats, which tends to build escalation on top of escalation. Unrestrained escalation causes participants to become more concerned with injuring one another than in managing the conflict productively.

Threats are especially unproductive in conflicts where the participants are of equal power or presume that they are of equal power. As Tedeschi (1972) has noted, because threats are so damaging and escalatory in dyadic interactions the parties usually invoke contracts or informal rules against their use. One couple that we know exemplifies this. They both are professional people and have relatively equal power. When they are involved in a conflict they often say things like, "Well, you make me so mad that I want to threaten you with leaving. But if I do, I know that you will probably call me on it. So, I won't issue any threats even though I feel like it.'' The partner has expressed that she is capable of threatening but that the two of them have agreed that threats are counterproductive—they adopt a norm against threats.

As the intensity of a conflict increases, the frequency with which threats are used also increases (Tedeschi 1972). As a result, the unbounded use of threats makes successful management of conflict extremely difficult. Giving credible threats presupposes that there is a chance that they may be used, and the use of real threats by both parties cannot go on unabated in a conflict without unproductive results. At some point, the threats and intensity of the conflict have to subside so the participants can effectively manage their differences. Threats signal, move toward escalation, and build power, but they cannot, by themselves, *resolve* conflicts.

Constricting the Other

Constricting the other person in a conflict is usually escalatory in nature. For example, constricting the amount of time you will allot to another to be heard often frustrates them and makes them want to fight harder for a hearing. Similarly, controlling access of the other person to you is a further reduction of their power and frequently produces hostility and escalation. When the supervisor refuses to see his employees about their grievances, it is not unlikely that they will go to the next union meeting and find ways to escalate the conflict for their purposes too. And, the intimate who refuses to deal with the other person by restricting her or his access (''Honey, I've told you not to call me at the office even if it is an emergency'') is feeding the escalation drive. Finally, to limit the escape of the other person from your influence is an escalatory act. The parent who forces the young child to eat hated vegetables or the friend who won't let you go from an unsatisfying conversation is serving to escalate the conflict. People fight for freedom of choice.

Breaking the Relational Rules

The final escalation tactic is breaking the relational rules. The most common forms of this are close friends lying to one another in the heat of a conflict, engaging in personal attack, or hitting ''below the belt'' during conflict. The clearest example of breaking relational rules comes from the Edward Albee play, *Who's Afraid of Virginia Woolf?* when George and Martha shatter the illusion of a dead son they have collaborated in fabricating for many years. All participants in relationship with one another develop sets of shared rules for the conduct of their time together. When the rules are broken, escalation usually follows. Betrayal is a dramatic and frightening experience.

Sometimes, breaking the rules is productive for the parties. A man and wife may have a rule that the wife is not entitled to hold a full-time job. If, however, she breaks the rule and becomes employed, she and her husband will have to renegotiate the rules of the relationship. The rule breakage will escalate a conflict, but it may also serve productive ends. In ongoing relationships, such as friendships, the participants also develop rules for how to engage in conflict. For example, two buddies may adopt the rule that it is fine to shout at one another during a heated conflict over any issue. Then, when one of the friends refuses to fight verbally, he can be signaling to the other that it is time for the old patterns to change.

The list of possible escalatory tactics is endless, but we have presented those that we have observed that occur most frequently in numerous types of relationships. Escalatory tactics, just like any other tactics, may serve either productive or destructive ends depending on the goals of the parties, how the tactics are actually used, and how the other party responds.

Maintenance Tactics

When people develop maintenance tactics, they use moves that neither reduce nor escalate the conflict to any significant degree, but keep the conflict at a level of tension that works for one or all of the participants. Sometimes parties have a vested interest in *not* resolving or reducing the conflict and, at the same time, not blowing it up so far that the other party withdraws. Persons using maintenance tactics, by definition, gain something by keeping the conflict where it is. Couples sometimes find they have nothing in common when they quit fighting or business people find they do not produce as well when their competition goes out of business.

All maintenance tactics share a common base. They involve equalizing the power of the participants, thus allowing the participants to gain symmetry. They can promote fair dealings between the parties for the issues at hand and, when appropriate, promote effective conflict management.

Of course, all maintenance tactics can be applied at inappropriate times and places thereby maintaining conflicts that should be managed in other ways. For instance, if one of the parties has a stake in maintaining the conflict at its present level (like a rebel group that gains its power by having to "fight the establishment"), then maintenance tactics can be just as ineffective and inappropriate as any others.

Quid Pro Quo

A *quid pro quo* is a maintenance tactic that consists of "getting something for something" (Lederer and Jackson 1968). In usual cases, one can strike a *quid pro quo* with the other party by outlining what each has to gain and lose from the conflict and then offering something for something. If an aunt wants a college student to come and visit her more often, and the college student wants time to study rather than visit the aunt every other day, the two of them can strike a bargain. For instance, if they are arguing over whether the niece "loves" the aunt, the niece could specify that she wants to show love for the aunt and also have her free time. She could point out that she only loves the aunt when she feels free, not compelled, to see the aunt. And, if the aunt would not push so hard for the niece to come and see her, the niece would feel freer about coming over more often, or less frequently, for longer periods. The niece explains that the aunt can accomplish her goal by giving her room to accomplish her own. The agreement will not necessarily "solve" the conflict, but it will keep it from escalating until the aunt can see that trading something for something will indeed gain long-range results. The key to a successful *quid pro quo* is that the parties treat one another as equals in order to consummate the trade. It is the process of equal power activation that makes the *quid pro quo* work, regardless of the specific agreement reached. If both parties are full participants then the agreement will be of like value to both of them.

Quid pro quos can, however, be used for maintenance of conflicts past their necessary stopping points. If conflict participants are of unequal power, and the one in the high power position wants the conflict to continue unabated, then a *quid pro quo* can be reached that will maintain the conflict but not lead to long-range productive results. For example, a couple may reach the point where they find it difficult to manage a conflict. They can reach agreement that they will come back to the conflict again and again until they manage to resolve it. However, the key may be that they are fighting with one another in order to test their interdependence and rather than continuing to keep the conflict at a given level forever, they would be wise to seek third party consultation on a range of issues.

One can maintain a conflict by issuing a *thromise,* a combination of the tactical elements of both threats and promises (Bowers 1974). The thromise is a message that combines the escalatory effects of a threat with the reduction effects of a promise. It is a double contingency that allows the participants to signal their interest and desire to inflame the conflagration with a desire to reduce it by giving a reward to the other. If a woman says to man, "I can only stay with someone who allows me equal participation in decisions," she is signaling both a threat ("I'll leave if you exclude me") and a promise (I'll stay and love you if you include me"). Assuming the man wants her to say, the message is a thromise. The joint tactic, if it successfully balances the two opposing elements, maintains the level of the conflict where it was before the tactic was issued.

Agreement on Relational Rules

Agreement on relational rules is a tactic that can serve to maintain a conflict at its present level of intensity while carving out areas of disagreement on which the conflict may center. For example, facilitators of small groups

frequently impose relational ground rules on participants who are conflicting by urging such things as, "you can say anything you want within the
limits of (1) reporting your own feelings and (2) not casting aspersions on
the other person's character." As a result, a party in the conflict can express
what is bothering her without escalating or avoiding. Similarly, the other
party will know that his turn to answer will arrive shortly, and that he will
be given the same opportunities to be heard. Participants can also establish
their own ground rules without the intervention of a third party. Two participants can say to one another, "OK, it is difficult for me but I'm going to
stay here and talk with you until we find out what the problems are between
us." Establishment of the ground rules helps maintain the intensity of the
conflict so the participants are motivated to manage it. Without the effort
to engage (maintain), needed information probably will not be shared.

Combining Escalation and Reduction Tactics

Many combinations of escalation and reduction tactics can serve to maintain a conflict at a desired level. For instance, if participants combine issue
expansion (escalation) with fractionation (reduction))they can maintain the
conflict so that important issues can emerge during the course of the conflict. An example of such a combination would be between a man and wife
who are arguing over income tax deadlines the evening before taxes are due.
She starts the triggering episode by saying, "Harold, you always leave income tax to the last minute. I just wish you would sometime in your life do
something on time" (expansion). Harold replies by noting that he has com-
pleted all important projects on time during the last month (answering the
expansion), but that the only important issue tonight is how to do the income tax (fractionation). She answers by saying that it isn't the income tax
per se, but his style of pretending that he wants to do things on time but not
doing them, that angers her. And, she notes, his exemplary behavior of the
past is not the usual thing (expansion). John, then, counters by asking his
wife why it bothers her so much (following up on the expansion). After she
has had a chance to explain, she then says, "Well, I guess those issues will
have to be settled later. For now I am really bugged about this income tax"
(fractionation). This example demonstrates that parties can effectively
alternate between expansion and fractionation in order to keep the conflict
maintained without escalating it too far beyond manageable control. Expansion tactics can serve valuable functions. For instance, they show commitment to your goals balanced with a desire not to harm the other party.
Issue expansion used by a group representative can demonstrate that the
representative is "doing his job" by making the other side work for any
gains they achieve. Many a negotiator has decided to maintain a conflict for
the purpose of proving his ability in making the other side come to grips
with his position. Finally, maintenance of conflicts can serve valuable func-

tions in training people in ongoing relationships how to manage conflicts. A departmental faculty, for example, that learns how to maintain and work through minor conflicts can then build a sense of faith that they can also manage large, threatening conflicts. Similarly, intimates can gain practice and a feeling of "we can survive conflict" by maintaining conflicts long enough for other tactics to be used to manage them.

All of the maintenance tactics mentioned here can be used for either productive or nonproductive purposes in a given conflict situation. They all serve to continue a conflict at a prescribed level for a longer period of time than would happen if they were not used. Maintenance is a middle ground between escalation and reduction.

Reduction Tactics

Many texts and articles on conflict management equate deescalation and reduction tactics with "conflict resolution," which suggests that an end, or resolution, can and should be reached in all conflicts. Although we do not agree with this position, it is a very common one. Most of the people with whom we work have a good idea of some of the reduction tactics available. Three of the most common tactics to reduce conflicts-negotiation, mediation, and arbitration will be discussed at greater length in the next chapter. Briefly, however, in the negotiating process parties come to the table (although the negotiating process often takes place very informally, not in board rooms) prepared to represent themselves or their group as to what is and is not acceptable to give away. In negotiation, people do not expect to get something for nothing—a bargain is struck. In the mediation process, a third party is called in, whether formally as in labor-management mediation or informally with friends, family, or counselors to help give insights about the management of a particular conflict. The participants are not tied to any decision of the mediators; the mediator helps the participants come to agreement and helps them "see" the conflict in new ways. In the arbitration process, the participants are legally bound to abide by the decision of the arbitrator or board of arbitrators, who act in a quasijudicial role, making evaluations about how conflicts should be resolved when the participants are unable to come to agreement. All of these tactics can be used to reduce conflict, as well as to escalate it, avoid it, or maintain it at the present level.

Fractionation

The basic reduction tactic is usually some form of the device known as *fractionating,* a phrase coined by Roger Fisher in his seminal essay, "Fractionating Conflict" (1971). He suggests that conflict can be reduced by focusing attention on the *sizing* of disputes. Simply stated, conflicts can be broken down from one big mass to several smaller, more manageable conflicts. Fractionating conflict does not make it disappear, of course, it simply makes component parts of large conflicts more approachable by parties who are trying to manage their disputes. Even though we often forget the idea, conflicts "do not have objective edges established by external events" (Fisher 1971, p. 158). Conflicts are more like a seamless web, with indistinguishable beginnings and endings. Choices are almost always available as to how the conflicts are sized for management. A group of ten townspeople recently met at the instigation of one of the members to determine what should be done about the deteriorating quality of the town's air. They were determined to do something to improve the quality of air after the recent inversion caused several persons to be hospitalized and other residents suffered from respiratory problems, allergies, and asthma attacks. In the group's opinion, the major culprit was the large papermill in the town, which had, they suspected, been violating air quality standards. One way to size the conflict would be to mount an all out attack on the very existence of the plant, contacting everyone they could think of to try to get the plant closed down. One step down from that mode of attack would be to conceptualize the conflict as being between the citizens of the town and the management of the company. Defining the parties in this way suggests a negotiation device to try to resolve the conflict. An even smaller sizing might be to conceptualize the conflict as being between some concerned citizens and city council and the county conmissioners who enforced the air quality standards. If the conflict were conceptualized in this way, yet another plan of management would be appropriate. The smallest sizing of the conflict would have been one seen as between the committee of ten and the engineers who monitor the air quality machinery at the plant. The group reached success in reaching reduction of the conflict (at least the conflict of which they were most aware) by defining the conflict carefully, assessing their resources, talking to the "other side," and carefully planning an incremental campaign to get more citizens involved in the issue. By fractionating the conflict for purposes of analysis, they were able to later escalate it to fit their purposes.

Fractionation also implies making small conflicts out of larger ones. This simple idea might possibly be one of the most useful tactics a person could use. Almost all conflicts can be made smaller than they are, without, we might add, trivializing or devaluing them. In a student-teacher conflict, for instance, the students might come into the classroom one day and ask for the abolition of all the grading in the course. The teacher could escalate the issue by becoming defensive and polarizing the issue or resorting to rules or external authority. But the issue could be reduced in size by the teacher asking the students about what they most objected to in the tests and then talking about those features. Or the teacher could look for other subissues, or small issues in the "Let's don't have tests" statement, and might find that the tests were misscheduled, unexpected, unclear, too long, or some other small issue. Then the parties can handle the small issue instead of losing all their relational power by fighting an issue that is too extreme and probably would not be resolved.

Negative Inquiry

Negative inquiry is a form of fractionation that is discussed in the assertiveness training manuals we mentioned earlier. In negative inquiry, when a person is criticized, he or she responds by asking for more information, not less, about what it is that the other person finds objectionable. Then the person being criticized tries to solve that part of the problem that is solvable. For instance, in a large university office the boss began a process of calling in the department heads one by one for private conferences with him. The conferences were unscheduled, and the tension level was rising considerably in the office. Finally, Shirley was called in. She reported that she used negative inquiry to great effect. When the boss mentioned that "people weren't getting all their work done and they were spending too much time on coffee breaks," Shirley asked for more information. She said, "Have you been unhappy with some part of my work?" The boss said he could not think of anything right then. She then asked how he thought she could improve her work. The boss, who really was not angry or upset at Shirley at all, mentioned a few things, which Shirley accepted, and then they turned their conversation to other problems in the office. If Shirley had bristled, gotten defensive, or refused to hear what the boss was saying, she would have jeopardized her job and their relationship. By *asking for more information* she fractionized the conflict. A caution is in order when using this tactic—be sure you want the negative information and that you are not simply using the device as a ploy—you could get more than you bargained for!

Metacommunication

Metacommunication, or talking about communication as it is going on, is another tactic that often is used effectively to reduce conflicts. If you can talk about what is happening, often you can change the system to one that fits the needs of the relationship more fully. For instance, when people *talk about tactics that they do not choose to use,* they are using metacommunication to reduce the conflict. The "fictionalized move" can be vitally important. For instance, the teenager who finds herself pregnant, decides to talk over the situation with her parents, and reports to them that she considered running away from home because she was so afraid of their reaction is using a fictionalized move. She really means what she is saying, but talking about the move not taken deescalates the present conflict—or at least it can if she is believed and the parents really want to help. Couples often tell each other that they "might leave," but then say they do not want to if they can resolve this dispute. This is a temporary escalation (using a threat) to reduce the conflict to a more manageable level. Also, if you can represent fairly to the other parties tactics that you considered but did not choose, your credibility is enhanced by showing that you are a person of good will who can see all sides of a problem (Rieke and Sillars 1975).

Another way to use metacommunication is to ask the other party for possible options for resolution. Encourage the other party to discuss freely options that you might find unacceptable. Then this "safe" period of talking over a hypothetical resolution will give the other party enough information about your reaction to the conflict so that he will be aware of many options.

Response to All Levels of the Conflict

Reduction of the conflict can be accomplished by asking the person to represent both "facts" and feelings—that is, to give you information about the content and the relationship levels of the conflict. A group of family members were discussing whether the aging mother and mother-in-law should be placed in a retirement home, move in with one of the children, or be left alone in her apartment. The volatile issue was reduced when one of the women asked her brother, "You seem almost totally opposed to having her stay in the apartment. Would you talk some more about how you feel about that?" The brother then responded, "It would be *ok* with me if she stayed in the apartment, but I'm the one who goes over there each day to do little things for her, and I might be transferred next year. I don't want to have to make any decisions about moving totally dependent on whether Mom needs me near." The other family members were able to identify with his fears and his affection for his mother and got involved in coming up with solutions. If the group had stayed with facts only (objectively verifiable data believed by most people), they might never have reached resolution of an issue charged with emotional content.

The Position Paper

In doing research for this book, we noticed a curious phenomenon. When people draw themselves up, get stern, and make a strong, nonnegotiable statement that is highly polarized and sounds cut and dried, they often change their minds quickly afterward. We began to call this communication pattern the "position paper" and started looking for its use in our own in-

teractions and the interactions of our friends. Sure enough, the flat statement often was followed by qualifiers or softening statements. We
hypothesized that the act of making a polarizing statement, having it
register in the minds of the other parties, and seeing the potential for all out
relational war served to reduce the conflict in the long run. Of course, we
see this tactic work in the opposite manner, also. But watch for it—you will
be surprised how often in intimate relations it becomes possible for people
to compromise after they have made a strong statement explaining how they
could not possibly compromise!

Compromise

Compromise is so well understood that we need not go into great detail
about its use as a reduction tactic. Along with fractionation, compromise
probably reduces more conflict than any other pattern of interaction.
Especially when participants can learn to see compromise as a situation in
which everyone *wins* something as well as *loses* something, the device can be
effective. Compromise has taken on a negative connotation, as in "I don't
want to compromise my principles." But compromise with other people can
often be the only way a conflict can be reduced—the alternative is no resolution, no win.

Establishment of Outside Criteria

Another helpful reduction tactic is to agree ahead of time on how the
decision is going to be made or on criteria for making choices. For instance,
in most organizations when a job opens up, the manager would be foolish
to ask people whom they think should be hired. Instead, a careful list of job
qualifications is drawn up, so that some of the power plays and persuasion
goes on before the choice is being made about who should fill the slot. Then
when tempers become heated, the chair of the committee can point to the
outside criteria. This tactic buys distance from the conflict and often builds
in time to make a decision. And if people can agree on criteria, they can,
perhaps, agree on some kind of final choice (Filley 1975).

Many other reduction devices could be discussed. Most conflict deescalation attempts that turn out to be successful are based on good faith moves,
respect for the other parties, and facing the issues on all the levels possible
instead of ignoring part of the problem. Reduction shows people in important relationships with each other that conflict does not have to be destructive and that people can express differences without tearing their relationship apart. A healthy relationship has a wide repertoire of reduction
patterns instead of relying on good will or fate and hoping that conflicts will
not happen.

Summary

We have discussed in this chapter the concept of the large, overall game plan in a conflict, or the *strategy,* and the *tactics,* or communication moves, that implement the strategic direction chosen. There are at least four directions for any conflict to take—avoidance, escalation, maintenance and reduction—and tactics facilitating each of these strategic directions were discussed. In the next chapter, we will discuss third party intervention. Then intervention in conflicts in which you participate as a primary party will be discussed.

Bibliography

Apfelbaum, Erika. "On Conflicts and Bargaining." In *Advances in Experimental Social Psychology 7,* edited by Leonard Berkowitz, pp. 103-156. New York: Academic Press, Inc., 1974.

Bach, George R., and Wyden, Peter. *The Intimate Enemy.* New York: Avon Books, 1968.

Bowers, John Waite. "Beyond Threats and Promises." *Speech Monographs* 41(1974):ix-xi.

———. "Communication Strategies in Conflicts Between Institutions and Their Clients." In *Perspectives on Communication in Social Conflict,* edited by Gerald R. Miller and Herbert W. Simons, 125-152.

Brockriede, Wayne. "Arguers as Lovers." *Philosophy and Rhetoric* 5(1)(1972): 1-11.

Caplow, Theodore. *Two Against One: Coalitions in Triads.* Englewood Cliffs, N.J.: Prentice Hall, Inc., 1968.

Filley, Alan C. *Interpersonal Conflict Resolution.* Glenview, Ill.: Scott, Foresman, & Co., 1975.

Fisher, Roger. "Factionating Conflict." In *Conflict Resolution: Contributions of the Behavioral Sciences,* edited by Clagett G. Smith. Notre Dame, Ind.: University of Notre Dame Press, 1971.

Frost, Joyce Hocker. *The Implications of Conflict Theories for Rhetorical Criticism.* Unpublished dissertation, University of Texas, 1974.

Gamson, William A. "A Theory of Coalition Formation." *American Sociological Review,* June 1961, pp. 373-382.

Gibb, Jack R. "Defensive Communication." *Journal of Communication,* September 1961, pp. 141-148.

Goffman, Erving. *The Presentation of Self in Everyday Life.* New York: Doubleday & Co., Inc., 1959.

Haney, William V. *Communication and Organizational Behavior: Text and Cases.* Homewood, Ill.: Richard D. Irwin, Inc., 1973.

Harsanyi, John C. "Measurement of Social Power in n-Person Reciprocal Power Situations." *Behavioral Science* 7(1962):81-91.

―――. "Measurement of Social Power, Opportunity Costs, and the Theory of Two-person Bargaining Games," *Behavioral Science* 7(1962):67-80.

Jamieson, David W., and Thomas, Kenneth W. "Power and Conflict in the Student-Teacher Relationship." *Journal of Applied Behavioral Science* 10(3)(1974):321-336.

Johnson, Wendell, and Moeller, Dorothy. *Living with Change.* New York: Harper & Row Publishers, Inc., 1972.

Jung, Carl G. et al. *Man and His Symbols.* New York: Dell Publishing Co., Inc., 1968.

Karrass, Chester L. *Give and Take: A Complete Guide to Negotiating Strategies and Tactics.* New York: Thomas Y. Crowell Co., 1974.

Laing, R. D.; Phillipson, H. and Lee, A. R. *Interpersonal Perception.* Baltimore, Md.: Perrenial Library, 1966.

Lederer, W. J., and Jackson, Don D. *Mirages of Marriage.* New York: W. W. Norton & Co., Inc., 1968.

Miller, Gerald R., and Steinberg, Mark. *Between People: A New Analysis of Interpersonal Communication.* Chicago: Science Research Associates, 1975.

―――, and Herbert W. Simons, eds. *Perspectives on Communication in Social Conflict.* Englewood Cliffs, N.J.: Prentice-Hall, Inc., 1974.

Phelps, Stanlee, and Austin, Nancy. *The Assertive Woman.* San Luis Obispo, Calif.: Impact Publishers, Inc., 1975.

Phillips, Gerald M., and Metzger, Nancy J. *Intimate Communication.* Boston: Allyn & Bacon, Inc., 1976.

Raush, Harold; Barry, W. A.; Hertel, R. K.; and Swain, M. A. *Communication, Conflict and Marriage.* San Francisco: Jossey-Bass, Inc., Publishers, 1974.

Rieke, Richard D., and Sillars, Malcolm O. *Argumentation and the Decision Making Process.* New York: John Wiley & Sons, Inc., 1975.

Roloff, Michael E. "Communication Strategies, Relationships, and Relational Change." In *Explorations in Interpersonal Communication,* edited by Gerald R. Miller, pp. 173-195. Beverly Hills, Calif.: Sage Publications, Inc., 1976.

Ruesch, Jurgen. *Disturbed Communication.* New York: W. W. Norton & Co., Inc., 1957.

Schelling, Thomas C. *The Strategy of Conflict.* Cambridge, Mass.: Harvard University Press, 1960.

Smith, Manuel J. *When I Say No I Feel Guilty.* New York: Bantam Books, Inc., 1975.

Swingle, Paul. "Dangerous Games." In *The Structure of Conflict,* edited by P. Swingle, pp. 235-276. New York: Academic Press, Inc., 1970.

Tedeschi, James T. *The Social Influence Processes.* Chicago: Aldine Publishing Co., 1972.

———. "Threats and Promises." In *The Structure of Conflict,* edited by P. Swingle, pp. 155-191. New York: Academic Press, Inc., 1970.

———; Lindskold, S.; Horai, J.; and Gahagan, J. P. "Social Power and the Credibility of Promises." *Journal of Personality and Social Psychology* 13(3)(1969):253-261.

Walton, Richard E. *Interpersonal Peacemaking: Confrontations and Third Party Consultation,* Reading, Mass.: Addison-Wesley Publishing Co., Inc., 1969.

Wilmot, William W. *Dyadic Communication: A Transactional Perspective,* Reading, Mass.: Addison-Wesley Publishing Co., Inc., 1975.

———. "The Influence of Personal Conflict Styles of Teachers on Student Attitudes Toward Conflict." Paper presented to Instructional Communication Association Convention, Portland, Oregon, April 15, 1976.

———, and Frost, Joyce Hocker. "Prisoner's Dilemma Primer." Unpublished manuscript, Department of Interpersonal Communication, University of Montana, 1977.

Yarbrough, Elaine. "Rules of Observation." Unpublished monograph, Department of Communication, University of Colorado, 1977.

Intervention
Principles and Practices

7

Perhaps you have engaged in some of the following conflict situations recently:

A father calls the police because his son insists on running away from home. . . .

Two neighbors engage in a dispute over their property line. . . .

A landlord and tenant argue over nonpayment of rent. . . .

A storekeeper argues with a customer over the exchange of merchandise. . . .

Two motorists confront each other over a minor traffic accident. . . (Bard and Zacker 1976).

Four department heads disagree angrily over the interpretation of a policy issue. . . .

A secretary feels she is passed over unfairly for a raise and discusses it with a friend. . . .

Your sister has an argument with her husband. . . .

All of the above incidents have at least one thing in common besides all being conflict situations. All *could* call for the intervention of a third party. We all are asked from time to time to enter into an "outside party" role for people engaging in conflict, or we decide to ask for outside help for our own conflicts. Intervention in conflicts is prevalent in both work and home lives, for people often seek and give assistance. Far from being "none of our business" that other people have disputes, often third party intervention is part of your job. Persons involved in telephone hotline counseling, drug abuse centers, therapy, social work, vocational counseling, legal work, peer counseling in dormitories, police work, politics, teaching, ministry, and many other professions all intervene, formally or informally, in conflicts.

The purpose of this chapter is to discuss the appropriate intervention tactics available to all of us in our everyday lives. The professional "helper" or manager will find useful principles here, but the main thrust of the discussion will be aimed at informal intervention—the kind many of our students and colleagues tell us is hardest of all. All of us are sometimes puzzled about when to intervene. We are not sure we can change the conflict, we do not know whether we are wanted in the system, and we would like to just not get involved. But because of obligations of the job, or simply being a concerned friend, we are faced from time to time with conflict crises—both crises in which we participate as a primary party and crises that we initially watch from outside the immediate system. Sometimes, the decision about whether to get involved has to be made instantly. "Conflict situations are frequently allowed to develop to almost unmanageable proportions before anything is done about them, by which time it is often too late to resolve them by peaceable and procedural means" (Boulding 1962). Often we do not have the luxury of careful analysis, deliberate tactical choices, and well-thought-through strategy sessions. Most of us function as intervention agents of some kind—*the choice is simply when and how competent we are, not whether we will intervene in other peoples' conflicts.*

One of the most common professions using crisis intervention is the police force. Disputes are among the most dangerous assignments for police officers. A family squabble can turn into a nightmare of violence and irrationality. An argument in a bar between friends or between a landlord and a tenant can easily become a shootout. About 25 percent of all police officers killed in the line of duty are intervening in a dispute of some kind (Bard and Zacker 1976). Police, however, rarely resort to physical force in dealing with disputes—they develop their own methods of intervention that fit their personal styles, the neighorhood, and the situation. They become instant arbitrators, who are legally empowered to *do something* here and now—that is, to prevent destructive escalation and restore some semblance of social order. Many police officers are returning to the "peace officer" concept of their job, which eroded through the years as the physical force of the policing function came to be used more than were verbal, nonviolent tactics. Several studies have shown that most police personnel spontaneously use subtle intervention tactics of the nonviolent kind despite their lack of formal training in communication and conflict management (Bard and Zacker 1976). The police typically separated disputants into different rooms, shuttled messages back and forth, articulated the point of view of an inarticulate disputant, or laid down rules for discussion and took the role of a referee (Bard and Zacker 1976). Systematic research has not been done for most professions, but most people who deal with other people daily have developed personal strategies for handling conflicts to which they are not a primary party.

Throughout the book we have discussed conflict situations, but we have not specifically discussed the concept of the *crisis*. Not all conflicts reach crisis proportions—people avoid the final confrontation, outside conditions change, compromises are reached, attitudes shift, and goals change with interaction. In this chapter we will be concerned with conflicts that have reached the crisis stage as well as those that have not. But, it is when conflicts have developed to a crisis point that parties are most likely to ask for help from an outside party or be receptive to help that is offered. When persons are in crisis, they become their own intervention agents, changing their norms, styles, goals, and messages quickly since they know that past attempts have not worked.

What is a crisis? Fink (1967) says that "A human system (individual, group, organization or other) is assumed to be in a state of crisis when its repertoire of coping responses is not adequate to bring about a resolution of a problem which poses a threat to the system." A crisis is precipitated by an identifiable event that moves the participants "over the edge to the point where they cannot cope." Arnold's (1977) definition emphasizes the role of the outside intervener in a crisis when he says, "crisis is defined as a decision-maker point when an individual, group, organization, state or nation is unable to cope without some form of assistance." A crisis point in a conflict, therefore, is a point at which outside intervention is needed to move the conflict toward some satisfactory resolution—even if that intervention is very informal, consisting only of a passing comment, a telephone call, a brief conversation, a book loaned to friends, or some other nontraditional intervention.

Many interventions, as we have seen, are highly informal. Some interventions into systems experiencing conflict are "one shot" communication attempts, others develop more formally over a period of time and involve many appointments, meetings, or other ways to bring the intervention agent into the system as a third party. Some interventions are carried out by persons legally empowered to act as a third party such as judges, attorneys, parole officers, social workers, police, legislators, or other elected officials. Other interventions are carried out by representatives of helping professions. People turn to them not primarily because they know the individual counselor, minister, teacher, social worker, or alcoholic counselor, but because that person *represents an institution* that is perceived as being potentially helpful to the persons in distress. And perhaps most commonly of all, many interventions are carried out by friends, coworkers, family members, neighbors, spouses, and "strangers on a train" simply because they are the persons most available to others experiencing conflict. It may also be that these people are less scary than legally empowered personnel or institutional representatives or that personal relationships of trust and confidence have been built between persons experiencing conflict and the third party.

Enter the Third Party

Asking for Assistance

Third parties enter conflicts through may diverse routes. Sometimes your position in a particular role demands involvement. Other times, however, the parties to a conflict ask for your intervention help indirectly and without a clear request. In these latter cases, the parties are typically involved in conflict that distresses one or both of the parties, and they search you out for assistance. Persons who are usually competent and function well also get involved in conflicts serious enough that they need temporary assistance. For example, Vincent (1972) discovered that distressed couples could function normally in other interactions. And, many models of counseling properly assume that the dysfunctions in a relationship are not permanent conditions because we all need help at times.

In cases where your prescribed role determines that you become involved in a conflict as a third party, your role is greatly clarified because everyone "knows" that you should be involved. If you are a counselor in a dormitory and one of your tasks is to "keep harmony" in the wings, when a disruption occurs other residents will seek your help—being fully aware that your role demands that you take action. Similarly, children seem to know intuitively that parents will step into the role as third party interveners when they have difficulties with their playmates. In cases where you are not in a prescribed role relating to conflict management, the ways you get asked to intervene are indirect. For instance, if you have a close friend whom you have known for four years, and she calls you on the phone to talk about an important decision, she may or may not be asking indirectly for intervention. A typical instance might be when the friend is in a committed relationship with someone (whom you also know), but is trying to decide whether to become involved in another romantic relationship outside the committed one. She may be using the phone call as a sounding board about her impending courses of action. Some cues to when people may be asking you to engage in being a third party without *directly* asking for outside assistance are as follows:

1. The person spends more and more time with you by seeking you out.

2. The person may be sharing more personally private information with you than usual.

3. The private information will involve some decision making situation; for example, whether to change directions of an existing

relationship; whether to get married; whether to get out of an unsatisfying relationship.

4. The person may make general statements such as, "I just do not know what to do about Lana, she . . ."

5. The key to most requests of assistance is when the person makes it clear that their life is not flowing as smoothly as he or she would like. Some element of distress or concern is present. The person feels as if he or she has low power, that things are "out of control."

The central key to indirect calls for assistance comes from the person in the conflict isolating his or her feelings of frustration and unhappiness. Obviously, when the person says, "Wes, I just do not think I can stand to live with Richard anymore," she is giving you an opening to ask what the difficulty is and whether your help is needed or not. But, often the determination that the person is in need of help comes from observing some dramatic change in their behavior or way of describing events changes. For example, if you are a teacher and you have established an ongoing friendship with a student who is usually happy and loves life, you may begin to notice that the student slowly begins to change his description of events in his life. Instead of the typical unbounded optimism, he begins looking for all the most negative things in his life. In the terms of Scott and Lyman (1968), the person's "accounts" for actions may be undergoing a change. Typically, if persons are involved in conflicts that are not productive for them, they give accounts of their own and the other's behavior, blaming the other person, pinpointing their faults, or castigating the other's motivations for actions. Any human action can be seen as desirable or undesirable depending on your point of view, so the key for the potential intervener is to watch for the point of view the person is expressing about the other's behavior. For instance, if Pat is saying, "I sure wish Roger wouldn't be so selfish with his time. All he wants to do is play with his stupid hobbies," you can guess that this account of Roger's actions expresses some underlying discomfort in Pat. She obviously has some goals that she depends on Roger for that she is not attaining.

Similarly, accounts people give of their own behavior are a real cue to the existence of a conflict and a potential request for help. Two major types of accounts for your actions are *excuses* and *justifications*. Excuses are offered when you do not accept responsibility for actions, yet admit that the act had undesirable results. For instance, the son who says, "Yes, I was out late Saturday night and got drunk and into a fist fight. But, it wasn't my fault because the other guy called me a chicken," is trying to excuse his actions by not taking responsibility for them. Excuses are socially approved ways to relieve oneself of responsibility when your conduct is questioned (Scott and Lyman 1968). Some of the techniques of excusing oneself are appealing to accidental causes ("I didn't mean to hit her, it was an accident"), appealing to biological drives ("I am just aggressive and cannot help it"), scapegoating (blaming someone else for your actions), and claiming you acted a certain way because of misinformation (Scott and Lyman 1968).

Listen also for people *justifying* their behavior. In these types of accounts, the person will use socially approved words to assert that the act they performed had a positive value, knowing that others see the act negatively. If a person is in a conflict with a friend because of "lack of commitment" on her part to the friendship, a justificatory account would be something like, "Well, if a person were to do everything their friends would ask, they would be totally controlled by the friends." As with excuses, justifications come in many forms. The most typical are a denial of injury to the other person, denial that anyone was hurt or harmed, asserting that others do it too so it cannot be a bad act ("everyone steps out on their lover once in a while"), and an appeal to the loyalties you have to others. In this last case, you defend an act by demonstrating how loyalty to another person prompted them to do it. For instance, if someone is saying, "I hated to lie to George, but my first allegiance is to his mother because she helped me out once a year ago, "the acts are justified because of some overriding commitment to others.

The important element to look for in both excuses and justifications is *what the person is saying about their conflict behavior* by using them. Often the accounts are translatable into, "I did this awful thing. Please be my friend and reassure me that what I did will not destroy the relationship I had with her." In short, accounts can be signals that the person is involved in a conflict and trying to find some way to deal with the negative consequences of their own behavior. People who seek out interveners are part of a system and should be dealt with not only as individuals but as persons-in-relationship.

Negotiating Your Role

Crucial questions facing a potential third party to a conflict are when to intervene, what your role and style of intervention will be, and what skills you will bring to bear on the conflict. In the next section, we will discuss the specific skills that one can use in intervening as a third party, but the first question is when to intervene. Questions facing anyone who is planning on intervening are:

1. Is the person or are the persons ready for intervention? *What evidence do you have* to indicate they are or are not?

2. Has the person requested your assistance, either directly or indirectly? If the request has been indirect, *what information leads you to believe that your help is being sought?*

3. *Do you have the necessary skills* to intervene in the conflict that others are having? Should you refer them to other resource persons?

4. *What choices do you have in negotiating your role* as a third party?

Often, choices for acting or not acting as a third party are limited. For example, if you are a supervisor and your two managers have a conflict regarding company policy, they will turn to you for help. Or, if you are a policeman or policewoman who handles domestic disturbances as part of your job, you will be in a third party role when you answer the call for help. Similarly, you may be in an informal role that also puts great pressure on you to intervene. If, for example, you are a very close friend to a married couple and the three of you spend a great deal of your leisure time together, if a conflict is triggered in your presence the couple may expect you to jump into the middle of things and influence the conflict. Everyone *always* has a choice about whether to be a third party to a conflict; the only problem is whether you are willing to accept the consequences of your decision. If, as in the case above, you are the supervisor and you decide not to serve as a third party mediator, then it is possible that you could lose your job, if serving that role is a central part of your job description. But remember, someone else's conflict is not your conflict, and if you serve as a third party to a conflict, you are choosing to do so. You have a right to not be the solution to someone else's problem (Smith 1975).

Once you choose to be involved in a conflict as a third party, other important questions remain. Will you be relatively uninvolved in the emotional aspects of the conflict, and try to balance out both sides? Will you become so involved in the conflict that you become one of the parties instead of a third party force? Do you have a stake in the outcome of the conflict such that you want the parties to reach some conclusion that you have preset in your mind? Finally, the basic question is how much influence you want to exert on the conflict processes. Do you want to control the procession of events or be an observer who serves as a catalyst?

Whatever the degree of involvement in a conflict, it is clear that the presence of a third party has a tremendous impact on a conflict. In fact, many times, just knowing that someone will intervene is enough to move the participants significantly into different patterns. Anticipation of your intervention can give parties the nudge they need to try different ways of managing their conflict because they may wish to save face in your presence (Johnson and Tullar 1972). And, if anticipation is not a sufficient motivator, your presence will exert an impact on the participant's system. It has been shown elsewhere (Wilmot 1975) that whenever a third party enters into an existing relationship, one of two things happens: either the relationship is strengthened or it is weakened. As a third party you may be able to help the conflict participants build more commitment to their relationship or common goal. But, as sometimes happens in counseling situations, you need to be careful that their cohesion as a unit is not built at the expense of casting you as a common enemy. If you intervene in a conflict and make suggestions that offend the participants, then it will be easy for them to cast you as the "enemy" and release all their tensions toward you. Remember, you are entering an already existing system, whether it is two friends, two employees, or any two parties tied by common goals. The other option is that your presence will weaken their bond, interfere with their choices for conflict management, and one of the participants will identify and feel close to you. Thus, their energy necessary for managing the conflict may be diverted. While you cannot predict ahead of time what will happen as a result of intervening in an ongoing conflict, you do need to continually monitor the interactions to watch for shifts in coalitions or a destruction of the original bond.

To negotiate your role in a conflict as a third party is difficult because often people expect you to take whatever role they have assumed you would—friend and buddy, "objective" third party mediator, or an outside person who can clearly demonstrate to the "wrong" party why he is wrong. But, you have to be willing to negotiate your relationship between yourself and the constituents, for it is a key part to the process (Haccoun and Klimoski 1975). At times you may be asked to perform a role that you must decline because of ethical reasons. One of us, for instance, was hired by a manager to find out the sources of conflict in his hundred-person department. After much research was done, it became obvious that the manager was only committed to supporting ideas that showed that specific groups were "wrong." In this case, the role as a third party had to be renegotiated.

Effective Intervention

Any effective interventionist, whether a friend of the disputants or someone in an official role as conflict manager, must have at least three major sources of strength. The person must have sufficient analytical ability to understand the processes of conflict, must manifest a communication style that can be used effectively in the interventionist role, and must have some tactical choices available that will facilitate the management of the conflict (Walton 1969). Although during an actual intervention in a conflict all of these components will be activated almost simultaneously, we will discuss them one at a time in order to provide some perspective on their contribution to effective third party intervention.

Analytical Ability

One of the most challenging aspects of a third party role is that you must make quick decisions regarding the state of the conflict and respond in helpful ways to the moves and countermoves of the parties involved (Rusk and Gerner 1972). If you are visiting two friends for an evening and become a central part of their ongoing conflict, it is not appropriate to say, "Just a minute. While I want to help you with this difficulty, I'll need three days of calm reflection before I can say anything." Of course, in some situations it is feasible to use time to diagnose the conflict, but often time is a luxury that the parties cannot give to you. And, whether you are in need of split-second decisive action or not, you must possess sufficient analytical ability to understand the processes of the conflict as they unfold.

Unfortunately, because you are placed in the role of a third party mediator or facilitator, you are not necessarily willing and able to be an effective analyst of the conflict. A common confusion is that elected officials think they are born mediators—"I'm responsible, therefore I will figure it out." Whether your role is officially or unofficially determined, you must possess analytical abilities so that you will not (1) contribute to the conflict by becoming a party to it, (2) analyze the conflict in unproductive ways so as to block effective management of the conflict, or (3) be unaware of the relational issues that overlap with the content considerations of the conflict.

As we noted in the first chapter of this book, any effective participant must be able to see the relational aspects of all conflicts. This also applies to any third party. When two participants are shouting at one another and using derogatory language by hurling insults, you can rest assured that the conflict hinges on the issues of power and self-esteem. People maintain their self-esteem and power through content—being a better worker, being an effective mother, and others—and act out the relational aspects via the content. For instance, two intimates who are arguing over "who contributes the most to this relationship" are not arguing exclusively about money or emotional worth, they are arguing about who feels important and worthwhile. An effective third party would be able to detect the relational messages inherent in all content arguments and assist the participants in dealing with both the content and relationship issues.

A second major kind of analytical ability that interveners need is the ability to stop the direction that a conflict is going by sensing the destructive patterns that emerge. For instance, the familiar pattern of blaming and counterblaming will usually not move the participants to the point of being able to manage the conflict successfully. As Leary (1955) noted long ago, hate begets hate and hostility produces even more hostility. In fact, the "interpersonal reflex" that most of us have is to return the same emotion to the other person that was sent to us. The effective third party intervener, therefore, will be sensitive to the patterns of conflict styles that are not productive and will be aware of the need for a change. If a couple is locked in the hate-begets-hate pattern, the third party obviously has to exercise control over the process to alter it significantly. Similarly, the mature intervener will be aware of more subtle patterns, such as patterns of mutual avoidance, and will understand that to counsel the participants to "just let it cool down and fade away" would be a disservice in this case. The third party must be able to understand the notion of "second-order change," where the structure of the interaction is changed. "First-order change" involves just calling for more of the same, more hostility or more avoidance, whereas "second-order change" involves a complete restructuring of the interaction (Watzlawick, Weakland, and Fisch 1974).

Altering the structure of interaction patterns involves assisting the participants in changing the payoffs they receive for their behaviors. As we noted in Chapter 4, the structure of the payoffs for conflict behaviors partially determines which behaviors will be activated. In the case of two parties being caught in a cycle of charge and countercharge, the third party can alter the payoff schedule by refusing to let the participants respond to negative barbs of the other. Anytime the intervener makes a suggestion like, "The next time he says such a negative thing to you, just ignore it and move on to what you find to be more important," he is altering the structure (Baumgartner, Buckley and Burns 1975). The structural change makes a difference because "in cooperation the parties jointly explore a wide range of alternative approaches and solutions, rather than each searching for the conditions under which the opponent will have to yield" (Fisher 1972). The parties stop punishing one another and begin cooperating because the third party has altered the structure. Such approaches have been suggested by a number of persons, most notably Blake and Mouton (1961) and Blake, Shepard, and Mouton (1964). A restructuring of the interaction of conflict participants involves an accurate understanding of what the current patterns of interaction are that contribute to the lack of effective management of the conflict. We will make specific suggestions below on communication techniques that can be used to directly affect the direction that a conflict takes.

Communication Style

The people we naturally turn to when we desire help in conflict situations all have something in common. They are persons we trust, to whom we are willing to risk ourselves in moments when we do not look admirable or when we may lose emotional control. They may be calm and deliberate, and almost certainly they are persons who listen well and respect the rights and personhood of other people. The following section discusses the communication style of persons who make effective third party intervention agents, whether in informal situations or in structured, large-group, conflict interventions. We are not suggesting that people can easily change their communication style to become instantly credible, but we are suggesting that you can emphasize those parts of your own communication style that are effective in the intervention situation. As we have discussed in the preceding section, many persons have little choice about whether they will intervene at some time or another in the conflicts of others—the choice is how effective that intervention will be.

Empathic Understanding of the Interpersonal Process

One of the crucial characteristics of third party interveners is their ability to attain and communicate empathy in the process of relating to other people (Carkhuff 1969; Rusk and Gerner 1972; Brammer 1973; Arnold 1977). The helper tries to see the world from the frame of reference of the participants in the conflict—not from his or her own frame of reference. The effective intervener knows that "only the parties themselves have experienced the full complexity of their situation, and only they know most of the determinants of their behavior" (Fisher 1972). Some of the principles of participant observation research are helpful in describing this process. It is important to gain an understanding of the social, internal reality of the participants themselves and not to impose outside categories of experience, belonging to the third party, onto the situation (Lofland 1971). When helpers listen fully and completely to the participants of the conflict, they are more likely to be able to feel empathy and understanding for those participants. No one wants to be judged, evaluated, or misunderstood—especially by someone who changes the system of the conflict by his or her presence in it. The participants should be able to "tell their own story" without evaluation or undue hurry. Then, third party perceptions can include an accurate estimate of how the participants see the conflict.

Some of the questions that help a third party to gain empathetic understanding of the conflict process are, "What are the people feeling right now?", "How do they separately view the problems?", "What does the situation look like right now to them?". Combs (1969) found that helpful intervention agents used this kind of internal frame of reference instead of outside frames of reference such as, "Why is he so upset?" or "Are the resources really scarce?'' or even "I'd better do something quick—this conflict is getting out of hand.''

It is of utmost importance that the helper not move too quickly into the empathetic role, and that he or she not move closer to one coalition or party than the other if effectiveness is to be maintained. Direction and objectivity are lost if the third party immediately "takes on" the attitudes of the persons in conflict (Brammer 1973). A balanced view of a conflict necessitates an accurate reading of how both parties perceive the conflict.

Congruence, Openness, and Genuineness

Many researchers point out the importance of genuineness and opennesss for persons taking the third party role (Carkhuff 1969; Rogers 1951; Brammer 1973; Combs 1969). Too much personal revelation and self-disclosure are not helpful; the third party must find a way of letting their own experience facilitate the expression of the participants' experience. Most of all, what a third party says should be congruent, genuine, and authentic. For instance, a friend might ask you if you mind coming over and helping her and her roommate work out some way to share responsibilities for the upkeep of the apartment. You have been a close friend of both roommates, they trust you, and they are in conflict over what each sees as the other one taking advantage of the good nature of the other. You and your roommate have a fine relationship about household duties, and the two people in conflict have agreed that they will ask you for help since you provide a good model for them to follow. Congruence means saying, "I'm sorry, Marilyn, I don't feel comfortable doing that since I want to remain close friends with both of you" if that is genuinely what you feel. Authenticity in response demands that your verbal and nonverbal communication reflect what you are feeling. If in the situation mentioned above you feel, upon being asked to intervene, "This is a setup. I know Marilyn really wants to move out and live with Janet,'' you then have the responsibility to reflect that with your answer. You might say something like, "I'm not comfortable with your level of commitment to each other. I want to help if you really want to be together, but I've noticed a lot of energy going elsewhere. Maybe you need to decide your level of commitment to each other first before we decide on how to divide up chores.'' Congruence means that your responses "ring true" to the conflict participants. You do not have to make things up and put on a phony role to help. You help most when you share your own genuine experience with people who want your help.

Regard and Respect for the Participants

Perhaps you have experienced being "helped" by someone who did not respect you as a person. The experience is demeaning and definitely unhelpful, since we all need to be respected as individuals before we can accept solutions or options from others. If you really think Frank and Sally are silly and do not deserve any better than they have (which at this point is a shouting match), then you are not the person to help them. Rogers (1961) called this condition "unconditional positive regard," meaning that even though the person in the third party role may not like what is going on in the conflict, he or she does respect the individuals involved and wants to help them. This attitude of respect is the opposite of a Machiavellian approach of manipulation—trying to get the conflict participants to do what you want them to do primarily so you can feel good about your own ability to exercise power. We have seen negotiators fly into a local situation from a distant place, work hard with a group of school teachers trying to negotiate a contract with the school board, and then judge their success on whether they could get the sides to do what the negotiator wanted. If the parties did not, they were labeled "recalcitrant," "ignorant'" "uninterested in a solution," or some other derogatory term. When we are respectful of the feelings and processes of others, we realize that they are the people who created the conflict situation and will have to live with the outcome, and we are there, whether for a short or long term, to *facilitate their own choices,* not to force them into solutions we might think are best.

Recently one of us was asked by a group of students in a class to intervene in a conflict they were having. Five students were in a special project group, the deadline was nearing, and they could not reach agreement on what to present to the class. They were to be given a group grade (perception of a scarce resource), and they had no choice about whether they were going to work together (they were highly interdependent). Yet one of their members insisted on trying to take charge, telling everyone else what to do, and judging ideas as they came up, calling them "unworkable," "stupid," or "impossible." The group asked for help from the teacher. At the meeting, the atmosphere was very tense. The would-be leader came in feeling obviously defensive, belligerent, and misunderstood. The third party, in this case the teacher, asked everyone to state his or her own perception of what was going on. Then the group came up with options. The third party said, "I will not choose the appropriate option for you. You are a group—you can come up with something that will work for you. I will try to help you identify what your choices are, and then you may choose." When the autocratic group member realized that he was being given a chance to stay in the group, he apologized for his bossiness, expressed frustration with the slowness of the group, and then began to listen to the perceptions of the other group members. The teacher stayed in the background, making sure everyone was heard and asking for clarification and restatement when necessary. Finally, the group came up with their own solution. If the teacher had said something like, "Obviously you can't work together. Every other group has been able to come to agreement, but this group can't," then the members would probably have felt so devalued as individuals that they might have united against the common enemy—the teacher! (A dubious way to resolve intergroup conflict.)

Active Leadership and Intrusiveness

The third party, especially the third party in crisis situations, should take over at times and actively change the structure of the conflict as it continues to take place. Sometimes it is quite a relief to a group experiencing conflict for someone to take charge, even if that leadership is going to be temporary. The frustration level might have risen to such an extent that a shift is needed. As we mentioned above, this active leadership is not helpful if the intervener does not respect the persons involved and wants to build his or her own self-regard at the expense of others. But often active leadership is paramount. This kind of leadership is risky and involves a calm confidence of the person taking charge—not a frantic scramble for power, which only aggravates the conflict that is already taking place. We will discuss in the next section some of the intervention tactics available to the leader who desires to change the structure of the conflict. The point we are making here is that the third party must sometimes be willing to take over.

Hopefulness

The third party can be most helpful if the attitude of hopefulness and optimism can carry through. We are not suggesting a naive, "all we need to do is talk to each other and then these ridiculous misunderstandings will blow over" attitude. We do suggest, however, that people need to be reassured that options are possible. You have seen people manage similar conflicts in the past, that the people involved are important and that you believe that they will be able to come to agreement. When persons are experiencing despair, they do not see all the options that are available. Two people we know recently experienced conflict when the wife was offered a fellowship to go back to school and the husband was not willing to commit himself to stay in the area for three more years since his job was unsatisfactory. They became quite angry with each other with counteraccusations flying until finally one of them suggested setting up a meeting with a counselor. The counselor knew them socially, not as clients, and did not perceive that the couple needed long-term counseling help. The first thing she said was, "I think you two can work this out. You have been through crises before, and you'll get through this one." When the couple told about the incident later, it was the attitude of hopefulness of the counselor that helped them stop escalating and begin to generate new options for what they might do.

Understanding Problems from Incomplete Information

Third party helpers are most able to help people when they can *infer* the reality of the situation for the participants from "cues" given by the participants, both verbal and nonverbal, instead of having to have the entire situation spelled out. Training in nonverbal conmunication is highly desirable for persons wishing to emphasize the communication principles in conflict management. For instance, tension shown in body postures, orientation away or toward each other, territorial markers, and dozens of other nonverbally communicated messages are often more important than the words that people use when they are explaining what is wrong. One of us intervened in a personnel issue involving a secretary who had been given a raise by her boss without having gone through the complex personnel system for the large organization for which she worked. In the meeting, which involved seven active, vocal participants, the man who had given the "illegal" raise sat slightly in front of the secretary. He answered for her, explaining "their" position. He challenged the personnel officer saying, "You don't know her work. Don't you think I'm competent to *judge my own people?*" From the man's defensive posture and choice of seating, it became obvious that he was more of a party to the dispute than the secretary was. In fact, the secretary constantly tried to soften her boss's statements with a shrug of the shoulders, a smile, and a gesture of self-derogation. The informal mediator was able to begin to separate the issues out from each other starting with the boss's identification with the conflict—for him it was a personal challenge of authority. The personnel officer saw the problem more as a larger organizational issue. This discrepancy was commented upon, and then the informal negotiations began. In this case and many others, nonverbal awareness was crucial to understanding the situation.

Safety

The third party needs to provide an atmosphere of safety in which people can risk and try out new solutions to conflicts without total commitment. The intervention situation can be one in which multiple options are generated without feeling that someone will jump on one of them, saying, "that's it!" and declare the conflict solved. A safe environment is emphasized by a person who projects an attitude of tentativeness and who is willing to be noncoercive (Burton 1968). The parties are encouraged to stand back and examine their role, images, and actions in a way that might be too risky if an accepting third party were not present. And the third party needs to be someone who will not misuse information by trying to trick the participants, catch them in inconsistencies, or overpersuade them to do a certain thing. The conflict intervention situation can be a "half-way house" experience of trying out possible solutions verbally before they are instituted formally.

Intervention Tactics

In the preceding section, we have discussed personal characteristics of third party helpers in conflict situations. It is difficult to separate personal characteristics from some of the most used intervention tactics—many of these tactics cannot be used unless the person has the characteristics we have discussed previously. They can be developed with practice, however, especially if you have a friend or colleague who can observe your interaction and give you suggestions about what part of your intervention behavior was most helpful to the people involved in the conflict. The following are some tactics that can be used productively in intervention.

Direct the Feedback Process

The third party should intervene in the communication process itself when it is apparent that the participants are not listening to each other, or that they need help in understanding one another. Some of the rules that might be appropriate follow (adapted in part from National Training Laboratories 1968 and Filley 1975).

1. *Be descriptive rather than judgmental.*

   Describe behavior in terms of what your reaction is to it, rather than pinning a label on the other person. For instance, try to get participants to say, "This is the fifth time we've tried to find a solution" instead of this is a "totally uncooperative group." Describe in terms of observable behavior instead of "mind-raping" (Bach and Goldberg 1974) the other person by saying, "I know what you're thinking."

2. *Encourage specificity.*

   Feedback is more effective when it describes specific instances instead of general feelings. For instance, instead of letting people say, "I'm sure that's not going to be acceptable to some people, encourage them to be specific by saying, "I'm almost certain that Sam will say no to that. And we need his cooperation." When dealing with painful feelings, there is a tendency to be abstract. People flounder when they are unsure; encourage them by saying, "Could you tell the group of an instance that illustrates when you get resentful of Sam's directions?" Try to avoid the use of such phrases as "most people," "they say," "it seems we" or "one might think" (Brammer 1973). If a statement is worth making, it is worth making specifically so its full power can be felt.

3. *Deal with things that can be changed instead of "givens."*

   Feedback is most effective when it concerns descriptions that are not inherent characteristics of persons or situations. Saying, "Mary just bugs me. There's nothing I can do to change that" is not very helpful. The leader could call a foul on such statements, asking for the participants to deal with issues that are *at issue.* Concentrating on things that cannot be changed is a waste of time and emotional energy.

4. *Encourage parties to give feedback when it is requested.*

   If Mary says, "I'm not sure how John feels. He never tells me," the third party might say, "Do you want to check that out? You could ask him to tell you." Or the intervention agent can ask parties to give feedback to each other when they need it, even if the need has not been articulated.

5. *Give feedback as close as possible to the behavior being discussed.*

   Feedback sometimes serves as a kind of "instant replay" to a behavioral pattern that has been observed by the third party. But it loses its effectiveness if someone says, "I was angry at your suggestion at our last staff meeting. I thought about it all week." The feedback would have more power closer to the triggering event.

6. *Encourage feedback whose accuracy can be checked by others.*

   In a group situation, sometimes people are unaware of their own word choices and behavior. A high school principal made a statement once at a workshop about wanting the facilitator to "make the faculty have more respect for each other." When the third party fed back that statement to the principal, he denied that he had said anything implying coercion. One of the teachers spoke up and said, "Mr. ___, when you talk about 'making' us do something, it makes me feel like a third grader. I feel resentment." He was able to understand her feelings since other people were able to corroborate the statement he had made earlier.

7. *Speak only for yourself.*

   Encourage persons in conflicts to not speculate what other people think, and to say "I think," or "I feel" often. Especially, check out coalitions by saying, "Mr. Jones has said you all agree with him. I'd like to check that out with the rest of you. Mr. Rogers, what are your feelings on the matter?" Often, coalition members will say, "Yes, I agree, *except,*" and then give a substantially different statement from the one made by a team leader or high power person.

Besides directing the feedback, other ways to direct interactions are suggested in the following areas.

Call on Quiet Persons in a Nonthreatening Way

Many times, persons in a group or even in an informal conflict interaction are waiting for someone to show an interest in what they have to say. They have opinions and strong feelings, but they do not feel comfortable or safe expressing them—often because someone of higher power is present. Or perhaps they feel they are alone in an opinion, when in fact a coalition may form around them when they muster up the courage to speak out. Many times we have seen a group struggle through a tense silence, then when the leader says, "Jack, you seem involved, but I'm not sure where you are on this issue . . . ," after a brief statement, several people chime in with, "That's what I thought but I was afraid to say it" or "I had no idea you felt that way." It is never a good idea to "catch" people, or point out in an abrupt way the nonparticipation of quiet members, but giving them a chance to enter in is part of the task of the third party.

Limit the Agenda and Keep People to It

Working toward agreement of the items to be discussed, especially when you suspect that there are multiple motives of some of the persons involved can be effective. For instance, one of us facilitated a meeting in which several rival groups from a low-income neighborhood were trying to decide where the community center, funded by the government, was to be located. Four groups sponsored a different location each; a small fifth, but vocal, group seemed belligerent about every suggestion, finding something wrong with each one. Finally, one of the men in the "opposed to everything" group said, "I don't know why we're building an expensive building for bums anyway. Those kids who drop out of school and people on welfare would just wreck the building and wouldn't appreciate it. What we need is a good job training center. That way we'd be doing people who want to work some good." In this case, the most effective intervention we could think of at the moment was to remind the group that they had agreed upon an agenda, which was to hear presentations of anyone wishing to suggest a location for the center *which had already been funded.* And, unless the group was willing to change their decision about the agenda, the group was inappropriately changing the direction of the evening. Then a mention was made of the lateness of the hour, and the rest of the group backed up the intervener. This was certainly not perfect, since the opposition group was disgruntled, but the intervention fit the primary energy of the group—to narrow down the choice of locations. Getting agreement ahead of time on the agenda is a safeguard against later subversion of the group process. Putting the agenda in writing on a flip chart or blackboard is a good idea—then the group can see how they are progressing through the discussion.

Set and Referee Time Limits

Even in a very informal conflict intervention, *make agreements about the time to be spent on the conflict and then enforce that contract,* if you can. Point out that every meeting is in some sense a contract to do something together, and that if the contract is to be meaningful, participants should plan to spend a certain time together and not much longer than that. Meetings are disrupted, to say nothing of dyadic conflicts, when one person or a group of persons suddenly decide to leave, without notifying the rest of the participants that they are going to leave. Sometimes leaving early, or keeping the rest of the group in the dark about how long you can stay is a power move, designed, however unconsciously, to keep the rest of the group guessing about your participation. In a staff meeting of a mental hospital, one older member of the group constantly warned the group that he was in a hurry and could not stay long. They rushed through decisions, not knowing that any decisions on which he did not have impact might be subverted later. Finally, the group leader said, "Mr. Jones, we want you involved in this decision about how to hire extra staff on the limited budget the legislature has given us. You are involved in much of the training of new people. We can't involve you if we don't know how long you're going to be here. Would you tell us when you must leave today, and then we can gauge our discussion accordingly?" Mr. Jones really did not want to be committed like that, but he reluctantly gave a time, and then stayed for the discussion.

Sometimes groups negotiate an open time limit—and if the limit to conversation is open, it should be negotiated so that people are not operating on different time clocks. A beginning church group, for instance, that operated on a "town meeting" democratic model, scheduled all business meetings to go on indefinitely until everyone had had his or her say, with the ending time to be negotiated at least half an hour ahead of termination. This practice made for some late nights and restless participants, but also maximized individual participation in the early, formative stages of the community-building. At that time in the life of the group, even in times of intense conflict, the full participation of everyone was a higher priority than getting home early. Of course, this model is not practical for most groups, but does serve to illustrate the point that starting and ending times can and should be negotiated in an open way. The leader can say, when the time draws close to the negotiated ending time, "It's almost 9:30. We agreed to end then—if we're going to talk longer, we need to decide that together, otherwise people will be free to go knowing no more decisions will be made."

Compare Parties' Positions

People who are in the throes of significant conflict often lose track of what they have said, of what the issues are, and thus lose areas of possible agreement and disagreement. One of the functions of the third party is to point out both kinds of areas. For instance, a third party might say, "I hear agreement on the issues on how we should allocate the travel money. But we are still in disagreement over how we will get the money for travel—from the supplies budget or from the summer school budget. Is that accurate?" Always ask for confirmation of your summation of the issues. The group needs someone to keep track of where they are. Also, the summation often provides impetus for compromise, for one party dropping a petty point, or for making an offer of a bargain. Point out inconsistencies as well, not to trip up people for being inconsistent (most of us in conflict are inconsistent), but to draw the lines clearly. For instance, the third party can say, "The two of you have agreed that you will complete the Environmental Conciliation grant bid together by June. But you also are arguing for the priority of the Land Management grant on the one hand, Steven, and the Planning grant for you, John. You may not be able to do both." Then the participants can decide what they will do with the inconsistent decisions they have made.

Restate Positions

One of the most effective third party tactics is to restate positions as you hear them being advocated and to ask participants to restate their own and each others' positions. One conflict exercise calls for the leader to enforce (if there is sufficient group interest and support) the restatement requirement—one person may not give his or her own opinion until the position of the previous speaker is stated to that person's satisfaction, including both the factual and the emotional content. One of us worked on an Indian reservation in South Dakota in the sixties. At a town meeting called to discuss different opinions on policies of rental of reservation land by non-Indians, the conflict (which at that time was bitter and not close to resolution) centered around two individuals, a large landowner who had, through the years, become dependent upon rental of Indian land, and the Tribal president. The two men yelled at each other for fifteen or twenty minutes, with coalitions forming around them, angry gestures being made, and tempers flaring. Finally, order was regained momentarily, and the leader asked the group to try an experiment—the restatement exercise. The group agreed. The Indian stated his position. He stated it with bitterness, anger, and some sarcasm. The communication requirement was then for the white rancher to restate the position of the Indian before he stated his own position. He tried. The group booed and cheered. The leader said, "Mr. Yellow Cloud, was your position stated correctly?" The man obviously said "no"—the rancher had been sarcastic and derogatory. The two men struggled for thirty minutes. Finally after a long period of silence, the rancher made a simple, honest restatement of the other man's position. There was more silence. The Indian touched him on the shoulder and said, "Thank you." The crowd clapped. This is an unusual example, but the group was able to move toward cooperative solutions after this attempt at understanding. Often people are quite surprised to find that their attempt at restatement does not meet the approval of the first party. They are unaware of the depth of emotion being expressed by the other side and downplay the feelings so much that they miss the whole point of what the other person is trying to say. This tactic can also be effectively used in business meetings when emotions are not so high. Restatement is a vital tactic of the third party intervener.

Provide Information for Persons in the Resolution Phase of Conflict

Sometimes the third party is called in to provide expert opinion or information so that the parties can make up their minds what to do (Arnold 1977). This request for information is different from an insincere request for advice that obviously is not going to be taken. At times when parties need concise information so that they can reach resolution, it would be inappropriate to reflect, restate opinions, or back up and summarize like the more nondirective tactics suggest. The people need information, and one of the qualities of an effective third party is that the intervener can give crisp, relevant, concise information when asked for, and then let the parties make their own decisions. It is a rare person who knows how to slightly undershoot the request for information instead of taking the opportunity to expound on their own personal opinion on what should have been done in the first place.

Reverse Roles When Appropriate

Similar to the tactic of restatement of another's position is role reversal. This tactic is only appropriate when the group is willing to experiment or in a highly personal situation when the persons involved trust the intervener, usually a person who is acting in the role of counselor. Parties are asked to take the roles of the other side, acting out, or stating as clearly as possible the positions of the other side or sides. Studies show that persons who successfully carry out this effort at understanding increase their level of cooperation when their positions are ultimately compatible or can be made so by relatively minor compromise or change of position. However, the drawback to this tactic is that if the positions are basically incompatible, either because the resources are indeed so scarce that no accommodation is possible, or because the parties are not interdependent enough to have to come to resolution together, then the level of competition is actually *increased* by the role reversal technique (Johnson 1967). Thus, the tactic is no panacea and can be used quite naïvely by the untrained leader. No tactics are sure-fire cures for destructive conflict: only the participants involved in the conflict can make the final decision to cooperate.

Spot Internal Conciliators

One of the principles of formal mediation, such as that carried out in labor-management disputes, is that the mediator looks for "lieutenants," or persons who appear ready to support efforts of conciliation and compromise. They may be persons who give verbal assent to good faith gestures, who try to point out areas of agreement, or who take any positive steps toward reconciliation of positions that have been presented as totally nonnegotiable.

The third party agent, whether he or she be on a formal board of arbitration, in the mediator role, or appointed as a negotiating representative, should look for signs of support from the group itself. Participants in a conflict are more likely to support measures proposed by their own members than by an outsider, especially if the outsider is there by force of law. One of us was empanelled to be on a formal board of arbitration for a dispute among transportation interests, in this case two taxicab companies, in a small, wealthy resort town. Both principles presented their cases, pointing out that the other side was totally without redeeming virtue and was wrong in every way. But one side consisted of three men, two of whom attended but did not speak. The arbitrator noticed that the vice-president of the company winced and grimaced when the president presented some of the more inflammatory statements about the impossibility of negotiating with the other side. When asked if all members of the company agreed, a discussion followed among the three officers, who then softened their position to be one with which it was possible to work. The arbitration board would have made a decision less likely to please either side because of the nonnegotiable nature of the position presentation. But with the inclusion of the other members, more information assisted in an equitable solution. Pinpointing the helpers is a wise move—the third party process is difficult, and all the help that is available needs to be called upon. Usually these conciliatory parties can be pinpointed by their statements such as, "I guess that's not such a strange request. I can understand why they made it" or other statements that show some understanding of the other side. These people then can be encouraged to function as "internal conciliators."

Recognize the Limitations of Your Role

The conciliator works with the parties but does not take an aggressive role in working toward resolution. The mediator takes a neutral position and has no legal power to force parties to reach resolution. The mediator has great interpersonal credibility and power since a person in that position is usually chosen by the conflict parties themselves, so they usually trust him or her highly (Keltner 1970). For instance, persons who are ministers, counselors, social workers, principals of schools, welfare workers, or lawyers out of the court situation often serve as mediators. Arbitrators have legal power of some kind. Often the participants have voluntarily agreed to be bound by the decision of the arbitrator(s), although their next choice may be to go to court if they refuse to reach agreement (Keltner 1970). Arbitrators usually are not chosen by the parties in the conflict, and they usually are not very close emotionally or in other ways to the participants. Arbitration is an efficient way to reach solutions when the parties wish to avoid a court battle, but have stopped talking to each other or have reached an impasse of some kind. Arbitration, however, is unusual in informal situations. In our opinion, arbitration should be used by hospitals, schools, communities, and family courts more than it is. It can provide a method of at least temporary resolution of potentially violent and destructive conflicts. Persons trained in communication who are appointed as arbitrators can do some of the same things we have suggested above, with the added responsibility of reaching agreement for the parties involved. In Chapter 5 we discussed the dual purpose of all conflict management: (1) to reach agreement and (2) to enhance the relationship for future conflict management. In arbitration situations, reaching agreement is more important than enhancing the relationship; in conciliation, enhancing the relationship is more important than reaching agreement. It is important to try to keep your role straight when you are acting as an informal intervention agent—especially when you are intervening with friends who are asking for informal conciliation, not mediation or arbitration. No one wants a friend to pronounce what should be done in definite tones. People in informal situations reserve the right to make their decisions by themselves, even when they ask for third party help.

Encourage Parties to Have a Range of Positions

Point out to conflict participants that if they are in a situation where intervention is appropriate (assuming that it is), then they are also in a situation in which it is inappropriate to announce that a wide range of positions are "nonnegotiable." For instance, if a husband and wife want to stay together, they have to be willing to limit their "bottom line" statements. Their interdependence enforces a wide range of position development if they are being honest and realistic about their situation. Encourage people who are not in formal negotiation (where it is often desirable to falsely represent a position at the beginning) to represent their most crucial issues honestly and sparingly. Openness and good faith are the cornerstones of effective informal conflict management.

Summarize and Get Commitment

It is crucial to the effective management of a conflict to gain the commitment of the participants at the end of the processing session. An effective conclusion to the management phase involves (1) summarizing where the participants have been and what has been decided, (2) asking and probing to see if there are any unresolved issues or concerns, and (3) asking the participants for clear statements about how the decisions will be implemented. With these interrelated tactics one has a much better chance of having the interventionist efforts pay off. Without them, all the effort could be wasted. Without asking the participants such things as, "How will you make this decision work?," "What areas do you feel are still not resolved?," "How do you feel about the decision?," and "Do you feel that this decision can be acted upon?," the conflict will likely reemerge later. In fact, all conflicts are episodic, they are noticed when triggering events bring them to our awareness, they then blossom and demand attention, they are reacted to, and finally they recede into the background. As a result, effective intervention must take account of the ebb and flow of conflicts by obtaining as much commitment from the parties as is practically possible. For, without the commitment, when another triggering episode occurs and the conflict comes to the forefront of the relationship, the workable agreements you have hammered out will not be brought into play by the participants. Conflicts do not begin and end, they emerge and recede. You need all the assistance you can muster to make sure the participants are clear about what the conflict was over and what their commitments are to the management of it.

Establish Superordinate Goals

One very effective interventionist tactic is to help the parties effect superordinate goals, goals that go over and above the ones they had originally. An example of superordinate goals comes from the field experiments of Sherif et al. (1961). The classic study used a group of young boys to demonstrate that the establishment of superordinate goals can bind previously conflicting parties together for a common cause. In this case, two groups were formed, the "Rattlers" and the "Eagles." After an initial period where the two groups (parties to the conflict) engaged in some rather hostile competition, the researchers began to sabotage some crucial functions of the camp. In one case the water tank malfunctioned, and in another a truck was out of commission. As a result of the superordinate goal, a goal that both groups had a stake in regardless of their prior competition, the boys from the different groups began to mingle and work cooperatively for the common goals.

Superordinate goals can usually be found for any group of conflict participants based on some need to cooperate. We noted earlier in this book that in every conflict there are both cooperative and competitive elements, and superordinate goals merely emphasize the more cooperative goals. If a marital couple, for instance, is involved in a series of conflicts, some possible superordinate goals that might be useful in the management of the conflict are appealing to "the marriage," "the children," or "your need of one another even during these difficult times." And, sometimes, as we warned earlier in this chapter, the defeat of the third party may become a superordinate goal for the parties. It is not unlikely that many conflicts have been helped by having a third party that the participants form a coalition against.

Finally, insincere attempts to establish superordinate goals that are used for gaining more power are usually readily apparent to the participants. If, for instance, two parties to a labor dispute call on an outside party who appeals to labor's "sense of fairness" and makes no reciprocal appeal to management, the labor representatives will be very aware of the one-sided nature of the appeal. A true superordinate goal is one that both parties can become committed to and are willing to work toward. It is a goal that requires cooperation between two antagonistic parties for some mutual benefit.

Equalize Power

The power balance between the conflicting parties is widely discrepant. One of the functions that a third party can serve in such a situation is to provide for more equalization of the power so that the participants are better able to conduct the management themselves. For example, marriage counseling often provides the distressed person with some insights and skills that will allow him or her to more effectively impact on the interpersonal system he or she is in. As we noted in Chapter 3, it is powerlessness that corrupts and produces a sense of despair and hopelessness.

Members of most of the Western cultures have a sense of equity, that people should receive some due rewards for their efforts. Often, a third party can appeal to this norm, ask for some change in the most powerful member, and be effective in getting some consideration. People often conform to the norm of equity (Lane and Messe 1971); (Gouldner 1960). Common sayings about imbalances of interpersonal power make it clear that people are aware of power differences when they say, "He just runs over her," "He is sure henpecked," "He is a bulldozer with her."

One of the ways to bring about a power shift is to help the participants know the costs they incur by their behavior (Brown 1968). If a man and his fiancee, for instance, are in a continual conflict where he seems to be giving orders to her, a discussion of the dysfunctional aspects of this for him would be enlightening. It may be that every time he acts in a bossy manner he feels guilty and unworthy, and if so, bringing this information to light will allow the parties to begin slowly shifting some of the balance of power. People need to save face, and if the third party can clear the air to let the participants fully discuss both the rewards and costs they incur from their behavior, power may be shifted (Brown 1968).

A shift in the balance of power will allow the parties to more effectively bargain with one another. They can establish the *quid pro quos* mentioned earlier and reach agreements that will work for both of them. Effective bargaining, where interests of both the parties has an influence on the outcome, will be a step in facilitating effective management of the conflict. With the stance of the parties being somewhat equalized, both will feel like what they say and do will make a difference (because it will) and will work harder for effective management of the conflict.

Produce Graduated Tension Reduction

This rather imposing sounding tactic is really quite simple. It is derived from the work of Osgood in international relations (1971). Osgood suggested that nations who found themselves in a balance of power, locked into an ever-escalating buildup of arms, perform a graduated reduction. Specifically, it calls for a nation to take a unilateral step to reduce some aspect of military might. The country risks a small step as a way to allow the other country to then take its own small step. Such a process can be suggested by a third party to conflict parties, whether they be individuals, groups, or institutions. For instance, if two friends are in a heated argument, one possible step toward graduated reduction of tensions would be for one party to say, "I'm still really mad, but I want us to solve this problem so I will not make any more negative statements about what you did that hurt me. Rather, I'll take five minutes and try to listen to what you are really trying to say." This and other forms of graduated reduction work best when the power of the parties is somewhat equal (Hamner 1974).

Siegil and Fouraker (1960) suggest an opposite approach, the "principle of toughness," as an effective management device. According to their advice (and this technique is used by many parties in conflicts), in a bargaining situation one should (1) open with a high request, (2) make a small rate of concession, (3) set a high minimum level of expectation, and (4) be unyielding. This advice, as appealing as it is to some people, has rather limited applications. If you are not interested in the ongoing relationship, like a personal relationship with someone, then such a tactic might well be effective. But in most personal conflicts the maintenance of the relationship is just as important as the specific issue to be settled. So, when you are in a position of power over the other, or the long-range relational feelings are of no importance to you, you might follow the four-step approach. However, most third parties will be intervening in cases where the graduated reductions will be more effective. Many an intimate has "gotten tough" and made demands on the other only to wake up the next morning and find the other gone.

Use the Institutions of Conflict Management

The third party intervention agent will often need to be knowledgeable about other persons who can help in the conflict management process on the interpersonal level. Our society is somewhat limited in institutionalized conflict management measures short of the court system. But most communities have people who are trained in aspects of interpersonal conflict management and are willing to help in times of crisis and intense conflict or who are trained in conflict prevention by planning and helping persons to identify possible future areas of conflict. People who are not trained specifically in conflict management, or counseling, need to refer their friends and coworkers when the problems being discussed are beyond the competencies of the potential third party. Peer counselors in dormitories, for instance, are alerted to suicide prevention centers, marriage counselors, job counselors, academic counselors, police, and other community agents who can help in difficult times. We do no one any favors if we try to handle problems that are above our level of competency or outside our province of expertise. Sometimes people are reluctant to refer because they do not want to send their friends or colleagues away—they want to be helpful. The role of a supportive friend, however, is crucial and should not be undervalued. While your associates may be seeking someone else for their more intentional conflict management needs, friends are necessary to give a sense of worth and importance. You can structure time with friends even after referring them to someone else.

If you are often in a position of being an informal third party, acquaint yourself with the facilities in your community for counseling and conflict management. Often university campuses have a student counseling center. Many ministers are trained in pastoral counseling. Lawyers sometimes act in a mediation role, especially in predivorce situations. Some teachers are trained in communication and conflict management. Private counselors are available, as are counselors at mental health centers, veterans administration hospitals, mental hospitals, retired senior volunteer programs, and numerous other community agencies. Sometimes the most effective intervention is a well-timed and helpful referral, then the persons needing help have the best of several worlds—friends who care about them and professional help.

Intervening in Your Own Conflicts

As we have discussed throughout the book, each individual is a participant in a system and changing an individual changes the entire system. Some interesting research on teacher-student interaction pointed out this fact in a particularly graphic way. Marginal students in an elementary school were identified and given special training to modify the behavior of the teachers who were most hostile to these students who often did not do their work, disrupted class, acted arrogantly, and other behavior considered unacceptable by the teachers. The students were taught to verbally reinforce the teachers for any positive attention and to point out to them in socially acceptable ways what teacher behaviors were harmful and helpful to the students. For instance, the children were taught to say things like, "I'd appreciate it if you would warn me about talking before sending me out of the room." The results, of course, were astonishing, with many of the students being socialized back into their classrooms, with large changes in their self-esteem and with the teachers feeling much more positively about the students (Gray, Granbard and Rosenberg, 1974).

In preceding sections, we have been discussing primarily the role of the third party in changing the system in which he or she becomes temporarily involved. But often we are participants in our own conflicts—no third party is going to be brought in, either because such action is impractical or because some of the participants will not agree to it, and if the conflict is going to move toward management, you as one of the primary parties will have to take some action. Three possibilities exist when you are in a conflict. You may:

1. *Try to change the behavior of the other party or parties.* Much of what we have discussed falls under this category. When you try to change the behavior of others, you perceive a goal, work toward that goal, and emphasize persuasion and motivation of the other parties to change. Often this process is necessary; sometimes it is shortsighted when we assume that if the other person would just quit doing whatever the target behavior is, then the conflict would cease.

2. *Try to change the structure of the conflict.* As we discussed in Chapter 4, all conflicts are structured around choices and potential payoffs for parties. Failing to make structural changes can lock participants into fewer options than they really have. A woman who was an administrative assistant to an extremely unorganized man complained bitterly that he unfairly dumped

work on her desk at the last minute. She bemoaned the fact that she would have to stay up all night to get the work done. She saw only the two choices mentioned thus far: accept the structure and resign or try to get the boss to change his ways (change the behavior of the other party). She needed to have more choices or alter the payoffs for the ones she wanted to exercise.

3. *Change your own behavior.* Parties in all genuine conflicts are interdependent, and, as a result, the best course of action may be to decide to emphasize change in your own behavior. This may be a process of changing overt actions or changing perceptions one holds. Ackoff and Emery note that,

What an individual perceives in a situation is not merely a matter of what is *given* to him by the situation, because much more is *offered* by it than he can possibly receive. Therefore, what he perceives is also a matter of what he *takes*. He enters such a situation with a set; the set is his model of the situation (1972).

In the situation of the woman who wanted to find another solution to having to do the work dumped on her desk at the last minute, she began to realize that she could choose to do the work (she needed the job), but at a lower level of competence than she ordinarily would. She could scale down her expectation level, and then point out to her boss that the work would be of higher quality if she had more time to do it. The option she finally chose was that of changing her own behavior—the least attractive option in many cases. Yet by changing your own interaction, the entire conflict will be different. One person is important in any conflict.

Changing your own behavior requires some perceptive answers to hard questions. The skills of participant observation research are helpful in analyzing your behavior as well as the patterned behavior of other persons in social systems.[1] The following questions will be helpful in analyzing your role before intervention (change) is attempted in a conflict in which you are a primary party.

Are You Involved Enough in the Conflict to Desire Change?

Confrontation and change means involvement. Confrontation should be saved for those times when you wish to increase the level of mutual involvement. Bach and Wyden (1968) discuss the importance of "not fighting unless you mean it." Conflict at its best means that the participants are

---

1. See Lofland 1971; McCall and Simmons 1969; Garfinkel 1967; Filstead 1970, for in depth discussions of the participant observation/qualitative methodology techniques of research that may be applied to analysis of situations before intervention is attempted.

struggling not only toward agreement but toward a relationship in which future decisions can be made more productively and toward a relationship of importance to each other. If you simply wish to get out of the conflict without working toward a more productive relationship, then one of the avoidance tactics might be most appropriate—or rapid escalation!

What Role Do You Play in the Conflict?

Try to identify patterns of interaction that recur. Are there themes that tend to emerge time and time again? How satisfied are you with your role? Could you describe your role to another person in fairly neutral terms, without running the other person down?

What Do You Gain from the Present Pattern?

Most researchers and communication scholars agree that if persons interact in patterned, predictable ways, there is something of value in the interaction or the participants would not continue to repeat the interactions. This is sometimes a hard truth to come to grips with, since persons often want to put most of the blame for a conflict on others, seeing themselves as innocent victims. But there are few innocent victims in interpersonal relationships; we participate in setting up most of our interactions. So the crucial question must be addressed: "What do I get out of this interaction?"

Do I Really Want to Change? Is It Reasonable to Change?

Often persons *want to want to change.* They see the dysfunction of present patterns, but change is difficult and threatening, so it becomes easier to stay in the present situation. Many couples stay together even though they complain angrily about each other; change is more threatening than the security of the present situation. Before you decide to intervene in a conflict, the question of desirability of change must be addressed. And then, the question of whether change is possible and reasonable must be answered. Persons who have participated in encounter groups might recognize situations such as the following. One individual dominated the discussion of one group we witnessed. He said he "welcomed the opportunity for others to point out his faults and problems, since that's the way I learn." He happened to have several highly obnoxious habits that greatly hampered communication between him and other members, such as excessive talking, and overgeneralizing about the other person without giving the other person a chance to respond. For instance, he would make a statement something like, "Most women are afraid to drive alone at night and would rather stay home." Upon being confronted with these habits, he would defend himself and say he did not want to abridge his integrity to present himself to be something he was not. After spending a large portion of group time, the group finally realized that he wanted to talk about his problems, but did not want to change. Furthermore, the likelihood of his changing was negligible. Then the group switched to more productive topics with other persons. They learned you cannot make a person want to change.

Many college students find, for instance, that they do not really want to change patterns in their interaction with their parents after they go away to college—they struggle for several years to change, often advocating dramatic change. But they then decide slowly through the years that the patterns are fairly set, and change is not likely.

Summary

Throughout the book we have presented various perspectives on interpersonal conflict—a philosophy of conflict, a discussion of personal styles of conflict, the structure of interactions, goals in conflicts, power relationships, strategies and tactics, and third party intervention. But the final resolution or management choice usually is up to the individual. The individual is the final arbiter of his or her own behavior. When we grow to value taking responsibility for our own behavior, when we can work toward mature interaction with others, and when we are able to see that our choices determine each instant of the rest of our lives, we will all realize that ultimately, we are the final conflict management agent of our own lives.

Bibliography

Ackoff, Russell and Emery, Fred E. *On Purposeful Systems*. Chicago: Aldine Publishing Co., 1972.

Arnold, William E. "Crisis Communication." In *Communicating Through Behavior,* edited by William E. Arnold and Robert O. Hirsch. St. Paul, Minn.: West Publishing Co., 1977.

Bach, George R., and Goldberg, Herb. *Creative Aggression: The Art of Assertive Living.* New York: Avon Books, 1974.

———, and Wyden, Peter. *The Intimate Enemy.* New York: Avon Books, 1968.
Bard, Morton, and Zacker, Joseph. "How Police Handle Explosive Squabbles." *Psychology Today,* November 1976, pp. 71ff.

Baumgartner, T.; Buckey, W.; and Burns, T. "Relational Control: The Human Structuring of Cooperation and Conflict." *Journal of Conflict Resolution* 19(1975):417-440.

Blake, R. R., and Mouton, J. S. "Union-management Relations: From Conflict to Collaboration." *Personnel* 38(1961):38-51.

———; Shepard, A.; and Mouton, J. S. *Managing Intergroup Conflict in Industry.* Houston, Tex.: Gulf Publishing Co., 1964.

Boulding, Kenneth. *Conflict and Defense: A General Theory.* New York: Harper Torchbooks, 1962.

Brammer, Lawrence M. *The Helping Relationship: Process and Skills.* Englewood Cliffs, N.J.: Prentice-Hall, Inc., 1973.

Brockopp, G. "Selecting the Crisis Intervener.: *Crisis Intervention* 4(1972):1-7.

Brown, Bert R. "The Effects of Need to Maintain Face on Interpersonal Bargaining." *Journal of Experimental Social Psychology* 4(1)(1968):107-122.

Burton, J. W. *Systems, States, Diplomacy and Rules.* Cambridge, Mass.: Cambridge University Press, 1968.

Carkhuff, R. *Helping and Human Relations.* Two vols. New York: Holt, Rinehart & Winston, Inc., 1969.

Combs, A. W. *Florida Studies in the Helping Professions.* Gainsville, Fla.: University of Florida Press, 1969.

Erickson, Bonnie; Holmes, John G.; Frey, Robert; Walker, Laurens; and Thibaut, John. "Functions of 3rd Party in the Resolution of Conflict: The Role of A Judge in Pre-trial Conferences." *Journal of Personality and Social Psychology,* 30(1974):293-306.

Erikson, Erik. *Identity and the Life Cycle.* New York: International Universities Press, Inc., 1959.

Filley, Alan C. *Interpersonal Conflict Resolution.* Glenview, Ill: Scott, Foresman, & Co., 1975.

Filstead, William J. (ed.) *Qualitative Methodology: Firsthand Involvement with the Social World.* Chicago: Rand, 1970.

Fink, S. L. "Crisis and Motivation: A Theoretical Model." *Archives of Physical Medicine and Rehabilitation* 48(1967):592-597.

Fisher, Ronald J. "Third Party Consultation: A Method for the Study and Resolution of Conflict." *Journal of Conflict Resolution,* March 1972, pp. 67-94.

Garfinkel, Harold. *Studies in Ethnomethodology.* Englewood Cliffs, N.J.: Prentice-Hall, Inc., 1967.

Gouldner, Alvin W. "The Norm of Reciprocity: A Preliminary Statement." *American Sociological Review,* April 1960, pp. 161-178.

Gray, Farnum; Granbard, Paul S.; and Rosenberg, Harry. "Little Brother is Changing You." *Psychology Today,* March 1974, pp. 42-46.

Haccoun, Robert R., and Klimoski, Richard J. "Negotiator Status and Account-ability Source: A Study of Negotiator Behavior." *Organizational Behavior and Human Performance, 14,* September 1975, pp. 342-359.

Hamner, W. Clay. "Effects of Bargaining Strategy and Pressure to Reach Agree-ment in a Stalemated Negotiation." *Journal of Personality and Social Psychology* 30(1974):458-467.

Ikle, Fred. "Bargaining and Communication." *In Handbook of Communication,* edited by Ithiel de Sola Pool *et al.,* Chicago: Rand McNally pp. 836-843, 1973.

Johnson, David W. "Use of Role Reversal in Intergroup Competition," *Journal of Personality and Social Psychology* 7(1967):135-141.

Johnson, Douglas F., and Tullar, William L. "Style of Third Party Intervention, Face Saving and Bargaining Behavior." *Journal of Experimental Social Psychology* 8(1972):319-330.

Keltner, John. *Interpersonal Speech Communication: Elements and Structures.* Belmont, Calif.: Wadsworth Publishing Co., Inc., 1970.

Lane, Irving M., and Messe, Lawrence A. "Equity and the Distribution of Rewards." *Journal of Personality and Social Psychology* 20(1971):1-17.

Leary, Timothy. "The Theory and Measurement Methodology of Interpersonal Communication." *Psychiatry,* May 1955, pp. 147-161.

Lofland, John. *Analyzing Social Settings.* Belmont, Calif.: Wadsworth Publishing Co., Inc., 1971.

McCall, George J., and Simons, J. L. *Issues in Participant Observation: A Text and Reader.* Reading, Mass.: Addison-Wesley Publishing Co., Inc., 1969.

National Training Laboratories' Summer Reading Book. Bethel, Maine: NTL In-stitute for Applied Behavioral Science, 1968.

Osgood, Charles E., "Graduated Unilateral Initiatives for Peace." *Conflict Resolution: Contributions of the Behavioral Sciences,* edited by Clagett Smith, pp. 515-525. Notre Dame, Ind.: University of Notre Dame Press, 1971.

Patterson, Gerald R. "Interpersonal Skills Training for Couples in Early Stages of Conflict." *Journal of Marriage and the Family, 37* (2), May 1975, pp. 295-301.

———. Cobb, J. A.; and Ray, R. "A Social Engineering Technology for Retrain-ing the Families of Aggressive Boys." Vol. II. In *Georgia Symposium in Ex-perimental Clinical Psychology,* edited by H. Adams and L. Unikel. Springfield, Ill.: Charles C. Thomas Publishers, 1972.

———. Hops, Hyman; and Weiss, Robert L. "Interpersonal Skills Training for Couples in Early Stages of Conflict." *Journal of Marriage and the Family, 37* (2), (May 1975), pp. 295-303.

Rogers, Carl. *Client Centered Counseling.* Boston: Houghton Mifflin, 1951.

Rogers, Carl. *On Becoming a Person.* Boston: Houghton Mifflin Co., 1961.

Rusk, T., and Gerner, R. "A Study of the Process of Emergency Psychotherapy." *American Journal of Psychiatry* 128(1972):882-886.

Satir, Virginia. *Conjoint Family Therapy.* Palo Alto, Calif.: Science and Behavior Books, 1967.

Scott, Marvin B., and Lyman, Stanford. "Accounts." *American Sociological Review* 33(1968):46-62.

Sherif, Muzafer; Harvey, O. J.; White, B. Jack; Hood, William R.; and Sherif, Carolyn W. *Intergroup Conflict and Cooperation: The Robbers Cave Experiment.* Norman, Okla.: The Institute for Intergroup Relations, 1961.

Siegel, S., and Fouraker, L. E. *Bargaining and Group Decision Making: Experiments in Bilateral Monopoly.* New York: McGraw-Hill Book Co., 1960.

Smith, Manuel J. *When I Say No, I Feel Guilty.* New York: Bantam Books, Inc., 1975.

Vincent, J. P. "Problem-Solving Behavior in Distressed and Nondistressed Married and Stranger Dyads." Unpublished doctoral dissertation, University of Oregon, 1972.

Walton, Richard E. *Interpersonal Peacemaking: Confrontation and Third Party Consultation.* Reading, Mass.: Addison-Wesley Publishing Co., Inc., 1969.

Watzlawick, Paul; Weakland, John; and Fisch, Richard. *Change: Principles of Problem Formation and Problem Resolution.* New York: W. W. Norton & Co., Inc., 1974.

Wilmot, William W. *Dyadic Communication: A Transactional Perspective.* Reading, Mass.: Addison-Wesley Publishing Co., Inc., 1975.

Young, Oran R. "Intermediaries: Additional Thoughts on Third Parties." *Journal of Conflict Resolution, 16* (1), March 1972, pp. 51-65.

———. *The Intermediaries: Third Parties in International Crises.* Princeton, N.J.: Princeton University Press, 1967.

Author Index

Subject Index